Edited by David E. Petzal

THE EXPERTS' BOOK OF THE SHOOTING SPORTS
THE EXPERTS' BOOK OF UPLAND BIRD AND WATERFOWL HUNTING

The Experts' Book of Upland Bird and Waterfowl Hunting

Edited by DAVID E. PETZAL

A CORD COMMUNICATIONS BOOK

SIMON AND SCHUSTER   NEW YORK

Copyright © 1975 by Cord Communications Corporation
All rights reserved
including the right of reproduction
in whole or in part in any form
Published by Simon and Schuster
Rockefeller Center, 630 Fifth Avenue
New York, New York 10020

Designed by Jack Jaget
Manufactured in the United States of America
By The Maple Press Co., Inc., York, Pennsylvania

1   2   3   4   5   6   7   8   9   10

Library of Congress Cataloging in Publication Data

Petzal, David E
    The experts' book of upland bird and waterfowl hunting.

    "A Cord Communications book."
    1. Fowling. I. Title.
SK313.P4 1975   799.2'4'0973   74-13202
ISBN 0-671-21884-0

For Arlene

ACKNOWLEDGMENTS

I would like to extend my thanks to John Realmuto of Abercrombie & Fitch, New York City, for the use of the Winchester Model 12 shotgun and the duck call that appear on the jacket. My thanks also to Drew Holl of Crossroads of Sport, New York City, for the duck decoy that graces the photograph. The over/under shotgun is my own—a pigeon-grade Browning Superposed, made in 1933. The photograph is by Irwin Horowitz.

DAVID E. PETZAL

CONTENTS

INTRODUCTION

THE HUNTING of upland game and waterfowl in the United States is probably as old an institution as any we have, although the meat-hungry colonist who leveled his blunderbuss at a turkey had motives quite different from those of today's hunter. (For those who are not familiar with the term, upland game consists of those birds that live in the fields, woods and forests. The other half of this book's subject matter—waterfowl—comprises those birds that spend their lives on water: ducks, geese and shore birds.)

The hunting of both upland game and waterfowl is now a far different pursuit from what it was a century ago. In those days, when existence for most Americans was a far more precarious matter than it is now, wild birds of any kind were simply a cheap and readily available source of food and were to be shot in the greatest numbers possible, either for one's own table or to be sold. Game was at that time wild meat, and it was extended no more courtesy than was shown a hog or a chicken.

Passenger pigeons, which once darkened the sky with their numbers, were slaughtered by the thousands and the tens of thousands and the hundreds of thousands until there were no more on the face of the earth. (The last one died of old age in a zoo.) Mar-

9

ket hunters who sought waterfowl developed an item called a "punt gun." This device was a giant shotgun—actually a smooth-bore cannon—mounted on a swiveling pedestal in the prow of a rowboat, loaded with a sizable charge of black powder, scrap iron, old nails, bird shot, broken glass and anything else that was lethal and cheap; it was fired at flocks of ducks on the water. When the smoke cleared, the hunters moved in, collected the floating bodies and sold them to the local supplier of fresh game.

By today's standards, these acts of wholesale killing seem hor-rifying, and no one would call them hunting in the sense in which we now use the word. But it must be remembered that in those times, natural resources—all natural resources—were present in seemingly limitless supply. No one could envision, as he pulled the trigger on a flight of roost-bound passenger pigeons, that someday they would all be gone. The South Dakota farmer, as he carried home half a dozen prairie chickens, could hardly imagine the day when the prairie chicken would be a rarity. The market gunner, scooping a score of canvasbacks off the water for the res-taurants of Baltimore, could not know that the canvasback would come very close to extinction.

Slowly, painfully, hunters have been made aware that life is a very precious commodity and that birds and animals exist very much at man's sufferance. The ducks and geese that we bag in the fall are those that have survived the gantlet of polluted waters and drought. They face hazards far more deadly than the hunter's gun, and we realize that we must not add to the difficulty of their sur-vival. Therefore, professional game biologists each year calculate the numbers of the various species that can be safely harvested, and only those numbers of birds are taken.

If the hunter, market or otherwise, has had a hand in the reduc-tion of this country's bird life, he has also played a major role in its restoration. The pheasant, which is now so common as to be the mainstay of American upland hunting, was imported from China. The Hungarian partridge was an import, as was the chukar partridge.

The wild turkey, once hunted down to a pitiful few, has made an astonishing comeback over the last two decades and is present in such numbers that the annual bag can safely run into the tens of thousands. The programs that brought it back were undertaken by state game departments, with funds provided by the sale of hunting licenses, arms and ammunition.

The fact that there are any waterfowl at all today is a towering tribute to the hunter's efforts at conservation. Ducks Unlimited, an organization composed entirely of hunters, can take much of the credit for preserving and creating the breeding areas that ensure new generations of ducks and geese.

As I stated in my introduction to the first *Experts'* book, no one else cares enough about wild creatures to make a real investment of time, money and effort in their survival but hunters. There are organizations such as the Audubon Society (which has many hunters as members) that do fine work, but the backbone of wildlife conservation is the men with the guns. The simple fact is that were hunting to be abolished tomorrow, most of our efforts to maintain wildlife would be gone the day after tomorrow.

But these are glum thoughts to be thinking on a beautiful Sunday when the first hints of autumn are in the air. It is hard, as summer fades, not to think of pheasant and quail and partridge and ducks and shotguns and dogs. They have been my good friends since an early age. I was lucky enough to grow up on a farm in what was then a rural part of New Jersey and can remember being awakened on many a morning by the raucous squawk of a cock pheasant leading his harem of hens across the backyard. In the evening, we could hear quail calling each other across the alfalfa fields. There was a swamp where the partridge would allow you to nearly step on them and then come thundering up practically in your face, scaring you half out of your wits. There were a stream and a very sizable pond where, before it was polluted with oil waste, ducks used to gather.

And there were the dogs: Colonel, an Irish setter of near-human patience, gentleness and intelligence; Major, an English setter who could not have cared less about people but lived only to hunt; Salt and Pepper, the springer spaniels who lived next door, and Wendy, a golden retriever who would climb straight up eight feet of chicken-wire fence if it stood between her and human companionship. They were all characters, some good, some bad, and I remember them all as if they were so many human beings.

In the trunk behind me (and in the handsome photograph that makes up the jacket of this book) is a Browning shotgun that belonged to my uncle. It was willed to him in the late 1930s by a hunting companion. And shortly before my uncle died, he passed it on to me. So I am now its third owner, and presumably there will be a fourth. Good guns never wear out if they're taken care of, and over the years the memories they engender and the hands that hold them make them priceless.

One's memories of days afield consist of isolated incidents—not of particular birds, but of happenings that were funny or exciting or frustrating.

There was, for example, the dark, rainy November afternoon that I found myself waist-deep in primal, sucking New Jersey swamp ooze (when it comes to primal, sucking swamp ooze, the Okefenokee has nothing on New Jersey). As I flailed around, trying to extricate myself, three grouse thundered out of a bush not three feet away. Now, it is an event to find two grouse together, and three at one time is a real occasion. But when you're waist-deep in the mire, it's futile to do anything in the way of bagging grouse. Self-preservation is the number one priority.

Or there was the day I spent in a duck blind built for midgets with 135 pounds of affection-crazed Labrador retriever in my lap. Gerry Gibbs (now Fishing Editor of *Outdoor Life*; I always knew he'd come to a bad end), George Haas (an associate editor of *Outdoor Life*; I must be more careful of the company I keep) and I were duck hunting on the South Shore of Long Island with an eighty-year-old gentleman named Captain Downs. The Captain had once been a market hunter, and he had built a beautiful box blind to his own dimensions. He was five feet three. Since I am five-ten, I found things a bit cramped, and matters were immediately complicated by Downs's enormous Labrador, Ace, who had not the slightest interest in retrieving anything, but who lay in my lap the whole day cadging sandwiches and chocolate bars. At the end of the day, Ace rode serenely to shore in the rowboat while the four of us pulled the craft against the outgoing tide.

Or there was the four-minute-mile pheasant who took refuge in a patch of uncut oats in a field in Illinois. The patch was about 100 yards long and 6 feet wide. My hunting companion, a portly Texan, and I knew that the bird could not get out either side of the patch, since the field surrounding it was bare. So all we had to do was chase him down to the end, one of us on either side of the oats, and he'd fly when he reached the end. The logic of this was flawless—except that someone should have told the pheasant. He ran to the end of the oats, stopped short and ran like hell in the other direction, with us in hot pursuit.

He reached the other end and reversed his field and, blowing like whales, we set out on our third 100-yard wind sprint. Again he swapped ends, and this time he was able to outdistance us sufficiently to take off at the end of the oats, while we stood there red-faced, sweating and wheezing.

In addition to the humor, and the stupid mistakes you make, there are the moments when, within your own small world, you rise to greatness. I have made a few good shots myself and have seen some marvelous ones by others. There was the duck hunter from Maryland with whom I hunted in Illinois. He had an AA rating as a trapshooter, which meant that during the past year he had hit at least 96.5 percent of all the targets he shot at, and his accomplishments as a leveler of waterfowl were no less. Three mallard, going full-tilt, flew past his blind, one behind another. His three shots were off in as many seconds and were so perfect that I saw three heads droop and three bodies tumbling crazily through the air, all in perfect sequence.

Or there was the Georgian who shot quail with the proficiency of a Raymond Berry catching passes. I saw him, on more than one occasion, wait for the paths of two bobwhites to intersect, snap a shot at that spot and watch the twin puffs of feathers as the birds plummeted. He did this not to save ammunition, but out of pride in his own ability. When you had hunted quail as long as he, there was a certain level of skill at which you operated, or else you lost your standing as a master of the art form.

Dogs too are capable of wizardry. If you have not seen it at first hand, you cannot appreciate, and will not believe, the intelligence and dedication an animal can bring to its work. I know an aged and gentle Brittany spaniel bitch who is the most affectionate of dogs. Yet she is a terror on woodcock. When searching them out among the alder thickets, she will not come near you, and when she retrieves, she will spit the bird out at your feet and not pause for so much as a pat on the head. Woodcock, you see, are her purpose in life.

Judy, on the other hand, was a pointer bitch with a temper that was less than angelic. On one occasion, a quartet of rabbit-running beagle hounds invaded a field where she was looking for pheasant. Without a thought to the odds, she pitched into the pack, and the welkin rang with the sounds of a screaming, snarling, yelping canine war. It didn't last long. The beagles decided within a few seconds that no rabbit was worth that kind of grief and scattered to varying points of the compass. Now, Judy was not necessarily a scrapper, but if something interfered with her work, woe betide it.

If you have any doubts as to the seriousness with which dogs take their work, hunt someday behind an old, cynical pooch who has seen it all, and miss an easy bird that he has pointed. Then take note of the look he gives you. You will be more careful about missing the next bird.

And there are sights and sounds and colors that you find nowhere else, and which you will never forget. There is the near-incredible tranquility of a pine forest in autumn, the only sound the wind hissing through the trees. Occasionally, if it is the right time of year, you will hear the rolling, muffled series of thumps a grouse makes in the mating season. It's called drumming, but the sound is more muted and subdued than any drum I've ever heard.

If you are lucky, you will have the privilege of accepting a grouse from your dog, or retrieving it yourself from the ground where it has fallen. No typewriter can do justice to that checkerboard tapestry of gold, brown, gray, black and white that comprises the bird's plumage. Not even the rainbow tail of the pheasant can match it.

Even the smells can be beautiful. I can recall hunting pheasant along the border of an alfalfa field that was edged by ancient hardwood trees. There was a sweet, dank, pungent smell of rotting leaves, laced with the smoke of distant fires where other leaves were being burned. (This was before it was decreed that leaf fires made an intolerable addition to the tons of pollutants created by automobiles and industry.)

The smell of a salt marsh where you hunt ducks is equally pungent. Over all hangs the heavy scent of the ocean, flavored by the rank odor of mud, and to this are often added the smell of a wet dog, the aroma of gun oil and the scent of rubber waders.

Like a piece of music that you have not heard in years but that can instantly bring on a rush of memories, these smells can also call back years, events, people and dogs past.

Although this book is instructional in nature, my introduction has obviously not been. Its purpose has been to show you how one person appreciates the sum total of what all the contributors to the book are talking about. If you are a hunter, you may or may not remember that on a certain day you knocked down a quail that was crossing at a hard right angle with a load of No. 8 shot from an improved-cyclinder barrel that threw 40-percent patterns and shot just a little high. What you *will* remember is the way your dog pointed the bird or, if you were among friends at the time, that you got a grudging compliment or two.

You will probably also remember if the day was warm, sunny October or if it was late December, when the ground was hard from frost and your fingers were numb and stiff around the gun. If, as they say, your head is in the right place, you will remember so many things.

I do, and I hope that you are equally fortunate.

DAVID E. PETZAL

New York City
September, 1973

PHEASANT HUNTING

BY BYRON W. DALRYMPLE

THE FIRST game bird I ever shot was a pheasant, and the incident was not only overwhelmingly exciting for a kid in his early teens, but uniquely dramatic as well. We lived on a small farm in the Thumb area of Michigan, and my father taught school in a nearby small village. I loved to roam the fields, which in those days were far from clean-cropped and were excellent cover for small game such as rabbits and squirrels and for the pheasant that had been brought into the region a few years earlier.

We had, in fact, watched the progress of the birds with great eagerness. An aunt of mine lived in Oregon, where the first successful introduction of the ringneck had occurred and where the first hunting season was held, way back in 1892. My Oregon uncle hunted pheasant and had sent us a cured skin, which hung spread out on the wall of our living room for many years, admired by everyone who visited our house. And of course, I dreamed of the day when I too would hunt pheasant.

I vividly remember when I saw the first one in our country. It was an arrogant rooster, crossing our vegetable garden to disappear into a sassafras clump at one corner where it could follow the cover of a zigzag split-rail fence back along our cornfield. At that time I was too young, my parents claimed, to shoot a gun; otherwise I'd undoubtedly have tried to bring it in. But later on, my brother and I came into possession of a single-shot .22 rifle. It was getting old even then, and our family was quite poor, so cartridges were by no means plentiful.

My brother and I took turns carrying the .22. I don't recall that we knew anything at all about hunting seasons. Certainly there must have been some regulations, but there was no enforcement officer in our area, and nobody among neighbors on other small farms would have given a thought to regulations anyway. If one saw a rabbit or squirrel and happened to have a gun handy—pop —into the pot. But in our case, a .22 single-shot and .22 Shorts, which is all we had, were not much of a combo for pheasant hunting.

One Saturday in early fall we were prowling around, my brother and I. Leaves were turning and it was one of those exhilarating days still fresh in my memory. It was my brother's turn to start out carrying the little rifle. Our agreement was that on any given foray, the one who started out carrying it was allowed to continue until he got a shot. If he bagged something, or missed, he then turned the gun over to the other.

We drifted back into the woodlot and had the great good luck to glimpse a big fox squirrel streaking up a beech tree. Finally my brother spotted it, took a rest against a sapling, sighted carefully and, wonder of wonders, brought it down. He was jubilant. I confess I was a little bit envious. Now it was my turn, but we'd have to go back to the house soon to do evening chores, and my chances looked slim.

We scoured the woodlot. No more squirrels. We started back across the field. We were possibly 30 yards apart, scuffing through hay stubble, when my brother flushed what looked to me like an absolutely enormous rooster. It hurtled up, cackling, and set a course that brought it crossing in front of me, broadside, perhaps 20 yards away. I was so thoroughly excited that, bug-eyed and watching the bird, I jerked the little rifle up beside my right hip, grabbed the barrel with my left hand, pulled back the hammer and jerked the trigger. Not much of a way to shoot a rifle, but to my utter astonishment the cock cartwheeled and fell.

We ran to it, still disbelieving. I was trembling harder than I

would be today at dropping a bull elk. And the fantastic part of
all this came when we finally cleaned and plucked the bird. It had
been shot through the neck!

From that day on I was a pheasant hunter. For years we hunted
pheasant in our area—and watched the birds' population there
grow literally to nuisance proportions. To give you an idea, after
my brother and I had shotguns to hunt with, many a neighbor
begged us to shoot every bird we saw, hens and roosters, to get
rid of them. I remember watching out our front window one day
in winter when food was scarce, especially with such a mass of
birds utilizing what was available, and counting exactly sixty-five
pheasant on one small open field of shocked corn.

Today there is no such thing as a shock of corn. But at that time
it was cut by hand and formed into shocks in the field. It was common to find shocks that had been torn to pieces by scores of pheasant. At times we ate pheasant more often than chicken—and it's
far superior to chicken, as all pheasant hunters certainly know.
This, the ring-necked pheasant, was the exotic game bird from a
whole world away that had "made it big" in the United States.

But what we were seeing then was nothing to what would occur
as the pheasant was introduced and flourished in some of the Central States, coming to peak populations of unbelievable numbers.
South Dakota is the prime example. There the ringneck became
for a time a wildlife phenomenon comparable in some degree to
the passenger pigeon of the previous century. I presume that few
readers of this chapter witnessed the heyday of the pheasant in
South Dakota. It is therefore worth describing as a vignette from
out of American shotgunning history, for without question it will
not be repeated.

When the first settlers came to the Dakota territory many years
ago, the region was almost solid grassland. Tales have been told
of the awesomely abundant prairie chickens then present. But the
tales aren't quite true. Originally the Dakotas region was not good
chicken habitat and, in fact, had few of the birds. Unbroken grasslands were short on the foods the birds needed.

It was not until the coming of the plow to the prairies that the
chickens began to prosper in that area. Then, with the sod broken
in patches and crops grown, they moved in, and they too were a
wildlife phenomenon, a virtual irruption. In August, when the

"squealers"—young of the year—abounded, hunters with team and wagon could drive out across the land and shoot until the wagon box was full.

But the plow, as more and more settlement spread out, cut too wide a furrow. In due time the croplands by far overbalanced the unbroken sod. The chicken declined and, as the imbalance increased, all but disappeared. Today only remnant populations remain. However, the ringneck had already been proved, first in Oregon and then elsewhere, to be a bird of croplands and their edges, an aristocrat of the farmlands. The plowing up of the grasslands, or most of them, had formed optimum habitat for the pheasant which was now introduced to replace the diminished prairie chicken. Soon tales began to drift out of the Dakotas—and from South Dakota in particular—that pheasant hunting there was sensational.

The news didn't get around as fast in those days (the '30s) as it does now, nor were hunters as numerous, nor did they travel as much or as easily. But presently South Dakota had become the mecca, the "Pheasant Capital of the World," as it billed itself without exaggeration. Pheasant had become virtual pests to many a landowner, but to some who illicitly market-hunted, they were a big money crop. During this period, although agriculture was being intensified, the Soil Bank was in operation, creating quality habitat balance between cropped and uncropped lands. It is not possible to state precisely how many pheasant were in South Dakota during the late '30s and early '40s, but the state flock in its best years has been estimated by reliable sources to have been at least 50,000,000 *birds*!

But the pheasant boom was not destined to last forever. Although good shooting is certainly still available in many places today, the peak has probably passed, in every state, forever. Some states are able to sustain a fairly stable population. But changes in land use have drastically cut into pheasant numbers. It is the same story everywhere. The fields I hunted as a boy, with their rail and stump fences and their small red willow swales and weedy fencerows, are now just about wiped clean. The small swales are nearly all drained and plowed up. There is no such thing as a weedy fencerow. Brush is cut or killed by spraying, and crops are grown right up to the wire. Modern farming practices have removed food and cover. There is little waste grain, and when one crop is harvested the field is immediately plowed and harrowed and readied for another.

In South Dakota the Soil Bank lands have now mostly been put back to work. No cover is left on them. Hundreds of old-fashioned windbreaks of trees have been destroyed. The ringneck steadily declined in that state after the big early-'40s peak. By 1947 it was considered at rock bottom, with no more than 7,000,000 birds. Of the next few seasons, some were good, some only fair. There were broad fluctuations, and then a swift drop. By 1966 South Dakota pheasants were drastically reduced, to an estimated 2,000,000.

Since that time, concentrated management and other factors have brought substantial recovery. Biologists have come to believe that if landowners are willing to raise the amount of permanent nesting cover by a small percentage, South Dakota can sustain a fair flock of 8,000,000 or more. But if agriculture continues its inroads, this state that once drew thousands of visiting hunters who poured millions of dollars into its economy, and which was the prime pheasant habitat on the continent, can hardly have more than 3–4,000,000 birds in any year.

I've used South Dakota to illustrate the general pheasant situation because it was the greatest and now represents rather typically what has happened to this grand game bird everywhere. After the ringneck had taken hold in a number of states across the North, every game department became interested. Almost every one of the Lower Forty-Eight experimented with pheasants. Some never were successful; a few had mild success; others finally settled hunter demand by offering released birds. There was a flurry everywhere—and there still is to some extent—to try other varieties of the world's hundred and fifty different pheasants, to see if any could be found that would replace the ringneck in habitat and climate situations where it was unable to colonize. The Reeves, the Japanese green, the Korean, the Iranian, the Afghan, the Kalij and many others have been tried. It is still possible that one or more may make it.

Today, at least thirty-six of the Lower Forty-Eight states have pheasant seasons. There have been experimental seasons in a cou-

If one word can accurately describe the pheasant, that would be "flamboyant." Everything about him is spectacular, from his brilliantly colored plumage to his rocketing, squawking flight. The bird shown below is an Afghan whitewing cock, a subspecies that has been established in New Mexico and Texas and is being tried in Arizona.

This is a day's bag in Wyoming. In the more northern states, the winter takes a heavy toll of birds each year, especially in the thin cover where this gunner was shooting.

ple of others—for example, Arizona for the experimental Afghan white-winged pheasant. Hawaii also has a season, for ringnecks and Japanese greens.

Few states can legitimately be rated as "excellent" pheasant-hunting areas today. Approximately half of them having seasons might be classed as "good." The remainder vary from fair to poor. Bear in mind also that in some states, pheasant just do not "take." In more than one locale, game departments and private citizens have tried mightily—and failed—to introduce the pheasant. No one knows precisely why the birds will not prosper in one spot, but that is the fact of it. Therefore, in my survey, some states do not appear.

I do not intend this as discouragement, but readers should be honestly informed. There is still some very good shooting to be had, but it is important for hunters to know where to find it. A regional appraisal is therefore in order. Bear in mind as I give a rundown of the pheasant-hunting states that how "good" hunting is may be difficult to assess. For example, a state with a high kill may have an ample number of birds, but it may also have an over-ample number of hunters. Thus success per hunter may be only average. A state considered to have good hunting may have it only in small areas. Wyoming is a prime example. What pheasant hunting there is can be rated "good," but not all counties have pheasant. Habitat is limited to irrigated valley croplands, and this bird gets the heaviest hunting pressure of any of the state's game birds. During one recent season, statistics gathered by the Wyoming game people showed 18,000 hunters and a harvest of 70,000 birds. By and large, however, you can tell by the size of the average annual bag the states that certainly have the *most* birds, and in general this means they will be found over a sizable range and that hunting will probably be good.

New England is basically not pheasant territory. Nonetheless, there is some pretty fair shooting there each season. Maine has a very small winter carry-over of birds but a heavy release program of as many as 30,000 in seasons past. Shooting in New Hampshire is mostly for released birds. Vermont has no wild self-sustaining flocks, but there is a small kill there each season, of releases. Massachusetts has the largest harvest in the region—as many as 100,000 in past years. But the flock is by no means self-sustaining. Heavy releases, as much as half the kill, are made. Rhode Island shooting is mostly put-and-take, with a low harvest, and Connecticut has only a few released birds.

New York is the most important pheasant state in the upper Northeast. It has a substantial breeding flock in the farming areas and a kill averaging in good seasons several hundred thousand. New Jersey stocks as many as 60,000 birds to add to the wild population and has had annual bags up to 265,000 birds.

A check of the Atlantic Coastal States shows very little available. Delaware makes some releases; Maryland has fair shooting but a very low wild population. Only privately released birds are shot in North Carolina. Virginia and Georgia still experiment with various pheasants but presently offer no hunting, and Florida has discontinued its experiments, which failed. The pheasant, in fact, of any variety has to date been a problem bird below the fortieth parallel, for reasons never entirely understood. There have even been experiments in the Deep South—Mississippi, for example—in which the birds were able to get along in good style but refused to breed. No one knows why.

Although Pennsylvania has a great many hunters, it also is a top eastern pheasant state, with a total bag in some seasons of up to a million. Included in this are many released birds. West Virginia has a few birds, but poor hunting. The kill is, in fact, negligible.

My old home state of Michigan was at one time one of the best pheasant states in the nation. The birds were spread across the southern half of the Lower Peninsula, and as recently as some seasons in the '60s kills ran to a million birds. But pheasant are in serious difficulty there, although in some locations good shooting is still enjoyed. Wisconsin's pheasant population has leveled off after a steady decline, and hunting there, with a bag some years well up toward half a million, can be rated as good. Minnesota has had many ups and downs with its pheasant, but management may yet make it with a substantial harvest. At present the average prospects are only fair.

The Central States, even the more populous ones, show an interesting pattern and furnish much better hunting than hunters realize. Ohio releases some birds and has an annual bag running to 300,000. Indiana also releases some birds and gets a kill of up to 100,000. Illinois is a real surprise, what with its heavy human population. Its farmlands furnish 600,000 to 1,000,000 birds most seasons. Some are released birds. And Iowa has long been the real sleeper pheasant state. How long farm practices there will allow a heavy bird population is debatable. But in recent seasons the kill has been as high as 1–1,500,000, beating once-prime South

This hunter is working a Wisconsin fencerow with his springer. The edges of cultivated fields are favored by pheasant when the pressure grows heavy.

Dakota by over 100 percent. Indeed, today Iowa is one of the top pheasant states in the nation.

Perhaps because of severe winters, North Dakota is an up-and-down state. Some very good shooting is there, if you run it down. The kill hangs around 300,000 in good years, and the number of hunters is not large. Once the undisputed pheasant capital of the world, South Dakota has had its ups and downs in recent years, but now appears to be at the top of a population cycle. The shooting in the 1972–73 season was very good, and if the hunting pressure does not build up too rapidly, it should remain that way for a while. In total number of birds, it is about equal to, or slightly better than, North Dakota. Missouri hunting is just fair, with a low kill. For a good many years Nebraska and Kansas also were sleepers. Both furnish very good shooting. Not too long ago I hunted both states on the same trip and we had little difficulty filling limits, which as I recall were three a day in each. The bag in each state runs from half a million upward. Oklahoma has pretty fair shooting over a restricted range, but the annual take is not very large—probably 20,000 birds on the average.

There is a bit of pheasant hunting even in Texas, located in a few counties of the Panhandle. This is probably about as far south as ringnecks have ever established themselves. However, the bag is small. Texas may eventually have other pheasant hunting. The Afghan white-winged pheasant has been stocked in some arid areas, and at present there is some hope for it.

This bird has shown promise elsewhere and then not really lived up to it. It is an exceedingly handsome pheasant, very colorful, with white along the wings. It is in my opinion much wilder than the ringneck. A few years ago New Mexico, which had been experimenting with whitewings in the southwest sector out of Lordsburg, near Red Rock, held its first open season. This was the first open season on pure-strain Afghan white-winged pheasants ever held in the United States, although I believe some hybrids (with ringnecks) had been hunted earlier in California.

Arizona also tried this pheasant, but in neither state has it colonized extensively. New Mexico has some hunting for it and some for ringnecks in scattered numbers along cropland river courses.

As we move up the Rockies, however, pheasant hunting picks up. Colorado offers fair hunting in restricted range, with a kill of

Nebraska, where this picture was taken, has consistently been a top producer for some years. The cover is typical of midwestern pheasant country.

up to 150,000. In Nevada pheasant are restricted to irrigated valleys and are not plentiful, but there is some fair shooting. Utah is a good pheasant state. Here again, the birds are tied to the valleys and river courses where crops are grown, but the kill runs a quarter-million.

I've noted that Wyoming has good, though limited, shooting. In Idaho the picture is somewhat better. Here the pheasant is extremely important and popular, and the annual bag goes to half a million or more. Unfortunately, the birds are having some difficulties in Idaho, again due to changing land use. Montana has good shooting in the eastern part of the state, particularly along the river courses.

On the Pacific Coast the picture is quite good, although hunters are numerous. California's pheasant are limited by suitable land available, but the kill goes to 750,000. Some releases are made. Oregon, where the pheasant was first hunted in the United States, offers good shooting, with the bag about a quarter-million. But here again, land use is upsetting the stability of the flock. Washington is an excellent state, with the bird exceedingly popular and quite plentiful and a kill of around 600,000.

The foregoing should give you an overall view of pheasant populations in the United States today. We should also look briefly at
Canada. There is fair shooting in southern British Columbia and
on Vancouver Island. Alberta has some very good shooting, especially in the central south, but severe winters cause rather drastic
fluctuations. Saskatchewan pheasant hunting has for some time
been restricted to residents. The bag is small, and severe winters
are rough on the birds. Ontario has a bit of shooting along Lake
Erie, and there is even some fair action in a few locations in Nova
Scotia.

The ringneck has always been something of a problem bird for
hunters because it is not entirely predictable. It is a runner, but
when the notion hits, it can also be one of the snuggest-lying of
upland game birds. I remember hunting one fall with a man who
had a springer spaniel that was eager and had a good nose, but
was a little too fast. I watched the dog jump a rooster and in fact
glimpsed the bird several times as it ran. It followed a weedy
dredge-ditch bank and literally ran for almost half a mile.

When the dog came back, we got into a field of dense clover.
Presently the dog hit a hot scent. The springer didn't run off, but
kept scouring a very small area in high excitement. This went on
for so long that we were about to call the dog off. There simply
couldn't be a bird there or, as we milled around, we'd have
stepped on it. Yet suddenly she found it and pounced into the
clover. The cock went zooming up with its tail brushing her nose.

During my early years of pheasant hunting, we simply walked
the fields and fencerows, without a dog. One learns a great deal
about pheasant habits this way—where they are most likely to
feed, roost and travel. This is a species tied to crop fields inter-
spersed with fallow lands. It hides and skulks in brush patches, in
weed patches and along marsh edges and the edges of woodlots.
But it is no forest or woodlot bird. However, at times I have known
pheasant, when hunted hard, to get back a surprising distance into
woods with understory cover. Marshes and marsh edges that are
not too wet are also prime pheasant cover.

In any given area, a hunter learns to size up quickly the various
spots the birds are most likely to use, and at what time of day. Except under specialized and uncommon conditions, ringnecks roost

on the ground. How much cover they require is to some extent dictated by the season. In warm weather I have seen them select a field such as cutover alfalfa. The cover is short there, but adequate. But in colder weather they will invariably seek deeper cover for protection. Most typical are patches of dense weeds, as in a patch, say, of wild sunflowers with grass beneath. Or perhaps the classic: swales that have heavy marsh grass but that are not wet throughout. The interior might be moist or even hold a bit of water, but the edges, with heavy dead grasses, are perfect hiding and roosting places. Even with snow on the ground birds will cling to such spots. In heavily farmed country, wheat and barley stubble and small willow patches make prime roosting places.

There are situations in which pheasant roost to some extent in trees. But these are so few that a hunter would be wasting his time looking up. I have also seen them burrow into corn shocks in cold weather, but of course in today's world corn shocks are few. Haystacks sometimes provide roosting cover, and ditch banks and fences with heavy weeds—the same lanes pheasant travel by day—will often serve as roosting spots.

Some of the finest shooting extant is to be had, either with or without a dog, by early combing of the roost sites. In summer pheasant may be active at first light, but in the normal hunting season they are usually, like quail, late risers. They do not leave the form until the sun is above the horizon and cutting the frost a bit. After having spent the night squatting in a warm bunch of grass, the birds sit very tight indeed. A walking hunter must cover every foot, wandering back and forth, because good roosting sites are not always abundant, and these birds, though not flocking birds or covey birds like quail, are nonetheless gregarious. A small patch of marsh grass may hold numerous individuals. They don't want to flush and give themselves away. And as I have said, nothing holds snugger than a pheasant that has its mind made up.

Although pheasant are, on the whole, difficult for dogs to handle, they are perfect when approached while still in the roost cover. But a thorough dog is required, and preferably one that works slowly. A dog that goes bounding around every which way is not much on pheasant regardless of where they are hunted. One of the finest dogs I ever owned was a small beagle hound. She was a problem, I'll admit, when she bumped into a cottontail. She

never chased a pheasant, but would begin to get excited and wag
her tail when she sniffed a sitting bird. We killed a good many
over her.

Shooting the roosts is short-term hunting. As the air warms, the
birds move out to field edges, along farm-road lanes and also along
public roads. They are often rather visible on this first movement.
They peck gravel briefly as they move to the feeding ground. Pub-
lic-road hunting is illegal in most states, but pickup-truck trails on
farms are not out of bounds, and hunting of such places after
sunup can be most productive.

However, after the birds have been without food all night they
are eager to fill their crops. Overall, the most popular feeding areas
across much of the United States have always been the cornfields.
Where corn is not a major crop, other grains such as wheat and
oats and, over much territory, redtop or maize or soybeans replace
it. It was in the crop fields, and especially standing corn, that the
popular drive method of hunting originated. Let me describe a
typical one made one season in the Midwest.

The cornfield was about half a mile long. Low wheat stubble
was on either side. There were an even dozen hunters. As we sized
up the field, which was about 200 yards wide, we decided that we
needed at least four blockers. (More might have been better.)
These men were to take their places at the end of the field, spaced

*Standing corn is just about
tops for pheasant cover.
When you're working where
visibility is limited, it's a
good idea to bell your dog in
order to keep track of his
whereabouts.*

In some states, redtop and maize replace corn and wheat as ideal ringneck cover.

evenly, and wait while the others drove. The rest of us were transported around to the opposite end of the field.

We lined up six men across that end. If the drivers are too few, birds duck back around them, just as white-tailed deer will do in a drive. This left two men. These, on opposite sides of the field, walked down the edge 50 yards or so before we started. Their job was to walk at the same pace as the drivers and to keep birds from darting out or flushing at the edges. Often birds will run to the edge and will fly when they come to the open. But if they see or hear the edge man, they duck back in.

Now, with the signal of the "boss," the drive was under way. It proceeded at a normal walk. Occasionally a bird flushed and flew off. Ideally it is best to agree not to shoot at such individuals—to hold fire until the end of the drive so as not to scare the birds. Now and then we could see a gaudy bird racing down a row ahead of us. As we finally came close to the end, everyone paused. We were sure a good many pheasant were pocketed between drivers and blockers.

"All right!" the drive boss called.

We moved ahead cautiously a step or two, talking now. A cock flew and was picked off by one of the blockers. Then another was up, and another. Guns laced their sounds across the field, and suddenly the air was a welter of bulky, long-tailed birds bursting up. Hens were, of course, among the blizzard of wings, and each shooter had to use care not to clip one. When the action was concluded, there were twenty-three birds in the bag!

If forage is ample, the birds will drift, or sometimes even fly, from the feeding location to varied cover by midmorning. They retire to rest in deep cover of brush patches, fencerows and dry swales. I have hunted them during the middle of the day even in dense cattail patches, although it is almost impossible to get them up from such a spot. During the resting period they dust and stay out of sight, taking their long siestas. The timing of the afternoon feeding period hinges on the weather and the food supply. If food is scarce and bad weather coming, they'll be out early. If food is plentiful, the best shooting hours will be the three right up until dusk.

Now the birds will be back in the same areas where they were during the morning feeding. But toward dusk they will be moving to cover. I learned early in my hunting experience that one can get some superb shooting during the last light—if legal shooting time doesn't cease before then—by checking out the travel routes of the birds. Some, in broad farm country, may fly from feed to cover. But undisturbed pheasant, like most upland birds, would rather walk than fly. So on small farms if you hunt the fencerows and weed patches again, you can often have exciting sport right up to the time when flame begins to be visible from the end of your gun.

I have noted earlier how snug a pheasant will sit if it takes the notion. But I want to emphasize also that a full-grown cock almost a yard long can absolutely disappear even in unbelievably short cover. I mentioned cutover alfalfa. It is prime pheasant habitat, for both feeding and roosting. Many insects (such as grasshoppers) are there before the frosts come. And there are seeds, too. I remember vividly, however, hunting this type of cover many times over the years and having a companion tell me a pheasant positively couldn't hide in it.

"They're too tall," one told me. "They couldn't possibly even squat that low to the ground."

Don't you believe it. A mature cock can lie flat in such cover, neck stretched out, or he can run through it crouched so low he's never seen. This phenomenon is one of the facets of pheasant hunting a beginner has to get used to. The bird looks so big and so gaudy it seems it could not disappear except in brush or high weeds. I have walked across a field of low wheat stubble and come upon a full-grown rooster that, apparently caught unaware, simply flattened out. I got past it in full sunlight before I noticed it, yet it had been practically under my boot. The moment I stopped and turned around, the bird flushed. The wise pheasant hunter should always be alert and aware of the game's hiding ability.

It can also run at amazing speed, and through cover that would seem to impede it. When a pheasant runs down a ditch, for example, it usually hits the bottom, if there's no water, and pours on the coal. I've watched in amusement many times while a group of hunters kicked grass and weed clumps in just such a place, because I knew that the bird was by then several hundred yards away.

Neophyte pheasant hunters often wonder how they could possibly miss such a big, lumbering bird. I've seen shooters who'd had experience even with ruffed grouse—difficult indeed—stand gawking after cutting not a feather from a cockbird spang in the open. There is at least one highly valuable trick to be learned. Anyone who has eaten a chicken knows that there is a small "spring bone" tied to muscle that runs up along the drumstick. It is practically vestigial. Domestic chickens have no reason to fly, and in fact are barely able to. If you have ever eaten a pheasant, you know that around the drumstick there are a number of small split but rather pliable bones tied to muscle.

The bird utilizes these "springs" to assist its takeoff. A mature cock weighs on the average between 2 and 3½ pounds. The long tail and heavy feathers also make it bulky. If it has a chance to run in the open, it can hop into the air and rise on an inclining plane, utilizing momentum. But pheasant flushed from hiding can't do that. The powerful legs must push the bird upward from a squat. The "springs" in the leg bounce it upward as the powerful wings push downward.

Thus it bounds straight up into the air, and as strobe photos have often shown, the body and tail of a rising rooster are actually in a ve˗ ˙cal plane—head up, tail straight down. The wings are

A good retriever will save many crippled birds within a few seasons. Almost any upland breed will do also.

beating partly horizontally and partly with downward thrust. Thus, between legs and wings, the bird is catapulted into the air. When it has attained enough height—from 10 to 15 feet as a rule— it literally tips over into normal flying position. What makes all of this so important to the shooter is that at the apex of the rise, and as the bird tips to horizontal flying position, it is for all practical purposes momentarily motionless. Right then, during that split second, is the time to fire!

Thousands of pheasant are missed each year because the shooter, startled at the noisy burst of the big bird rising practically under-foot, jerks up his gun and blasts away instantly—and shoots under it. Rattled by his miss, he stares as the bird levels off and zooms away, and either misses again or doesn't recover in time to shoot. So take your time on the rise. Time your shot to the peak of it. You will be shooting at a practically suspended target, and you'll collect every one with ease.

Going-away shots at pheasant cripple a lot of them by being offside and breaking a wing. A winged rooster will run like a racehorse and without a good dog is all but impossible to retrieve. The same angle also may break a leg or put shot into the body. The bird will die, but may not be retrieved. The more positive shots, the ones commonly presented when several people hunt together, are crossing and quartering shots. No one can tell you how far to lead, because "lead" looks different through the eyes of individual shooters. The important thing to learn is that a ringneck in full flight is a real sizzler. It may look like a lumbering freight train, but it is traveling much faster than you imagine.

In fact, the average speed of an undisturbed bird has been clocked at 40 miles per hour, and it is reliably estimated that pheasant are capable (under pressure) of double that! The bird that has had time to rev up to Full Ahead will be covering anywhere from 40 to 90 feet per second. Those statistics should make one aware that the ringneck looks like a slow target only because of its size.

The pheasant is not only clever and unpredictable and fast: it is one of the toughest game birds known. Even a mortally wounded rooster will somehow summon the strength to hide in a brush pile or run in cover until it drops. The bird is also deceptive in the air because it appears to be a lot of target. Two-thirds of it is no target at all. A hunter should train himself to shoot not just at the bird, but at the front end of the bird—the head, neck and wing-butt section.

There will always, of course, be many arguments about guns and loads. I've shot pheasant even with a .410. But I wouldn't recommend it. I've also killed scores with a 20—which, particularly in this day with so many husky loads available for it, is a perfectly legit gauge. By and large, however, the 12-gauge is the most popular choice for this endeavor. Years ago, when I could not always get the shells I wanted, I shot whatever I had, even No. 8 shot. But that isn't much of a ringneck load. No. 7½ may be all right at opening of season, but as birds mature and put on winter feathers, I am convinced No. 6 high-brass loads are as good as one can use.

In chokes, a compromise has to be made. Improved-cylinder and modified are good in a double. Although for a long time I shot a 20 with a full-choke barrel, and it brought down a great number of ringnecks, I wouldn't claim it to be perfect. On close-rising birds it patterned too closely, and out at long range it didn't allow much latitude for error. A modified barrel is a good compromise. And a variable choke, for those who like it, allows one to switch for situations in which most birds are flushed close or must be taken passing in full flight.

Trying to advise anyone what kind of dog to use for pheasant is a confusing matter. If you are wealthy enough to own several pointers or setters and have them trained by a pro on pheasant, you don't need any advice. If you have a dog that is excellent on quail, or on ruffed grouse and woodcock, I'd think long and hard before putting it through the frustration of pheasant. It is the general consensus that a pheasant dog, to work its best, should never know any other upland bird.

One of the best dogs I ever owned and worked on pheasant was a cocker spaniel. She was slow, because she couldn't go very fast in cover anyway. She didn't chase after flushed birds. I also hunted over a big springer a number of times. Dogs of this breed are fine, but often need to be restrained. If you can keep them from ranging wide and chasing flying birds, they are great. A friend of mine had a Brittany with a superb nose that was one of the slowest-working dogs I ever saw. It was almost painful to hunt behind it. It took one quiet step at a time. However, that little dog would be on a pheasant before the bird was wise, and seemed to prowl so gently it held an uncommon number of birds.

The various retrievers all do a good job, if they learn what to do. It seems to me the chief job of the dog *is* as a retriever. Unfortunately, on most pheasant hunts a substantial number of birds are crippled. They are just plain tough to put down to stay. A good retriever saves loss of these. There is the occasional and exceptional dog that just seems to catch on to pheasant, to know how to move swiftly around in front of a running bird and bring it up short. By and large, a dog that works close in, with utter thoroughness and with a cool head, is the one I'd pick.

There are purists who for years have scoffed at the pheasant, who stick with their beloved bobwhites or ruffed grouse and disdain the big, gaudy birds. But the pheasant has probably made a greater impact upon the average American shotgunner than any other bird anywhere in the world. The reasons are quite simple. It is first of all extremely appealing because of its colors and its regal, almost arrogant, bearing. But the chief impact over a vast expanse of the nation has long been that here is a bird for everybody.

A dogless hunter can successfully walk 'em up. Any hunter anywhere in pheasant range can get a chance at the birds, because this is not a wilderness species but quite literally a bird of settled country, from village edges to the small and large farms and even farmyards. I can remember so well how an uppity old cock used to come into our yard and drive chickens away from their feed until he got his fill. One summer we had thriving tomato vines right up beside the house, and the pesky pheasant would sneak in and decimate them. I taught a few of those a lesson, right out the kitchen window.

So here is a game bird for everybody. It is easily accessible, in most instances requiring no long trip. Thousands of pheasant hunters run out for a quick late-afternoon go at local flocks. But more than that, the average hunter, when he downs a bird or two, really has something very much worthwhile to take home. I happen to be one of those who believe the eating is often as enjoyable as the shooting. A fellow who brings in a brace of roosters has 3 or 4 pounds of dressed meat to put on the table. This has been an important attribute in the making of pheasant popularity.

Without question we'll not see the heyday of the ringneck repeated in this country. Nonetheless, in average seasons nowadays some 10,000,000 birds are collected across the nation. This, of course, does not include the numbers downed at scores of shooting preserves. The pheasant has proved to be a mainstay on all of these. And there is one very important reason why. You can raise pheasant in a pen, but you cannot tame them. Once they're released, although they may not be equipped to sustain themselves, they instantly revert to their inherent wildness.

This, indeed, is what brought the ringneck to fame among sportsmen. It is a bird capable of colonizing the very fringes of settlement, yet it has always adamantly preserved its heritage of wildness—never succumbing, as have many other game birds under similar conditions, to the gentling influence of close proximity to civilization.

QUAIL HUNTING

BY CHARLES F. WATERMAN

THERE are quail that run and refuse to fly. There are quail that hide in trees. There are quail that live to old age because they are protected by rattlesnakes, and there are quail that live amid cactus so menacing that it turns back most hunters. And then there are quail that behave as quail are supposed to—holding tightly for classic pointing dogs, flushing in compact coveys and spreading out as singles to be found and put up at the gunner's leisure. So quail hunters from various parts of the country have plenty to tell each other.

It's pleasant work, but it would take quite a while to sample all kinds of North American quail hunting. There are several species, of course, but much of the variety comes from the types of cover and the methods used.

"Quail" in the East generally means bobwhite, and I suppose that's the most desired of quail species, having adapted to the widest range of terrain and providing the widest variety of shooting. The bobwhite may be no better than a mountain quail or a scaled quail, but it has a greater following—partly because it performs best with pointing dogs and partly because it responds so well to game management. Fat and informative volumes have

38

been written about this one bird, and fortunes are spent in hunting it.

Adaptable? I have hunted southern bobwhites that never seemed to feed more than 50 yards from a swamp no one could hunt in. These are in "one-shot coveys" and go swerving off among the vines and brambles when flushed ahead of dogs—or run into the swamp while the dogs are still working out their route.

I walked up to a north-Florida point one day and missed birds that dived over a bank—and into a heap of old auto bodies where only a ferret could have followed. "That bunch always goes in there," my more expert companion commented.

A dog pointed rather uncertainly on a single I'd marked down, and while I was stamping about, equally uncertainly, my palms sweating in anticipation, the bird whirred out of a tortoise hole behind me, to the glee of a fellow gunner.

I have been forced to give up completely on a bunch that scurried around underneath tall weeds that had been flattened by heavy rain. That was in Kansas, and it did no good for either the dog or me to hear the scurrying progress of birds about our feet. They wouldn't fly.

In New Jersey, Pete McLain, of the ready gun and top-notch pointers, reports covey trails that go into woodchuck holes during a snowy winter. Even during a poor season it is common for flocks to stroll across suburban lawns and feed happily on the shoulders of main highways only a few feet from NO HUNTING signs. Add to these unpredictable performances the fact that quail feed on corn or camphor berries, grasshoppers or ragweed, and "adaptable" takes on special meanings.

It's to the bobwhite's credit that he can be farmed as a crop over most of his range. The big quail plantations of the Southeast are truly bird farms, the crops managed purely to accommodate a saturation population of quail. It is not unusual for field-trial com-

A native American species, the bobwhite quail is one of our "classic" game birds. In the South, where it is at its most numerous, astonishing amounts of time, money, effort and ceremony are put into its pursuit.

petitors to find more than 100 coveys a day in managed quail cover. That's where bobwhite shooting is done in the grand manner, often with rubber-tired shooting wagons (hydraulic brakes) and matched mules while the dogs are handled from Tennessee Walkers. The traditions of bobwhite quail shooting have kept it a sport of wealthy people as well as less affluent gunners, and the bobwhite has had the advantage of more professional management than any other game bird. But then, management works best with the bobwhite.

The Southeast, home of the plantations, is not necessarily the best hunting area for wild birds. Although the populations have their ups and downs, some of the best shooting may be found in Oklahoma, Texas, Missouri, Kansas or Nebraska—or other spots. Transplanting has worked clear up into the Northwest where the Pacific currents keep weather moderate. It's cold weather that establishes the northern boundaries of the range, and the greatest population fluctuations occur along the ragged northern edge.

The traditional method of hunting bobwhites is behind wide-ranging pointers or setters. The farther south you go the greater the percentage of pointers, mainly because of the warmer weather. The fast-going dog's popularity is not necessarily a matter of wide-open country, for the bobwhite is a bird of the edges of fields and forests. Knowing dogs seldom need to hunt out an entire field, but make most of their finds where one kind of cover breaks into another. It's often a matter of birds' using one terrain for feeding and another for escape. Escape cover doesn't necessarily mean a place where the birds live. In fact, some of the "swamp birds" (mistakenly labeled as those that *live* in the dark depths) are just hiding there until danger passes.

The wide-going dogs are used by those who hunt on horseback or with motor vehicles. The "brushpatcher" needs something else —a prober that's highly controllable and that squeezes in where cover is thick while a slow-moving hunter fends off the brambles with a scarred shotgun held uncomfortably at the ready until his arms ache. It's a hard way to hunt, but the very presence of open-country gunners nearby makes it profitable by crowding the birds into thick spots where the wheels won't turn. In these close quarters there's been a need for many of the "foreign" breeds, such as the methodical German shorthair, the cautious Brittany, the

The paramount quail dog in the southeastern states is the pointer. This big, rangy breed's light coat permits it to work in hot weather, and the pointer's tendency to "go big"—cover large amounts of territory—results in efficient bird harvesting.

springer spaniel or even the biddable Labrador. The guns are short and quick, and "choke" is a bad word.

A dog's range is an individual matter, and while there are users of English pointers who have carefully bred for close-working, pedestrian dogs, other experts have speeded up other pointing breeds into what would be called medium range if not wide range. The Brittany is often classified as a plodding old-man's dog, but I visited northern Texas and watched Jim Leverich's field-trial stock sift the hills and draws and came away more certain than ever that range and fire are a property of the individual instead of the breed. It's the same go whether it's an English pointer, Irish setter, Gordon, German shorthair, Weimaraner, vizsla, German wirehair, pointing griffon, English setter or Brittany. Nevertheless, you can get a head start on what you want by getting a breed that seems to fit your picture.

Without a dog? Well, I know very few bobwhite hunters who go for very long without getting one or the use of one, but some learn quail habits accurately enough to do surprisingly well alone. Invariably they hunt in very restricted areas and become acquainted with each individual covey and its habits. Bobwhites do not have a wide range when all is well, and the same coveys are found repeatedly within a 200-yard area if hunting isn't too heavy. People who know an area well and are familiar with local cover can spot the likely places almost instantly. Nevertheless, dogs make hunting more fun, find more birds and are invaluable for locating cripples and dead game. Most quail shooters consider them a necessity.

The bobwhite is a bird of civilization. Chances are there are more bobwhites now than there were when the white man came to America, laid out his little fields and left weedy and brushy fence lines. Still, probably fewer quail exist than there were before farming practices became efficient, resulting in large fields. Housing developments have erased much good quail cover, even though unhunted birds may prosper in the few weed patches that are left. Bobwhites love weed patches.

The basic requirements of quail can be broken down to simple things. Assuming that food is present, the quail also needs some room to walk and run, so the thickest and heaviest grass is out except for emergency shelter. Dense forests that shade out ground

In more recent years, the closer-working breeds have made inroads. Dogs such as German shorthairs and Brittanys (shown here) are becoming highly popular where the hunting is conducted on a smaller scale.

vegetation are no good for bobwhite residence, although the birds
may live along the edges.

The ideal day for quail hunting would be one of moderate temperature for the section you're hunting. If it's extremely cold, birds
don't move enough to put out much scent. If there's a lot of rain,
the scent will be washed away. If it's extremely dry, it's possible
your dog couldn't find a barbecued steak, let alone a few ounces
of hidden bird. Quail generally feed in early morning and again in
midafternoon. They may move very little on cold or wet mornings,
so an early start then won't help. If there's a lot of hunting pressure, they tend to scoot out just before dusk to fill their crops.
Some of my best hunting has been at such times.

The average unbroken bobwhite covey during hunting season
will be something like twelve or fourteen birds, although they may
sound like seventy-five or eighty. The roaring noise they make is
part of their defense and can unnerve predatory foxes as well as
nervous men with shotguns. Generally, though not always, the
resting covey will take off in a fairly tight bunch. This is less helpful than it first appears, because you're going to be shooting at
only one bird (I hope) and the others are simply added distraction. If a covey has flown together and alighted only recently at
the spot where you hope to score, the birds are likely to be a bit
more scattered.

But these covey rises are dependent upon a whole list of factors.
For example, let's say the birds are engaged in feeding and are surprised by a hard-charging dog that skids to a point and has them
glued when you walk up, checking your safety and feeling a little
unsteady in the knees. Now, the dog has arrived so suddenly that
the birds haven't bunched up in alarm but have squatted wherever
they happened to be. Such a rise is likely to be scattered. It's true
that when you kick up part of the bunch the rest will follow
shortly in most cases, but such circumstances make "sleepers"
likely, and you should be ready for a bird that decides to leave
long after the others have been missed.

It's no hard rule, but such a scattered rise is likely to result in
better hunting for singles, the covey sometimes landing all over
the south forty. I have seen a flustered bunch land in a fairly open
field, although heavy thickets were nearby, and they got up one at
a time right under my feet. By the count, I've seen a dog find every

single member of a covey. That doesn't happen often, but it's a dream situation.

In very cold weather bobwhites sometimes retain their "roosting disk" formation for warmth, even during daylight hours. It takes several birds to make the formation, which is a tight circle with the heads facing outward, and the covey of ten or more birds makes it highly protective. It appears about the size of a pie. From that position they take off in a pretty tight wad and can scare the stuffing out of some predators. There are times when you'll come upon quail loafing or dusting in plain sight and they will freeze into immobility at the appearance of a dog.

Although they have the reputation of being "gentlemen" and holding better than most other game, there are plenty of running bobwhites, many of which are never pinned at all. Some veteran dogs (I've seen a few) will deliberately circle the travelers and point from directly in their path. This usually stops the birds, and they're likely to hold. It's much more common for a dog to follow, alternately pointing and moving, while the quail go on ahead and eventually elude him. I don't know how far quail will hurry ahead of a dog, but I think a couple of hundred yards is a long run. Usually they either come to a spot where they feel flying is safer or get into something so thick they can stop and rest. Sometimes they scatter.

Don't believe that a single won't run. In Florida I once noted my dog was birdy, and I happened to see a single scooting across an open place ahead of him. It was on the border of an orange grove, and the quail started legging it down a row of trees just as I lost sight of him. The dog followed by scent, but as we neared the opposite side of the big grove I assumed we'd lost our prey, especially since a main highway ran along that side of the trees. I called in the dog to keep him off the road, but as he came in I saw our single flush from the fence line and sail over a speeding trailer truck to disappear on the other side. Incidentally, there was a small town on that side. He just didn't know all the rules.

I think heredity has a short-term role in quail behavior. It can be simply a matter of the flying birds' being eaten and the running birds' getting away. This may or may not be a matter of evolution. I suppose that if you stopped gunning in a given area, the running habit might disappear. I do know that many old-timers talk about "swamp quail," which are supposed to be larger and smarter than the others and insist on running instead of flying. There is much talk of "Mexican quail," supposedly more addicted to running. It's true that Mexican bobwhites have been introduced into the United States from time to time, but biologists tend to discount the running theory.

When it comes to the shooting part, bobwhites can best be described as easy marks that are hard to hit. Although he flies with moderate speed compared with some other game and holds pretty much to a straight line, the bobwhite has a lot of psychology going for him.

To begin with, a flush is likely to be the result of a dog's point, and the shooter may have had considerable time to figure out ways of missing as he walks up. If he's riding in a jeep or wagon or on a horse, the tension has that much more time to build for jumpy guys. This is a little different from the constant preparedness of other kinds of hunting; it all seems to come in a bunch.

The way to walk up to a dog in bobwhite country is to note where he's facing, assume the birds are probably near there, take a good look at the surroundings to figure about where the birds will be going and then check the locations of other hunters for safety's sake. I'd rather not have more than two shooters walking up to a point, and I feel much better when I do it alone—unless others are observing critically from a distance.

Now that you have the lay of the land, you walk up promptly; don't sneak up, because it's hard on the dogs and may cause birds to run. Don't run up, because any but a staunch dog will come apart and you'll be in no mental state or physical position to shoot. Just walk up promptly, and if they don't fly start moving around in the cover in the logical area. Many greenhorn hunters, and some not so green, go more and more slowly as they approach the birds and may come to a complete stop, hoping to be in a perfect shooting position. Don't worry about being ready to shoot. There'll be time. Focus your eyes a little above the ground and about 10 yards out. If you try to see the birds before they fly or just as they jump, you're asking for trouble.

Most of the good shooters I have watched carry their guns in approximately the port-arms position as they walk up. Now to touch upon the delicate matter of the safety: I see no reason for it

When walking up on a bird, most shooters carry their guns at approximately a "port-arms" position, keeping their eye on the spot where they expect the bird to appear.

to be pushed off until the birds actually fly, although many good shots take it off early. I've always contended that anyone who is familiar enough with his shotgun to go hunting with it should know it well enough to get the safety off as it comes up to his shoulder without extending his reaction time.

Okay, if it's a covey rise, you're supposed to pick a single bird and forget the rest until that bird is down or has disappeared. A lot of flock shooting is done at bobwhites, because they are small, sometimes go up close together and make considerable noise, but the idea is to select one bird and shoot it. If you happen to get another with the same shot it's because they just happened to be near each other, although some experts carefully select two birds close together and then shoot at one of them. Flock shooting at the whole bunch doesn't often work. If the main bunch distracts you, shoot at an individual on the flock's edge.

On any rise within 10 yards of your feet you should have time for two well-pointed shots unless the cover is thick, and whatever else an expert bobwhite shot may have going for him, he's nearly always a master of timing. Any birds that fly nearly straight away fall at about the same distance, time after time. He couldn't tell you just what it is, but it's likely to be around 20 yards for the first bird. A second one from the same flush is likely to be a little farther away, but not much, simply because the hunter tries to get one of the first birds out and then takes a second shot at one near the rear of the bunch.

Next to flock shooting, indecision is the cardinal sin. Walk in and the birds get up a little scattered. You have your eye on the first ones, but as you get the gun up (it feels as if it's swinging in molasses) you see a late riser right in front of your nose and appearing roughly the size of a condor. This, you decide, is the bird you'll kill before shooting all of the rest, so you miss it at roughly 6 yards. Then, likely as not, you'll give it the other barrel in the same place and stand there with an empty gun with all of the covey still within range and seeming to move in slow motion now that you have no more shells to fire. Some might say that the solution is a repeater instead of a double, so that you could still be shooting instead of watching, but that doesn't work, because a wild man with a lot of shells misses worse than a wild man with only a few shells.

Now, I don't always foul up quite that badly. I have even been known to double on occasion—but those are the times when I force myself to maintain some semblance of timing, generally with an early bird and a late bird. Most experts kill quail within 25 yards most of the time, and very few fall at more than 35 yards. Most beginners shoot too fast, especially with their first shell. Some of them are so amazed at their first miss that they then take careful aim with the second shot and wait too long.

In normal bobwhite rises there is time for two well-pointed shots and possibly three. Although I use side-by-sides and over/unders, simply because I seem to shoot better with them, I can see merit in the repeater, especially on sleepers and cripples. We'll get into guns a little later.

Experienced shots drop their birds at 25 to 35 yards. Snap shooting is a losing proposition, since most hurried shots are missed, and a hit at short range can ruin a quail for the table.

Part of relaxed shooting is being faced pretty much in the direction in which you're going to shoot. One of the common errors is to
walk around to a spot between the birds and obvious cover with
the intention of heading them off. This is especially unnerving if
the point has been made within 30 yards of heavy cover on one
side and far from concealment on the other. Since the quail are almost certain to fly into the heavy cover, your best bet is to come in
so that they will fly nearly straight away. If you walk halfway between them and the brush, you may be entertained by a swarm of
roaring missiles coming right at your head, too close to shoot at
(although you probably will). By the time you turn and take
them going away, your nerves and marksmanship are gone.

Quail often fly very close to shooters, and the most common
fault is blazing away at close incomers instead of turning and
shooting coolly as they go away. In brush shooting, this mistake is
easier to make than you might think. Incidentally, if things are
thick, quail are apt to fly for patches of daylight, and you can take
that into consideration when walking up to dogs.

All of this would indicate that they are difficult targets, but I
don't think so. Some old quail poppers who are mediocre dove or
duck shots can run up surprising strings on bobwhites. This is the
story: If you can whip the psychological problems, the actual
shooting isn't very hard. They go pretty straight, they don't go
very fast and they aren't very far away.

At any time when I kill a few quail and begin to think I know
what I'm doing, I am immediately humbled by the recollection of
the one I missed four times in succession in an open field. I guess
the bird was confused, for it headed straight away from a patch of
timber while the rest of the covey dived in. It looked so easy that
I missed it with a quick shot (having the other birds in mind, I
guess) and then steadied down and missed it a second time after
waiting until it was out of good range—but the bird evidently
found it had flown in the wrong direction and turned around to
fly right back toward me. After reloading, I missed it two more
times and went home for the day.

Now as to bobwhite guns:

The common and oversimplified description is short, light, fast
and open-bored. And you may read uncompromising statements
that the 12-gauge is too large and that the 20-gauge is the only

sportsmanlike answer. You may hear that real deadeyes turn to .410s to make it more challenging.

I want to dispose of the .410 first. It is not enough quail gun for most of us. A .410 simply does not throw enough pellets for long shots unless it is tightly bored, and if it's choked down the pattern is too small for average gunners. It is a bore size only for a master shooter who judges ranges meticulously and never gets overeager or sloppy. Otherwise, it is a crippler.

The 28 is an expert's gun, but with the heaviest loads in careful hands it's adequate for bobwhites. The 20, 16 and 12 are fine with appropriate loads, and I don't think there's a problem of sportsmanship, which is a property of shooters and not shotguns. Go to a 12 and you may lose a little speed of handling while you gain in power. Perhaps the most popular quail load of all is 1⅛ ounces of No. 8s in a 12-gauge. I think a 20 should carry at least an ounce of shot, and that goes for any quail gun that is capable of handling that much. Most of the guns are open-bored, and the birds are small. A patterning board will show that there are bad holes in most patterns out past 30 yards, and few are the gunners who can resist an occasional long poke.

I believe weight, within reason, is less important than balance. A quick, lively shotgun with the weight mostly between the hands and back of them—call that "muzzle-light" if you prefer—can weigh more than 7 pounds and still be a good quail gun. There are true featherweight guns preferred by extremists, but personally, I have always felt I shot better with a gun of about 6 pounds, although I've been happy with doubles as light as 5¼ pounds and as heavy as 7¼. Most repeaters feel too long for me, sticking out a couple of inches more than side-by-sides and over/unders of the same barrel length.

Although skeet guns tend to be a bit heavy for upland hunting, many of them are used by quail shooters, and skeet boring is fine in the larger gauges. I once used a 20-gauge skeet gun for a while and decided it was a little too open for me, so I traded it for a gun bored improved-cylinder and modified. A very good compromise, although not common in field guns, is skeet and improved-cylinder. That's close to what's known as skeet one and skeet two.

In repeaters not using adjustable chokes, I believe improved-cylinder is a pretty happy medium, although plenty of modified barrels are in use. There's no doubt about a need for the maximum of scatter in real brush shooting, and one of the best brushpatchers I know uses a 12-gauge riot gun (no choke) with 1¼ ounces of No. 9s. He doesn't mutilate his birds, and he doesn't miss too many. In his kind of cover you need all the help you can get.

There's an old rule of using 9s or 8s for early-season birds and going to 7½ shot or 6s later on, when the birds are wilder and have heavier feathers. That rule doesn't consider the chokes, though, and I have a dim view of large shot in skeet borings. It's simply a matter of the shot's being too scarce out at the ranges where big pellets are of any use. Shoot 9s or 8s in a skeet or cylinder boring. If you have a modified barrel you can make good use of 7½s. And the lighter the load, the smaller the shot should be in most cases. An ounce of 6s or 7½s is a little skimpy unless the choke is modified or tighter. These are things you don't have to take my word for. Just tack up a paper and do some shooting at quail ranges.

If you shoot a side-by-side or over/under with two chokes, double triggers have much merit, but they're becoming less and less popular. There are a few single-trigger barrel selectors that can be switched quickly to the tight barrel, and although this sounds like a good idea, not many gunners actually change once the birds are in the air.

Anytime there's talk of southern quail there's the bugaboo of snakes, and the big diamondback rattlesnake kills some fine dogs in southern Florida. Having hunted in the South and talked to many dog men, I think I can come close to breaking down the geography. In northern Florida—the part above the peninsula—and in other southern states, snakes present little danger except on especially warm days. It's different in the southern part of Florida, where a big snake can be active on almost any day of the year. Hunters there generally operate only on the cooler days.

No doubt a dog running downwind can land on a snake by chance. Some dogs never learn to stay away from snakes, and they usually don't live long where rattlesnakes are active.

Certain types of terrain attract snakes, and anyone hunting dangerous country in hot weather should inquire of old-timers as to just where the hot spots are. Rattlesnake danger isn't confined to the South, of course, when the weather is unseasonably warm. Dogs can be snakebitten clear up into Canada during early bird seasons. Last fall I shot a rattler under a dog's nose in Montana. Four years ago I set a long-jump record when I found a lively one under my feet in Alberta. Generally these northern snakes are not as large, and the weather is generally a bit cool for them to be at top efficiency.

Not many shooters wear snakeproof boots or leggings except in Florida. Down there you'll shoot better and walk happier if you know you have some protection.

The commercial game preserve is already important in bobwhite hunting and may increase in prominence as time goes on and public lands become scarcer. A game preserve can range from a sort of shooting gallery for barnyard fowl to a setup that very closely approaches wild gunning. Perhaps the finest compliment a game preserve can earn is for you not to be sure whether you're shooting pen birds or wild birds, but there's usually considerable difference.

I think the bobwhite is the best game-preserve bird of all. If properly handled, pen-raised birds can stay fairly wild. The problem is that raising them under such conditions is expensive, and the cost is passed on by the preserve operator, who must charge higher prices to his clients. The lowest-priced preserve isn't necessarily a bargain, and the setups should be studied before you draw conclusions.

Preserve shooting is the cheapest for most gunners in the long run. A good preserve furnishes dogs, handlers and vehicles, and probably food and lodging. If a man hunts no more than ten days a year, his expenses can easily run to more than $100 a day if he maintains his own dogs and hunting vehicle. Spend a similar amount at a preserve and you can get plenty of birds without the fuss and worry. But then, maybe the fuss and worry of getting an outfit together and finding a place to hunt are part of your fun.

Most preserve hunting is a put-and-take proposition, and the pen-raised birds do little to bolster the count of native quail. Most preserves are stocked heavily just before the hunters arrive, and where birds are expected to last for a while there are feeders to keep them in the proper areas. Sometimes caged call birds are

used to decoy them. If this sounds a little too artificial, be sure to
count your expended shells at a good preserve before passing final
judgment. Unless you're a mighty good shot, there'll have been
some misses.

Except as a means of supplying birds for new introductions
(many of which have been successful) and for helping out where
high mortality has taken a toll from natural causes, the big gov-
ernment quail hatcheries have been expensive failures. That's
been known for many years by biologists, but it's taken a long
period of public education to do away with them as large-scale
operations. A new pair of quail in a spot noted for lack of birds
won't mean a population boom, and the bobwhite generally regu-
lates his own numbers. Certain spots have held coveys for human
generations. In good years extra bunches may be on the periphery
of these ranges. In bad years there may be only a single small
covey, but we can't gain much by turning out new, pen-raised
birds to compete for food. Improving habitat is something else, of
course. That's the key to bobwhite plenitude, as it is with other
game. A good thing about bobwhites is that they can go from
scarcity to plenty in a year or two.

Quail vary in color and size in different sections of the country,
the southern birds being consistently lighter in weight than those
farther north. This seems to be a matter of climate and forage
rather than heredity, and the same kind of size variation is found
in other birds and animals. The fact is, the very largest bobwhites
are found near the northern edge of the range, where populations
fluctuate greatly with the weather. Since the birds seem to be
adapted to their ranges, there doesn't seem to be much point in
shuffling them around except where brand-new populations are
desired in quail-less areas or where local birds have suffered severe
setbacks.

I haven't found that bobwhite hunters are particularly eager to
go after the western quail. Most of them figure they have the best
bird of the bunch and are not inclined to look for something new.
It's true the bobwhite has the reputation of being the best "dog
quail," but some of the western quail are very exciting game. Some
hunters like them better, and the persistent stories that you can't
use a dog on western species are completely false. I'll admit that

most of the Westerners run a lot and could be hard on a dog's character, especially if he's used to quail that don't come unstuck until kicked up.

No treatise on American quail should skip the harlequin, or Mearns, quail found down along the Mexican border and farther south. It doesn't look like a bobwhite and has very different feeding habits, but I can find no difference at all in hunting methods. A bobwhite dog should feel right at home, and the harlequin holds well; some say it holds too well, but it'll take a hike now and then, with the dog close behind.

It's easy to lump the Mearns with "desert quail," because they are both found along the border in Arizona, New Mexico and western Texas; but although the Mearns lives near true desert, it is found at higher altitudes, where the vegetation is grassy uplands and often oak ridges. In that country, you find a little colony of hunters who look and act a lot like bobwhiters. You don't hear very much about them; their hunting grounds are extremely limited and couldn't stand heavy pressure.

Since they hold unusually tightly, Mearns quail have been called "fool quail" for the very reasons that have made bobwhites famous as "gentlemen." The first harlequins I ever saw were within a few steps of a southern-Arizona hunting camp we'd set up for them, and I immediately decided it was going to be too easy to be fun. I'd turned a dog out for a little exercise, and he pointed a small covey in a little rock outcropping amid heavy grass and a few scattered oaks. I hadn't even taken my gun with me, and I watched them fly off with clinical interest. The next day, I thought, we'd really have them cold, but it didn't work out that way. Using an Arizona Brittany with a reputation for harlequin efficiency, we scoured the shallow draws and heavily grassed ridges, but never had a shot all morning. I *did* hear some birds fly and once saw a gaudy little rascal sneaking between grass clumps while the cautious dog worked close behind him and pointed at intervals. That one went out behind us somewhere. When we met some other hunters with several birds, we learned that it was a poor season in that particular spot, and a local expert offered to take us to a better place, almost within rifle range of the Mexican border.

The harlequin leaves considerable sign, since much of its food consists of bulbs and tubers and it scratches deep grooves with its long claws. Down there against Mexico we quickly found sign, but when our dog finally pinned some birds, we had to look for him in hip-high grass along a ridge. When they flew, the birds buzzed downhill into the oaks. After I had killed a couple and was feeling cocky about the whole operation, I got hasty on my second chance, scoring a perfect Dutch double and watching the covey buzz into the trees, still within good range. They scattered in a draw, and down there cooler heads prevailed. It turned into a wonderful day. However, I hope you won't hunt harlequins too hard. There aren't that many. Theirs is a beautiful country on the shoulders of highlands that bulge out of the desert, often within sight of snow patches on even higher slopes.

There's another quail that once disappeared from our southern border and may be making a comeback with careful reintroduction. That's the masked bobwhite, a bird with bobwhite habits and outline that seemed to be extinct at one time but was rediscovered through careful scientific sleuthing south of the border. The masked bobwhite has a smoky-dark head, but looks like our old friend in other respects.

Then there are true desert quail. The Gambel quail, wearing a perky topknot, lives in the true desert of the Southwest, a land of temperature extremes and giant cactus. Hunting him is another ball game, because he is a runner. Many gunners feel a dog is out of place in his habitat and will say the only way to score is to outrun the bird on the ground, make him fly and nail him with a

Hunting Gambel and scaled quail in the southwestern deserts is an especially tough proposition. In addition to coping with the heat, both man and dog have to learn to steer clear of cactus, which is everywhere.

tightly choked gun. It's not unusual to see Gambels scooting along through the open spaces up ahead. I simply don't agree about the no-dog concept, however. Granted, hunting is often fine with no dog at all, but there are times when dogs can make your day.

Vegetation of the desert country sticks, tears and clutches, but the very nature of the land means considerable distance between large plants, and a smart canine can work through these avenues, a procedure he must learn. It's surprising how quickly a dog can learn to avoid most of the spears and stickers, just as his master learns. At first you wonder how it's possible to walk through that stuff without becoming a pincushion, but you'll do it.

I don't know if *all* dogs can learn to operate in the desert. I'm sure that any of them will collect thorns now and then, but I have watched one learn to handle himself within a few hours, despite some early defeats in cholla balls. I think it's a poor place for a wide ranger, because you'll want to check your dog constantly. At regular intervals you should go over him to make sure he hasn't collected something bent on impaling him; but if he'll be reasonable, he can make it.

The Gambel covey usually flushes wild the first time up. That's no hard-and-fast rule, but I have had few shots on the first rise. After that the drill is to mark them down and then use your dog, for they tend to scatter, and the singles may hold tightly. I'll admit that only a small percent of a large covey will give you shots, but you'll nearly aways find a few. Steve Gallizioli of the Arizona Game and Fish Department took me and Bill Browning of Montana on our first Gambel expedition and seemed to have the Gambel itinerary memorized. The first bunch went over a ridge and out of sight, but Steve simply walked up on top, pointed to a draw where brush was a little thicker than elsewhere and announced they'd probably be there. They were—widely scattered, to be sure, but available to our dogs. In that case I doubt if we'd have had a shot without dog help.

The Gambel may fly as fast as the bobwhite, but he gives the impression of being slower—partly because of what seems to be a slower wingbeat and partly because of a longer tail and less noise as he goes. Gambels sometimes make up very large coveys. Since the first rise is likely to be out of range, there's a premium on marking them down. Although they may first take off from a ravine, it's good to have one hunter on a ridge as a spotter, even as another stumbles through the lower brush. Maybe a dog will do the low-level work.

Desert air is likely to be so dry that scenting isn't good. All of us have experienced upland days when dogs seemed to have stoppers in their nostrils, usually during hot, dry weather. On one afternoon after Gambels I could have sworn my dog had lost any nose he'd ever had, but a more experienced one wasn't doing much either. My dog had birds getting up behind him and couldn't tell a dead one from a cholla ball that afternoon, but he'd done pretty well until about 11 o'clock, and I think the desert air had dried out the scent. It had become pretty hot after a crisp morning.

I doubt if the Gambel is in much danger from overhunting in his more hostile habitats. Saguaro cactus, cholla balls (I don't know how many kinds there are) and prickly-pear don't encourage casual gunners.

The scaled quail, or blue quail, called cottontops in the Southwest, often live alongside the Gambel bird, but they go farther north and into plains country that can't be termed desert at all. They run more and seem to fly higher. I never noticed the latter characteristic until Gallizioli pointed it out. Where I've hunted them they were harder to pin than Gambel quail. Athletic gunners run them up afoot, and quite a few scalies are shot on the ground. When you see a bunch moving ahead of you, it is possible to follow while they peel off until none are left. Retrace your steps and you may be able to do well with singles.

The cottontop has a reputation for preferring thin vegetation, the better to do his running act. In some places birds of this species like to live around abandoned farm buildings. Their range extends well up through the Central Plains, spreading to cover most of our side of the Mexican border. They eat many more insects than do other species. Like any dry-land quail, they're most likely to be found in the neighborhood of waterholes, even if they can subsist without a drink.

Except for the harlequins, these dry-country birds are shot at a wide variety of ranges, certainly tending to longer distances than the bobwhite. Thinking of this, I have a short 12-gauge double bored improved-cylinder and full with two triggers. The idea is that I can select the barrel after the birds are in the air. That

Valley, or California, quail are residents of the grassy slopes. At one time they congregated in huge flocks, but years of hunting have brought a halt to this habit.

choke combination isn't common in off-the-shelf guns. Although some very good shots prefer full-choked models for quail of the wide-open places, I think most of us would do better with modified in a repeater and improved-cylinder and modified in a two-piper. There are some close-range shots with any of these birds, and only the more accurate gunners can take full advantage of a really tight choke.

I believe a 20 is as small as you should go for desert birds, and I think anything less than 1⅛ ounces of shot is cutting it pretty fine. I've used 7½s more than anything else. In my experience, the careful timing of the bobwhite marksmanship doesn't work out West, as rises are so unpredictable, especially if the game has been worked over pretty thoroughly.

The names "valley quail" and "California quail" are freely applied to the same bird. Plenty of these quail are still around, although they aren't in the multiple thousands that were market-hunted around waterholes nearly a century ago. They've been the most puzzling game of the whole tribe as far as I'm concerned.

Valley quail sometimes form huge flocks, but when guns and dogs arrive they can follow a policy of every bird for itself. Those that take off and go like hell (and they certainly can) present good targets. The ones that hop around on the ground, cling obstinately to the lower branches of sage bushes or run around on tree limbs are the ones that fluster me.

When they're in good cover, they're reluctant to leave. I had a good bunch in a brushy creek bottom once and kept chasing them back and forth for two hours in a 300-yard area. Each time I'd find fewer birds, and finally they'd all disappeared. Where had they gone? Well, not very far. Some of them had simply settled high off the ground in streamside trees, some had flown or walked out to the surrounding sage and rock slopes and it may be some were on the ground in the creek bottom and had been missed, for one reason or another, by the dogs. The general rule is to go to the heavier cover, but on some days they'll scatter into open country.

I recall the time I was about to give up on a female pointing dog that refused to bust brush along with a more energetic hunter. While the good one scoured a brushy draw with a tiny creek at its bottom, the loafer slouched along the hillsides, where sage was dwarfed and cover skimpy. Finally, she stopped, apparently in boredom; but when she didn't move on, I went over there—and you know the rest. The little rascals were all over the hillside. I don't think they were feeding. I think we had moved them out of the draw. I've caught valley quail in this act on other occasions, and I've known mountain quail to do the same thing.

Mountain quail are the biggest of American quail and are found in the Pacific Coast states and inland through part of the Northwest, where many casual observers simply lump them together with the valley birds. Sometimes they're found in the same cover, but they're a different species, with a long streamer for a headpiece instead of a perky topknot. They aren't found in large coveys, and they tend to migrate to lower elevations when the snows are heavy.

When you follow mountain quail into thick brush, you'll often have trouble making them fly. They can travel at amazing speed with only short flights of a few feet, using windfalls and low branches to run on. Like the valley birds, they can be hard to flush out of a tree, and a man throwing sticks or stones at a spooky bird on a high branch is seldom in position for accurate shooting. When found on steep hillsides they tend to fly downward like other upland birds, and if you can get them coming out of a very steep and very narrow mountainside gulley you can have some open shooting. It happens.

One little bunch of mountaineers fooled me not once but three times, and I never got a shot. On each occasion I sighted them just off a jeep trail. I'd kick out my dog, grab my gun and shells and hurry after them. It was on a nearly barren hillside with only a narrow ditch, perhaps 20 feet across, with a few bushes. Twice I saw them running up ahead, only to disappear, and once I heard them fly out behind us. I haven't drawn a bead on one of them yet.

But that's why I go quail hunting.

WOODCOCK HUNTING

BY GEORGE BIRD EVANS

AGAINST the light of the window at my elbow, a beauty of an aquamarine pressed-glass bottle (of the type known as a "chestnut flask") displays an early-nineteenth-century gunner with a plump game bag shooting one of a brace of woodcock flushed in front of a bird dog who appears to be breaking shot. If this flask, which came from Vermont, held old brandy it couldn't warm me more than the design pressed into its glass—the two woodcock, the dog, the flintlock fowling piece and the man shooting by the limitation of the single-barreled muzzle-loader only one bird from a flushed brace (something I usually do by choice).

Woodcock go back as far as retrievable time in gun diaries, and prints show English sport with the European relative of our bird shot over spaniels. Lithographs depict velveteened and bearded gunners dropping woodcock over braces of American native setters, or setters in mixed brace with bulging-eyed pointers, in an unlikely Adirondack kind of setting; but who am I to question Arthur Tait and Messrs. Currier & Ives? Ours to reason that "in those days" things were that way.

Shooting reports indicate that woodcock became extremely scarce in the late 1800s and the early part of this century. In 1918,

61

rigid bag and season restrictions brought woodcock back in a way that leaves little doubt that overshooting, especially by market hunters, had been responsible for the decline, considering that weather factors cannot be legislated. Woodcock today are flighting in numbers that are bountiful enough to furnish grand sport for the select group of gunners who hold them in esteem. The annual bag of woodcock in terms of wings sent to the Patuxent Wildlife Research Center may reflect higher kills rather than higher woodcock populations, or it may reflect the increasing number of gunners shooting 'cock, but the study is important research for woodcock management.

Most woodcock enthusiasts live a gunner's dichotomy, having equal involvement with ruffed grouse; but there is an elite coterie of woodcock purists—men who commit their bird-shooting year to the short season during which this lovely small game bird moves south along the eastern portion of the country in fall migration. I had a friend who expressed the urge to start in the South and move north with the strawberry season with a good Jersey cow. I have fondly considered beginning in New Brunswick with a brace of good 'cock dogs and following the woodcock south through the open seasons, but I know this would pall. With the wealth of dog and gun action in a good woodcock year, I have all the 'cock shooting I care to do by the time hard freezes arrive and send the birds from my coverts, though the end of each season never fails to move me with the old yearning. But the fleeting charm that makes autumn precious—"the glory of flame in the glory of embers"—lies in each day of woodcock gunning to be lived to fullest savor.

As the bobwhite belongs to Dixie, the woodcock is a Yankee bird, a special property of New England gunners. This is a generous concession on the part of a man who shoots most of his woodcock just below the Mason-Dixon Line. It is true that woodcock are shot in Louisiana, and during the past fifteen years, because of decreasing numbers of grouse, a growing number of gunners in the Alleghenies have been turning to woodcock for exciting shooting. There have been generations of woodcock gunners in New York, New Jersey and Pennsylvania, but when you "go for woodcock" you go to New Brunswick, Nova Scotia or New England—particularly to Maine.

Among my shooting friends I have the *compleat* woodcock fowler—a Vermonter who guns exclusively for 'cock. He shoots mostly in Maine and New Brunswick over an eleven-year-old setter bitch. Chatting here before the fire, he mentioned decisions he and his companions face on their trips to northern woodcock range—whether to go while native 'cock are there, when you can be sure of birds but must deal with flies, hot weather and heavy foliage (difficult for shooting and observing the action of a young dog) or to wait for the flights with cooler weather and thinned foliage but be subject to change in weather that may push the flight birds through so rapidly the shooting will be over in a few days.

I may not be blessed with woodcock in the numbers encountered in the northern ranges, but I am within two hours' driving of my top coverts and am in touch with developments, taking a cabin and staying over when the flights are in. Any gunner may experience woodcock hustled out of his coverts by rough weather, but we, farther south, have flights coming over for a more extended period than men shooting in the higher latitudes nearer the "starting point."

However, I'm not certain all that phoning ahead and consultations to preguess flight patterns by the full moon and weather forecasts isn't part of what woodcock gunners enjoy—the imponderables of the sport. I used to have an old colleague in West Virginia's high woodcock terrain whose communiqués were helpful and succinct: *You had better come up the woodcock are on the move.*

We all like to feel we know when we are gunning flight birds. To oversimplify, if you gun far enough north, all woodcock are "natives," there being no migration from farther north. Conversely, in the extreme southerly wintering grounds all birds might be considered "flight birds" or they wouldn't have reached there. But woodcock chicks have been seen in Louisiana, posing the question as to where else these Louisiana "natives" go in spring migration, banding records having pretty well established that woodcock return to breed in almost the exact covert where they were hatched.

Wintering woodcock concentrate in Louisiana, Mississippi and to some extent Florida. Yet comparatively few are shot in marginal areas of this range. My friend John P. Bailey, whose Quail Hills Plantation is in northern Mississippi, has kept an accurate gun diary for years. He writes:

"We hunters in northern Mississippi never go woodcock hunting. There just are not enough of them. For the past fifty-one years I have hunted quail about fifty days per year and some years I don't see a woodcock. In all that time I have killed an average of only three a year. One February my dog pointed a woodcock and when it fluttered off the ground I saw four eggs. Another time in March I saw a woodcock with four young ones. These are rare instances."

During the past two years, concentrations of woodcock have been reported in Georgia, with recommendations that gunners should go there for exceptional sport, much as 'cock are taken in large numbers in parts of Louisiana. I am of a turn of mind that doesn't relish shooting for ease of shots among enormous numbers of birds, but instead likes sporting handicaps. I love to strike a flight of 'cock, moving perhaps two dozen in a few hours, but to have this be a common experience would take away from my pleasure. The mere fact of woodcock's wintering in an area is not reason to send gunners scurrying there to kill them under easy conditions. It would be equally feasible to gun the nesting grounds in New Brunswick, or to reopen spring-migration shooting (closed in 1918). Game management should not consist of offering birds to be shot simply because they are present. Instead of subjecting wintering woodcock to shooting, it should give the birds more than normal protection during such concentrations.

In the thirty-four years I've lived at Old Hemlock, I have not seen one young woodcock here in the mountains of extreme northern West Virginia. Two years ago we found one woodcock egg, grayish tan with brown splotches, nearly as large as a grouse egg but more pointed at one end. William Sheldon mentions that woodcock eggs are split lengthwise when hatched, unlike the eggs of other species. Breeding woodcock described to me in this area usually turn out to be singing males passing through in spring migration. The breeding woodcock populations in West Virginia are found in the higher elevations.

Banding records indicate three major migratory routes, with 'cock from New Brunswick, Nova Scotia and New England generally following the Atlantic route along the eastern coast, those from the St. Lawrence and Great Lakes following the Central route and those from Minnesota and Wisconsin following the Western route due south to Mississippi and Louisiana. There are crossovers, such as my woodcock, which move southwest along the ridges of the Appalachians, and some Atlantic Flyway birds that cross northern Pennsylvania to the Central route.

In my home coverts, which can be ignored as breeding areas, I occasionally see dribblings of fall migrants as early as late September. When these "outriders" turn up early, it indicates earlier-than-normal flights to come. When they appear in conspicuous numbers, woodcock can be found in unusual areas such as the lowlands to the west of our mountains.

Flight birds, especially during early flights, are often found in cover natives do not appear to use; late flights frequently follow river valleys. Throughout the flights, 'cock may be found in numbers in some coverts and be almost nonexistent nearby—characteristic of the spotty manner in which they travel. There is a tendency to think of woodcock as departing from their native areas as a group, remaining together along the migratory route south. Actually, they fly as individuals, dropping in singly where cover attracts them. That others have been attracted to the same covert does not mean they have been together before. Birds that shared a covert in Pennsylvania may select different portions of the Canaan Valley to stop in the following week, grouping with new birds at each stopover. Flights are obvious, with a sudden appearance of 'cock in coverts that held only a few or even none earlier in the season. Late flights seem to tarry a shorter time at stopovers.

In well-known woodcock areas where hunters concentrate, it is possible to misjudge a covert as blank or to think the flight has moved on if one or two good areas prove empty. This is sometimes the result of a party of gunners having worked it too hard just ahead of you—not necessarily having killed all the birds, but having pushed them into recesses such as dense thickets of spirea (hardhack) where they cannot be reached. You may find them back in normal cover after a day's rest. One of the disadvantages of gunning famous woodcock terrain is that its reputation attracts too many gunners who either pound the coverts and the birds too steadily or by their presence get into each other's way. A remote, lightly gunned area can make up for perhaps fewer birds by the pleasure of privacy. Some hunters enjoy noise and confusion; I do not, and most dogs share my view.

Banding returns have shown that native woodcock are sometimes shot in their home coverts after most of the flights have passed through, indicating that the birds do not move out simultaneously and emphasizing the woodcock's individual behavior.

Clear nights and cold weather to the north combined with favorable winds will bring the birds south like Gypsies. The length of time a covert will hold flight birds is unpredictable. Fine weather seems to entice them to linger, but, like opinions as to what kind of cover at which time of day, no rule is infallible. Warm, pleasant days after a rain make for almost perfect 'cock shooting during the flights; I have done well with a light snow clinging to thickets but with sun and blue sky. Shooting in a fog that verges on a drizzle can be equally fine, though not so comfortable. Every season I have great shooting in the Canaan Valley on "Canaan days"—wet, with fog like white smoke obscuring the surrounding mountains halfway down their slopes.

Strong winds are generally considered adverse, but last season on October 17, sunny and almost cold with a wind that took my cap off, Kay and I put my dog Briar out of the station wagon and he immediately pointed a group of four 'cock, then a single, and a group of five in twenty minutes and within 100 yards.

During wet periods the birds are inclined to scatter, but a prolonged dry spell will concentrate them in damp lowlands or thickets dense enough to keep the soil moist. In 1965 even the bottomlands in my coverts were baked hard, and the dried cowpats gave off a smell like that of tobacco. Woodcock seemed almost nonexistent until I ran into them by chance while looking for grouse on the Dolly Sods, nearly 1,000 feet higher than the Canaan Valley, where frequent fogs had kept the soil moist in spite of the long drought. The 'cock were there; so were Kay and I with three setters, Shadows, Dixie and Bliss, and in that isolated piece of misplaced Canadian terrain everything was beautiful in a way that only a woodcock gunner can know.

The notion that you can distinguish a flight bird from a native by size or marking, other than to identify sex and age, is, I think, false. All woodcock are natives before they begin their fall migration, flight birds after they start. A sudden appearance of 'cock in large numbers usually indicates flight birds. Concentrations of natives before they start south can be misleading, but in a sense even these are flight birds. My gun diary shows that when obvious flights have begun I usually shoot more hens in the first flights, having taken a relatively even mix of hens and males from birds that, judging by time and cover, were natives. During the end of the flights my woodcock are predominantly males. Bill Goudy, supervisor of woodcock research in West Virginia and formerly with the Patuxent Wildlife Research Center, tells me that immatures migrate south before adults, adding another possible clue as to flight birds.

Sex can be determined by size: the large woodcock are females with mandibles about ¼ inch longer than those of the males, wider wingspread and greater bulk evident in the hand and in flight. The outer three flight feathers on the female are wider than those of the male, with a more concave curve on the trailing edge.

Age is determined by the tip marking on the outer five secondaries: a buff tip with a sharply contrasted dark subterminal band indicates a yearling; a tip blending in a cloudy or smoky edge, usually lacking the dark band, is an adult. A yearling female quite often has a slightly shorter mandible than an adult female, but still longer than an adult male's. I seem to shoot more yearlings than adult males, bearing out the contention that adult males are a bit more elusive than adult females and yearlings. Much more so than with grouse, it is difficult to accurately count woodcock, replacement by flight birds and the greater number of flushes making it nearly impossible to distinguish between separate woodcock and reflushes.

Making a technical thing of your observations can detract from the color of 'cock shooting, but I think it worthwhile to examine your bird to see if it is a hen or a male, yearling or adult, as part of admiring it, just as I like to hang my birds for a day or two at home for the pleasure of looking at them as well as to enhance their flavor. Woodcock are too gamy for some people to enjoy—a pity. This may come from preparation of the bird too soon after shooting (I can't imagine eating them the same day). Another cause of strong game flavor in 'cock is rooted in the traditional insistence upon plucking the bird instead of skinning it. Game flavor in any bird is concentrated in fat deposits, some of which remain under the skin when the bird is plucked. Skinning 'cock and removing all visible fat not only does away with undesirable strong flavor but removes any residual pesticides that are retained in the fat and organs of birds, places where they occur. The pesticide scare has quieted, with restrictions on use of the chemicals, but it is not absent. Pesticides do not appear to have affected woodcock populations, but there is no assurance that they may not have some effect on those who eat woodcock in large quantities. Glutting myself on woodcock is something I wouldn't care to do, aside from principles of sportsmanship.

Flight birds are thought to use hillsides with birch, aspen and hawthorn more than natives, resting there until they move into feeding cover late in the day. It is difficult to say that natives would not have been using this same cover at this time of year, had they not already left. One of my favorite coverts is a hillside covered two-thirds to the top with hawthorn, part of a large valley used by migrants in November. Curiously, I haven't found the birds in this covert until about an hour before sunset, suggesting that it is a feeding and not a resting site.

The woodcock may be many things, but it is not a lover of open country. Alder and aspen thickets are its favorite haunts, and the bird likes the ground to be soggy rather than hard. (Photo by Jack Gates)

I've never been able to locate any game bird by strict guidelines as to what cover at exactly what time of day, finding my birds more by experiment and experience. Each woodcock gunner's experience varies as to good cover, especially in different portions of woodcock range. Of all types, I think alder and aspen are the most frequently used throughout the latitudes. William G. Sheldon has stressed in *The American Woodcock* (which I consider the woodcock equivalent of *The Ruffed Grouse* by Bump, Darrow, Edminster and Crissey) that "pure alder or aspen stands are not so attractive to woodcock as coverts where alder and aspen are mixed." This is clearly indicated in the best areas in the Canaan Valley, where alder, spirea, aspen, hawthorn, crab apple, red spruce, hardwoods and grass occur both in solid stands and in combination.

My shooting friend Dr. Charles C. Norris said that 80 percent of the woodcock he found in southern Nova Scotia were in alders, while the 'cock he shot near Ellsworth, Maine, were on briery hillsides. He described a guide's method of locating the birds' daytime resting cover by "lining" woodcock as they flew into feeding grounds, much as a bee tree is located, except that the woodcock's flight direction was sighted in reverse so that the guide could estimate where it had come from.

The "dusking flight" of woodcock approaching feeding grounds is a thrilling spectacle, with birds materializing in numbers beyond what the cover might seem to be able to hold. Actually, they are coming from areas that may be distant from the feeding site. Shooting woodcock at this time is an unsporting and deadly practice and is illegal, being after sunset. This is occasionally done by novices, but once a man knows better it is unforgivable, and reputable 'cock gunners hold themselves above it.

As the years pass, the gunner becomes familiar with the "look" of woodcock cover. For me it is alders, aspen clumps, hawthorns, crab apple thickets, old apple trees, a lack of deep wiry grass and moss and, very attractively, cattle grazing about. The heavy black soil laced with and redolent of cow manure that is found in the Canaan Valley is a type for me to judge by. White birch is absent from my coverts, but open forest floor along a small stream, or grassy spring seeps on edges or in woods, or leaves flattened in moist ground pack under hawthorns beckon me, along with alders and aspen, to such a degree that they can be considered specifics for 'cock. And always, moisture to attract worms.

But of all things to look for, woodcock whitewash tells me most. Any bird has rapid metabolism to dispose of excess weight, but I have the impression that a woodcock exerts no control whatever over its bowels. This does the gunner a good turn, for if you see whitewash, juicy, marbled with black, you can expect a flush momentarily, for the bird that put it there is likely to be not more than 10 yards away unless it has just flushed. I cause raised eyebrows when I say that even dried splashings indicate that 'cock have been there since the last slight precipitation. It has been my experience that whitewash disappears with the first mist, fog or heavy dew.

Whitewash may, without boring holes—especially in unlikely cover—indicate resting sites where the birds loaf during the day. I've found it in abandoned lanes too stony to permit probing, and I recall a late-season afternoon when I found splashings on a rocky forest floor together with a group of flight birds resting.

When you see holes, singly or in clusters, you can identify that area as feeding cover. Some of these holes in dried cowpats look at first like open spots on the surface, but if they are round and about a quarter of an inch in diameter they were put there by a woodcock probing through to earthworms underneath.

I have flushed woodcock that left whitewash floating on inch-deep water—not one, but two or three splashes—contradicting the statement that woodcock don't use actual wet areas. These birds may not have liked getting their feet wet, and they may not have found earthworms under the water, but they were wading in water trying.

A friend wrote that he had been shown what was said to be woodcock whitewash last November in Nebraska, an unlikely place to find woodcock. Robin droppings and even isolated splashes of owl droppings can be mistaken for woodcock whitewash by a man not familiar with it. But there is something about woodcock whitewash, once you've known it with all its implications, that makes the real thing unmistakable.

The man who feels that woodcock are blest when accompanied at table by a Pouilly-Fuissé, Chablis 1er Cru "Fourchaume" or a nice Rhine wine would find 'cock shooting nothing without a

Woodcock are not especially difficult for a dog to handle, but the canine that is to be truly efficient on timberdoodles must be started early and trained intensively. Woodcock have a distinctive scent that some dogs find unpleasant—so much so, in fact, that they refuse to hunt the birds at all. (Photo by Kay Evans)

woodcock dog or even a brace of dogs. A fine 'cock dog has almost always been developed from the start by a woodcock gunner and not arrived, full-blown, from a trainer specializing in quail dogs or one aiming to produce field-trial stars to work on several kinds of game birds. There have been rare cases, but specialists do not often come from culls in another specialty.

Woodcock are not nearly as difficult as grouse for a dog to handle, yet it does not follow that 'cock coverts are a place for inferior dog work. The close-working woodcock dog has been lauded for so long that it has become almost a standard, possibly because too many men have attempted to gun 'cock over offspring of trial champions. A dog that has won in big trials will do what it was bred to do—reach out. Finding a dog that works almost underfoot and will heed a voice or whistle so delights the man who has been treated to one of the wild ones that he thinks he has the perfect 'cock dog if it does no more than assume a comatose atti- tude on point and finds only those birds the gunner would have walked into on his own.

To compare one of the slow-moving, close dogs with a stylish, fast-searching 'cock dog can be enlightening. The woodcock dog many gunners never know is the individual who weaves a rapid ground pattern left and right ahead of the gunner, sometimes out of sight but checking with the gun and always within hearing. In widespread clumps of aspen or hawthorn he saves you walking the entire area by covering one birdy spot after another, and if he hits a 'cock at the far edge he will hold as solidly until you reach him as he will on a point 20 yards in front of you.

Partly because feeding woodcock walk considerably in their search for worms, and partly because they are often found lying tightly just ahead of scent, dogs learn to put their noses to the ground more than is desirable. On damp days in particular, wood-

The timberdoodle is an ungainly-looking bird with pop eyes, a long, slender beak and a plump body. Its camouflage is so nearly perfect that you can see one on the ground only within a few feet.

cock scent hovers low above the ground like smoke from a camp-fire. The potterer trails this like a hound, usually bumping the bird as he comes on it unaware. At times, the high-headed dog pins these birds with points as stylish as a grouse specialist; at others, he works them with head extended, sucking in the aroma a couple of feet off the ground as he homes in on the scent bloom-ing richer around the bird. The slow dog rarely brightens into an inspired point when he comes on 'cock. Compared with a drooping crouch, the point slammed into at full tilt, often with a sudden 90-degree turn, is something to remember after a day's shooting. In past years I saw this many times with my setter Bliss and regularly have points with the same character by Briar, grand-son of Bliss's mother, proving what can be achieved by line breeding.

I am told of woodcock's running from a pointing dog, requiring the dog to relocate. I see woodcock so frequently on the ground I can't believe I would have missed seeing a runner. The incidents reported to me may have occurred when a dog struck hot scent where birds had been feeding, then drew over the scent-saturated ground to the bird, which had been out ahead all the time—the dog, not the bird, doing the moving.

Without exception, a woodcock dog must retrieve. A woodcock air-washed in its fall may be difficult for a retrieving dog to locate, but it is almost always found. A man without a dog may search within feet of a dead bird and never see it, and he is at an almost equal disadvantage with a nonretriever, which may find the bird, nose it and walk away. Thousands of woodcock are dropped and lost every season.

There have always been dogs that find woodcock repugnant, refusing to pick them up or even point them. In *Natural History of Selborne* the British author Gilbert White (1720–93) wrote, "No sporting dogs will flush woodcocks till inured to the scent and trained to the sport, which they will then pursue with vehemence and transport; but then they will not touch their bones, but turn from them with abhorrence, even when they are hungry."

Mature dogs, not introduced to woodcock until experienced on other birds, are the ones more likely to turn them down; young-sters usually find them fascinating. You can often get a dog over his indifference to 'cock by stimulating a competitive urge, letting

If one good woodcock dog is good, two are far better. A pair of noses can scour heavy cover with great efficiency. Sometimes a "backing" dog honoring a point will be visible where the pointing dog alone would be obscured from view. (Photo by Kay Evans)

him see other dogs point and retrieve them. If no trained dog is available, hold your dog steady after the kill, making him stand while you go and retrieve the bird, taking it to him and letting him smell it. Toss it out and repeat the retrieve in the same manner until he becomes excited enough to mouth the bird. If he does this, toss it out once more and try for a retrieve by the dog. Like most "cures," this does not always work.

Not even in quail shooting is dog-brace work so effective as in woodcock cover. In thickets so dense both dogs are obscured from view, the backing member of the brace often locates the point. I shot for years over a brace of "snow beltons"—Dixie and her daughter Bliss—and I can think of no lovelier sight than those two. The use of the dog bell, originated, I am sure, by woodcock gunners, is carried one step further with a pair of bells with individual pitch, one on each bracemate, making it easy to distinguish the action and location of each dog.

No woodcock dog is finished until he is steady to wing and shot. I was moved to perfect this in Briar by a situation during his third season. Shooting 'cock only over points, I was confronted with impossible shots when putting up the birds in hawthorn thickets where I was doing much of my gunning. On one point I was blocked by a wall of thicket where, with Briar holding rock-solid, it became an impasse. On an impulse, I sent him on with two blasts of the whistle; he obeyed and flushed the 'cock, which topped the cover and gave me a grand shot. Having a dog flush on command was common practice fifty years ago, and the idea appealed. For the balance of the woodcock season Briar held his points, loyally staunch until ordered on, when he performed his duty with glee. My average on woodcock climbed, and all was lovely.

Afterward, on grouse, I saw no reason, nor did Briar, to alter our arrangement, except that he added what he considered a refinement. After holding his points, if I arrived and did not move in and flush immediately, Briar gave me about ten seconds and then took over without waiting for the two-blast whistle. When he started moving the bird before I reached him, I scratched the dog-flushed-bird program and made him hold while I flushed, regardless of the quality of the shot. To completely wipe out any residual desire to put up birds, I set out to make Briar steady to wing and shot as the final phase, perfecting it with an electronic collar. It makes for a beautiful performance on woodcock, when a second or third bird lying after one 'cock is flushed may be bumped by a dog lunging after the departing or falling bird. Time lost in holding the dog steady before putting him onto a retrieve is minimal and at the gunner's discretion. Friends have asked about exposing a dog that is steady to a companion's dog not trained in that respect. A well-trained dog will have the integrity to stand solid while the other dog breaks, and each time this happens the training is set that much more firmly, though resisting temptation with more than one bad example might be too much.

It is my contention that woodcock, like grouse, deserve to be gunned by not more than two men as a matter of sportsmanship. If you shoot with a group, divide into pairs; the experience is too fragile to spoil for sociability, which can be savored after the shooting and before the evening fire, and gunning with no more than one companion enhances dog work.

Woodcock offer a gunner a chance for his top shooting performance, demanding a bit less than grouse yet presenting exacting opportunities in thick cover, and once it gets into your blood

When walking up on a point, the intelligent hunter keeps an eye on the surrounding terrain. The man circling to his dog's front is maneuvering to get a shot unobstructed by trees. Note that the man behind his dog is not staring at the ground, but is watching the area where he thinks the bird will first fly. (Photos by Jack Gates)

you are not likely to give it up. No intelligent man will blast at a 'cock a few feet from his gun muzzle, but some of us have done just that. I remember one poor bird that disintegrated like a clay target. Usually the surest way to miss is to fire at a bird as fast as you can get your gun to your shoulder, as any desperate gunner in a shooting slump can tell you. A slight pause to see the bird clearly before mounting is the control that sets the eye, brain and gun in coordination. And yet, in thick cover you must take the shot at the first reasonable opportunity; if you wait for the 'cock to clear cover and make a level flight, you are almost always too late. Because a climbing woodcock is frequently too close, some men try for it as it changes direction at the top of his rise—a subtle moment when it seems to hang, but one difficult to judge. I find it effective to shoot immediately after the bird makes this change in direction, holding just under the overhead going-away form silhouetted against the sky.

Chances at woodcock are almost as varied as the number of birds flushed. Low flushes when the 'cock appears to twist give it its reputation for zigzag flight—an inaccurate one, to my mind. What seems an erratic motion is often a rolling from left to right but in a path surprisingly straight. The rapid mount for going-away grouse that I described in *The Upland Shooting Life* handles these straightaway flushes woodcock often make in open cover. Take a one-second look at the disappearing bird; then cover it with your hand holding the fore-end of the gun, bringing the stock to your shoulder and firing as it touches. The actual mount-and-fire requires about half a second and is amazingly accurate, provided your gun fits you as it should with none of that nonsense about throwing its pattern higher than it points.

Burton Spiller insisted that he found woodcock more difficult to hit than grouse, then went on to tell of shooting seven straight 'cock, which leaves me unconvinced. On a three-day trip in 1967 I made eleven straight hits on 'cock—a chance grouse would never give me or many men, if they count every shell fired. When gunning grouse I carry eight shells—not because I am a brilliant shot, but because in my coverts grouse have never offered eight bona fide shots in an afternoon. Perhaps from pathological optimism, I can't bring myself to go 'cock shooting with less than a pocketful of shells, in expectation of the fast action woodcock almost always provide.

Certainly, along with grouse, woodcock require the instinctive fast swing. Forget sustained lead and *see the bird*; then mount and overtake and fire as you go through—about one and one-half seconds will do it. It is not that woodcock are so fast—some are, while others seem to float—but it's a long way from the skeet field, where the gunner calls for the target, knowing where it is going to sail, to the woodcock coverts, where he may or may not get a glimpse of the bird.

Woodcock rarely fly more than 100 yards on the first flush. Some, when missed, will sideslip to the ground at the shot as though hit, later flushing at the approach of the gunner. The slow ones that "float" usually do this on the first rise, but woodcock become increasingly "flighty" after a second and especially a third flush, taking off for distant parts. The gunner who shoots only at first flushes, feeling it sporting not to follow the bird farther (and it is a nice thought) may not, however, subject himself to the most difficult shots. For all their apparent lack of wildness at times, woodcock become a very fast bird when they get their feathers ruffled. Which suggests my nearly one-man crusade against the term "timberdoodle"—a name that implies a simpleminded bird flapping brainlessly through cover.

It is thought best for your shooting not to look at the bird on the ground, on the principle that your eyes will hold to that spot after the bird flushes. At times I find it impossible to avoid seeing woodcock under a point, but I don't think it affects my shooting unless the bird stares back at me. There is a saying in our mountains: "Don't let a lizard look you in the eye; it will turn you into a witch." A woodcock looking me in the eye turns me into a sentimental fool. Once we've become that well acquainted, I can't shoot.

Woodcock shooting is a place for light guns, light loads and small bores, but not smaller than 28-gauge. Using a .410 for game birds is closing your eyes to what cannot be avoided with such a thin pattern—crippling. The 20-gauge gunner considers a 16- or 12-gauge gun brutal for 'cock, much as I would view a 10-gauge. I am dedicated to the theory that a man shoots one gun better than he can shoot two, and I must also plead a hopeless devotion to my 12-gauge Purdey, which at 6 pounds 7 ounces makes a grand 'cock and grouse gun. Being custom-built, Purdeys are rarely alike, which I was made particularly aware of when a collector brought one to compare with mine. Laid beside the gun proofed for 1½-ounce loads, mine, proofed for 1⅛-ounce loads, not only was lighter but had a frame perceptibly smaller, reminding me that my gun had been designated as "the little Purdey" before I inherited it. It has 26-inch barrels, it is "lively" and it throws its patterns exactly where I look—my definition of a woodcock gun.

No. 9 or No. 10 shot makes a nice woodcock load in the smaller gauges, providing adequate density. In the 12-gauge, one ounce of 8s will obviate too dense a pattern at the close range at which much of my shooting in thorn thickets must be done. On the principle that wing shooting consists of centering your bird, not spraying it down with marginal pellets from a wide-open tube, I use nothing wider than improved-cylinder for grouse and woodcock. But on woodcock, I feel the true cylinder would be entirely sporting at between 10 and 20 yards, where almost all of them are taken, and would be worth trying.

Tables of shotgun chokes do not classify them exactly the same —one specifying "improved-cylinder" as 50 percent, others as 35 to 45 percent. Robert Churchill, who built beautiful guns and knew chokes, defined improved-cylinder or "quarter-choke" as 50 percent at 40 yards, with a killing circle of 26 inches at 20 yards. This is effective for grouse, but at 15 yards, where many woodcock are shot, the killing circle is reduced by 6 inches. To obtain a 26-inch killing circle at 15 yards you must go to true cylinder (40 percent)—a pattern that when centered is less likely to destroy woodcock for the table.

I thought I achieved wider patterns for woodcock in my improved-cylinder barrel by using loads without plastic shot sleeves until I made tests at 20 yards, when I learned that I obtained the same 26-inch circle with or without plastic sleeves. In my guns, the wider patterns without shot sleeves occur only beyond 20 yards, where the mass of pellets without the sleeve begins to flare like a trumpet bell until, at 40 yards, it is about 10 percent more open than the sleeved load.

Woodcock shooting is too colorful to view only in terms of chokes and shot sizes. Days with cold wind or drizzle, or skies incredibly blue with a sun that brings out a bead of oil on a gun-stock; lemon-yellow pungency of aspen leaves trembling in the big alder flats; immense quiet broken by a tinkle of a dog bell link-ing you with a setter, a shorthair, a pointer or a Brittany make it fine for each of us in his own way.

For me it is the last retrieve of a grand old setter, or Briar's impeccable style, or my well-trained wife dropping to give me a clear shot at an incomer that darted over my shoulder; the day I shot the first of a brace against a setting sun and watched the second 'cock fly on, with pleasure in knowing a sense of enough; the element of luck accompanying the unpredictability of the flights; a lost bird found three days later in perfect condition in the high-country cold; the gratitude Kay and I knew when Dixie, after lying through the summer of '67 nearly dead from postopera-tive complications, opened the season with us by hunting three and a half hours. And the *Through the Looking-Glass* experience of discovering a new woodcock covert.

In 1971 we had several times gunned a small covert, stopping by at end of day after shooting in other areas. It held few birds, but was good for a point or two. A low hill cutting off the view at the far end stirred the 'cock shooter's eternal curiosity, but each time we let sunset turn us back without exploring. On October 25 of the following year we drove south from a Canaan cabin, reach-ing the small stand of alders about 2:30 P.M.

For Kay and me, the "Glorious Twenty-Fifth" of October has become a date to view much as British gunners look on the "Fa-mous Twelfth" of August on the grouse moors, for it has seldom failed to produce outstanding flights of woodcock. This day was cloudy after a morning fog, with a temperature of 35 degrees. Crossing to the end of the alders, we heard a grouse drumming and flushed four woodcock with no shots, the birds holding poorly for points.

We climbed the gradual rise and stood looking at a basin that stretched for nearly a mile. From a top fringe of second-growth woods, separate clumps of hawthorns covered the slope almost to the bottom, where a little stream ran through scattered alders for the length of this dream of a covert, with black birch, thorns and second growth on the far side, broken by openings that looked from there like spring seeps. We had not conceived of woodcock cover on a scale like this, and it was ours.

Briar hit a point at the nearest group of hawthorns. I shot and I at first thought I centered, mistaking a shower of leaves for feathers. He found nothing when I sent him on, but soon pointed below us. When I walked in, a 'cock flushed and dropped at my shot a split moment before it rounded the thorns, tumbling out of sight. I reloaded and, in my excitement, lost both shells from my open gun as I leaned over to accept the retrieve from Briar.

Working our way around the near side of the basin, we found woodcock, not in great numbers but in nice distribution, as far as we hunted without reaching the end of the thorns. Soon after we started we had seen cowpats and found what appeared to be a hundred Angus grazing beyond the curve of the hill. Each spring draw, each choice clump of thorns seemed to produce a bird, as though the 'cock selected the most dramatic spots, and I gloried in Briar's quartering, covering the slope in broad swaths.

His last point was a honey, slammed into and held with head rigidly thrown back to the fullest extent possible over his left shoulder. The bird gave me a fine left-quartering chance well out and dropped the way we all like—without a flutter. It took a moment for Briar to locate it and deliver—a male, the only adult bird of the five. The night before had been densely foggy. If this covert had been as barren the preceding day as the Canaan area we had hunted to the north, this flight must have settled there during the night fog.

My pedometer indicated that we were about two miles from the station wagon, but our trek back was gay with talk of covering the entire periphery of the basin on our next visit. We had not seen one empty shell other than mine or a footprint other than ours. Most of us like to give our coverts names, and the phrase that seems to best suit this one is the name of an old-fashioned variety of apple once found on these hill farms—"Seek No Further."

There is a fever in every woodcock gunner's brain, like Masefield's "quarry never found," for just one more perfect covert. Nash Buckingham inscribed one of his books: "To live as tho' a pleasant Land lies just beyond our door." We who gun woodcock enter such a land with each October.

GROUSE HUNTING

BY FRANK WOOLNER

INITIALLY, I am not going to tell you that a ruffed grouse is the world's greatest game bird, because enthusiasts *always* say that— to the intense disgust of woodcock hunters and the harriers of quail, pheasant, white-winged doves or you name it. Each bird happens to be "the greatest" at that moment in time and space when it is silhouetted against the sky, a shotgun is swinging smoothly and time stands still.

Having said this, I nimbly hedge and offer a few qualifying phrases. Ever since upland gunning became a joyous mania in our new world, *Bonasa umbellus*, that brown bullet with the thunder-making wings and iridescent ruff, has been considered a classic quarry. There are men who scorn all other fliers as unworthy of serious attention; they are citizens who covet fine guns, breed aristocratic pointing dogs and know paradise only in a frost-touched upland covert where pats are resident.

Woodcock are mystic little gnomes, and quail test tickers when they explode in a covey flush, yet a shooting gentleman cannot make comparisons or offer argument unless he is acquainted with the bird that has come to epitomize all that is wild and wary and remarkably deceptive in flight. Therefore, in order to boast acceptable intelligence about upland gunning, one simply has to arrange a confrontation with grouse. Don't be surprised if you are humbled.

So—*Bonasa*! The drummer, fantail, thunderwing—often declared king of game birds: the name is partridge, pronounced "pa'tridge" in New England, birch partridge in some southern Canadian provinces or just "pat." Along the southern Appalachian slopes it may be a mountain cock or mountain pheasant. "Grouse" is most prevalent now, thanks to greater use of that word in the literature. Only a dolt prefixes it "ruffled." Old *Bonasa* may have his faults, but he is seldom ruffled!

Here is a hardy native American, ranging over almost precisely half a continent, from the northeastern section of the United States and southern Canadian provinces down through West Virginia and then across this vast land of ours to the Pacific. Wherever, within this range, one finds fringe woodlands, there will be grouse. Moreover, look for sport supreme where civilization threatens the wilderness. This seems contradictory, but our grand quarry needs competition to hone its skills. Those native to remote, overgrown and almost forgotten farmsites of New England, New York, Michigan, Pennsylvania and West Virginia have evolved into the canniest of adversaries. Away up in the bush of southern Canada or along the willow-thicketed creeks of the Rocky Mountains, grouse sometimes earn the title of "fool hen" by perching in a conifer until shot down, or naively flying a straight course away from the gun.

Such targets are possible, but improbable, in well-hunted areas. Indeed, the expert shooter often misses so-called sucker shots because he expects something flamboyant and aerobatic. Geared to swing fast and shoot quickly once proper lead has been established, a deadly marksman tends to overcorrect on the slow boat —and places his pattern far ahead. There is a lot of empty air in any grouse covert.

First, a gun. Classic shooters prefer side-by-side doubles and ferociously scorn pumps or autoloaders. Some even run an elevated temperature when companions show up with over/unders. This is patently ridiculous, but grouse hunting is bathed in a patina of tradition. To old hands, there are things no gentleman will do, and no argument will sway them. The fact that a few of us

Part of the game is the admiration of a magnificent bird. The gun is the author's customized 12-gauge Winchester Model 59 autoloader. It offers three quick shots, weighs less than 6 pounds and is lightning-fast to get on target.

cannot master a side-by-side, and therefore require single alignment, is brushed aside. But there are areas of agreement.

A grouse gun must be light, because a shooter will spend long hours trudging over some of the most exasperating terrain short of a moonscape; he'll plunge into hidden seeps, stumble over camouflaged rock piles, push through an assortment of apparently cast-iron brush and malicious briers. Most of the time, even late in the season when temperatures plummet, our hero will be sweating and swearing, made aware of summer-softened muscles he never knew existed. As fatigue accumulates, it is increasingly difficult to swing a heavy smoothbore—so the ideal grouse gun will be a piece that weighs 6½ pounds or less. Always prefer "less," if that is possible.

Side-by-sides have much going for them: they are trim and slim and beautiful to behold. You have a choice of boring—perhaps improved-cylinder, for that first poke, and modified, to anchor a bird well out, on afterburners. Over/unders boast the same choice of pipe, but are generally clubbier and heavier than the fine double.

There is nothing degrading or otherwise wrong with the pump or autoloader that is light enough to carry. Ithaca's Model 37 corn sheller weighs 6½ pounds in 12 gauge and is an excellent choice. I personally work with a customized Winchester Model 59 auto that scaled 6½ pounds in cosmoline and now, with my cropping, weighs less than 6. This is the famous (or infamous) glass-barreled shotgun that Winchester discontinued because almost nobody bought it. The gun was far ahead of its time, and I hold that my conversion is the deadliest upland piece in the world.

A big-bore is most efficient. However, a grouse hunter can do very well with 20, or even 28, gauge, and these can be had in lightweight packages. Make no mistake: as you progress down the gauges there is an efficiency loss. A low-brass 20-gauge shell does not contain as many pellets as a comparable low-brass 12, so the shot string suffers. If the 20 is beefed up, you get into recoil problems.

About twenty years ago there was a flurry of interest in the 16-gauge. It is an excellent boring, quite right for ruffed grouse, and a host of old-timers still swear by it. Nowadays there may be difficulties in obtaining fodder at country crossroads shops—another argument for the 12, which remains America's favorite shotgun.

Over the years I have found it dangerous to make flat statements, but I make one now. The little .410 shotgun should *never* be used on flying grouse: it simply doesn't throw enough flak, and it is sure to lose birds through wounding. Some idiots insist that miniguns are "sporting," whatever the hell that means. We shoot to kill clean or miss clean, not to ensure lingering death with a single, misdirected pellet. I can see a .410 on a skeet field, but not in the uplands.

Next, boring. Long ago, William Harnden Foster declared that the average grouse is tumbled at approximately 23 yards. In early-fall foliage Foster's figure may be excessive, because you will either score quickly or lose the bird in a jungle of green and gold. Twenty yards is 60 feet, and it's probable that most of our kills are made within that range. Therefore cylinder, or improved cylinder, is logically best. Today the plastic shot sleeve ensures good patterns with true cylinder—a wide-open pipe.

Arguments about one open tube and another modified are telling, yet the gentleman who shoots a piece so bored may handicap
himself in the taking of a double at close range. If I could shoot a
side-by-side, which I cannot, both barrels would be either wide-
open or skeet. This choke is excellent at 30 yards or less, and good
out to approximately 40 yards. I will not shoot at a grouse beyond
that mark. Forty yards is a long poke in thick upland cover.

Granting that there are areas in which long shots are feasible,
the double that features one wide-open tube and one bored modified cannot be faulted. Perhaps this combination is best for all-
around upland gunning, even though it will prove a handicap in
the close-range belt at a brace of birds. We also exhibit a wisp of
ignorance in scorning old-fashioned double triggers: they are—in
split-second action—far superior to the single trigger with its
choice of boring dictated by a button that must be pushed. A gun-

*Grouse and woodcock often share the same cover, and a day's bag
may well include both species.*

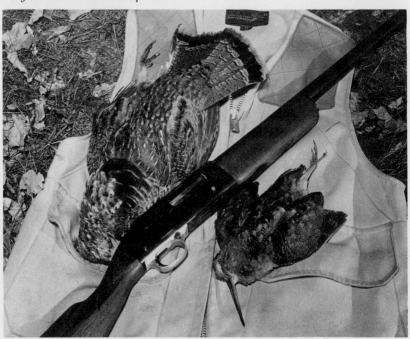

ner who is familiar with his piece can swiftly select the boring for a specific job. In some cases the old double trigger cannot be topped.

Ruffed grouse are spectacular fliers, but not too hard to down when hit. A couple of pellets are enough, and they needn't be oversized. In early-season, close-range shooting, 8s are excellent —efficient on pats and the occasional woodcock found in a grouse covert. Later, when trees are bare and longer shots may be necessary, 7½s suffice. You want a wide, even pattern on target, not the clout of a load designed for pheasant or ducks.

Pattern is, in itself, a deceptive word. We have always absorbed the garbage that so many pellets within a 30-inch circle at optimum range guarantee success. While there is a necessity to keep the charge concentrated, academic gunners forget that those pellets do not arrive en masse. We deal with a shot string, and in the business of intercepting flying game it is the duty of the gunner to place a long sausage of speeding projectiles in such a position that a part of that string will collide with the fleeting target. There is a hosing effect, not a concentration, and this is particularly true in a sharply angled shot, in which a bird will be caught by a very small segment of the string. Obviously, a big-bore shotgun is most efficient because the sausage is longer and contains a greater number of pellets.

Lots of grouse hunters lean toward "brush guns," which means abbreviated barrels. This is logical only up to a point. In the boondocks one must swing fast and avoid tangling with assorted birch whips and tree trunks. Still, there is a necessity for an adequate sighting plane. My own feeling is that you need approximately 36 inches from the eye to the muzzle; therefore, barrel length depends on the type of smoothbore employed.

If you stick with side-by-side doubles or over/unders, then this sighting plane is best ensured with 26-inch barrels—standard, since manufacturers are far from dolts and have figured all the odds.

Barrel length can be diminished on a pump or autoloader, because these pieces feature 5 to 7 inches of receiver behind the tube. Theoretically, with some of the repeaters, you could go to 20-inch barrels, but there is another factor to consider: under

The partridge delights in dense, tangled cover. This one is being retrieved from a tangle of grapevines and poison ivy. Shooting glasses are necessary for eye protection here; this man is taking his chances without them.

23½ inches there is an infinitesimal loss of ballistic efficiency. Better copper all bets and make 23½ inches minimum.

Variable-choke devices aid the shooter who will use one gun for many purposes. Most of them add a "muzzle bulge" effect, which is no handicap and may even prove beneficial; indeed, there are enthusiasts who swear that the "bulge" is a definite aid to pointing. I do not find it so, but I respect the opinions of colleagues.

Any grouse gun should be light; it should be very familiar, so that the piece feels like an extension of one's arms. In action there will be no time to think things out and work by the numbers. You will react almost immediately at flush, and you will either move quickly or fail abjectly. This is one of the reasons why ancient, flat-bellied old-timers usually humble bright young athletes in upland hunting—they're always ready, often moving at the first sound of wings.

You dress for this sport. This means comfortable, brier-turning pants and long-sleeved shirts, plus well-broken-in boots that are tough enough to prevent stone bruises. The game is all fluid motion, from hip twisting through tangled alder runs and birches to slogging along swamp edges. The best pants will be light in weight, but reinforced at thigh and knee to defeat thorny growth. Some get along with denims, and others like ordinary chinos. I find the denims too tight-fitting for comfort and the summer khakis delightful—until I push into the first brier patch. Stagged (shortened) pants ensure less attrition on cuffs, but allow all sorts of juniper needles and other itching nasties to work down into a man's boots.

Early-season grouse hunting is hot work, but the long-sleeved shirt is important because, again, it turns briers. Light flannel is probably best, and choose either red or bright orange so that companions can spot you while you're working a covert.

Until late in the season, eschew all hunting coats and favor a vest featuring shell pockets and an abbreviated game bag aft. I feel that canvas coats are always handicapping, but the quilted garment—often one designed for duck hunting—affords warmth and reasonable mobility after temperatures have plummeted in late fall and early winter. The coat then becomes a necessary evil.

Boots are important. I like rubber-bottomed pacs, such as the L. L. Bean type, but there is much to be said for the Russell Birdshooter in dry going. Indeed, Vietnam combat boots are excellent if you don't mind occasional wet feet. Some favor short, all-rubber models; I can't stand them, but maybe you can. At the very least, be sure that boots are well broken in before any trip afield: it is no fun to acquire blisters. Worse, if feet become tender, then reflexes suffer, and you'll find it very difficult to swing properly when the chips are down.

Proper uniform includes a cap, not a hat. This will protect a tender headbone from the caresses of thorny growth and provide an eye-shading visor. Stetsons and other wide-brimmed types may be attractive, but they are snatched off by every whipping twig. The baseball cap is about right—better if it is made of a porous blaze-orange material that can be seen by a comrade.

Shooting glasses are really essential. Some gunners cannot abide them, but grouse hunting is conducted in thick cover and there are switching menaces. It is painful to be "twigged," and it can be downright dangerous if the twig is armed with thorns. Usually the yellow lenses favored by trap and skeet shooters are best. They ensure contrast, especially under inclement light conditions. If these impose eyestrain, go to a light neutral gray or green—but always wear glasses. You have but one pair of eyes, and they are intended to last a lifetime.

Brambles are going to tear your hands and wrists in thick cover. I cannot feel comfortable in gloves, but some wear them happily. Perhaps the best are designed for golfing; they are very thin and flexible, offer little protection against cold weather, but will turn ordinary briers. A few enthusiasts wear a glove on the left hand, but none on the right. It's a matter of personal conviction, and scratched wrists plague every upland gunner during a fall season. I always worry when I meet a lean old-timer whose wrists are bloodied in one of my favorite coverts. That character, especially if he is accompanied by an alert pointer or setter with a tail tip crimsoned by thorny growth, is more lethal than a dozen ardent youths armed with the latest autoloaders and magnum shells!

All of the literature on the sport extols great grouse dogs, and they do exist. Unfortunately, I must report that truly great performers are exceptional. The problem lies in specialization: too many of today's sportsmen think that a dog must be able to do everything well, and most of them cannot. True, we see an occasional canine genius shift gears in handling different game, but the majority are mediocre on all. A minority exhibit maximum efficiency on one bird but are troubled by others. This shouldn't be very surprising.

A dog, unless it is a truly remarkable animal, is likely to be confused by the diametrically opposed tactics of ring-necked pheasant, grouse and woodcock. A pheasant runs like an ostrich, but can be pushed and will usually hold to the point. Quail skitter through low cover and are somewhat more nervous than the skulking ringneck, but they also permit a rather close approach. Woodcock usually—and never say always—scrooch down and practically wait until you nudge them out of cover: therefore a dog can almost put his nose on a crouching timberdoodle.

Grouse are different. They won't be pushed, and they regard all of the world as hostile. A biddy in any well-shot-over territory skitters along like a nervous mouse on a cat farm—alert, glistening eyes suspicious, ears attuned to unnatural sound in the whispering hush of an upland covert. A pointing dog must be careful or it will be a loser. One simply does not sail in on old *Bonasa* and then anchor him with a flash point while he cowers like a

The traditional grouse dog is the English setter. Note the bell that enables its master to keep track of the animal's progress.

woodcock or hides like a pheasant. All of the better performers respect grouse; they point at a safe distance and, if the bird is a runner, move "as though walking on eggs."

Most of America's handlers will assure you that the champions they peddle are equally adept on all flying game—and they lie in their teeth. These gentlemen are engaged in the business of breaking gun dogs for sale to well-heeled sportsmen. While it is quite possible to offer acceptable performance on quail, pheasant or woodcock prior to the two-year mark, it takes approximately twice that time to finish a grouse dog. The name of the game is specialization, and it is even unusual to find a setter or pointer able to handle pats and woodcock with equal skill.

Therefore, most of America's truly great grouse dogs fall into very narrow categories: they are brought along either by astute handlers lusting for field-trial honors or by private citizens who go for broke and desire only the feather finder of a lifetime—that canine genius so remarkably endowed with nose and brain that he will be recalled for his owner's lifetime. Perfection in any discipline is a matter of specialization and precision. More than any other bird, the ruffed grouse demands the ultimate in finesse.

In America the English setter is traditionally associated with grouse hunting. I am fond of setters because I love their grace and beauty, yet it would be ignorant to bad-mouth the pointer, a highly competent breed—and perhaps swifter to absorb knowledge. These two lead the field, even though the Brittany spaniel has made inroads in recent years. German shorthairs are excellent, as are Weimaraners and many other breeds. I have gunned grouse over springer spaniels and frighteningly intelligent Labrador retrievers.

Flusher-retrievers are fine, so long as they work close to the gun —but Americans prefer pointing breeds in a grouse covert. There is something indescribably fine in a solid point. Enthusiasts always get psyched at that moment, while the dog is a statue in the flickering shadow and shine of a covert. One's heartbeat revs up, and buck fever is quite possible when it is reasonably certain that a hurtling brown bird will soon thunder out of concealment and go twisting away through the thickest of brush. An easy shot is the exception to prove a rule. Every fantail seems to have a new trick to exhibit.

Backwoods cracker-barrel sessions always argue the merits of a close-working dog against a "big-going" field-trial type. Certainly there is a nice compromise; all dogs used in brushy uplands must be belled, and the ranging animal should not progress beyond hearing. A putterer is as bad as an unguided missile, although he has the saving grace of pointing or bouncing birds within the gunner's sphere of efficiency. Nothing is more exasperating than the big-going bumbler who flushes bird after bird far ahead of following guns.

Grouse hunting appeals to incurable romantics; hence the sometimes illogical allegiance to fine double guns—only because they grace a tradition. For the same reason, legions of bristle-chinned old-timers abhor the sight of a stub-tailed pointing dog. While aristocrats of the uplands accept basic pointers and setters, they often sneer at mention of Brits, German shorthairs and Weimaraners—only because all of these sport abbreviated tails! A great old sportsman once told me that his son-in-law had a great Brittany, but he couldn't enjoy hunting over "the thing" because it reminded him of a pink-nosed rabbit pointing a head of cabbage!

Still, Brits are coming on strong. They are intermediate between the setter and the spaniel, combining natural hunting instinct with a predilection to point. Many of them have the brains to differentiate between a close-lying woodcock and a wary ruffed grouse. Nobody will convince an advocate of the pointer or setter, yet there is little doubt that Brittany spaniels may be as close to the all-purpose upland feather finder as current breeding permits.

It is quite possible to hunt grouse without a dog, although there will be times when you'll wish for a vest-pocket retriever. Actually, the clever jump shooter will account for more birds than his blood brother who uses a mediocre feather finder. Quite naturally, this assumes a working knowledge of coverts and the ability to shrug off panic and get into action with a minimum of false motion. The slow jump shooter will lose birds.

Some years ago, while researching a book called *Grouse and Grouse Hunting,* I kept meticulous records of the ratio of birds lost to birds pocketed. For four successive years my figures showed one wounded biddy lost to every twelve knocked down in a smoke stream of downy feathers.

Then, having written the book and fatuously assumed that my statistics were correct, I had a disastrous year in which the "lost" column climbed to three out of twelve. One horrible morning I knocked down two in rapid succession and found neither. This

Despite the condescension with which traditionalists view it, the Brittany spaniel is a first-rate upland dog and is a talented performer in the grouse coverts.

sort of thing leaves a raw scar on the soul of any honest upland gunner. It is one thing to harvest a precious renewable resource, and quite another to wound birds and leave them for the foxes. Quite certainly a good retriever would have found those biddies, and I offer no instant-expert alibi.

Eyebrows raised, I have read that a downed grouse is easy to find. This has never been my experience; the birds are well camouflaged, so they blend into the stuff of a covert's understory. Slightly wounded, every pat will run into the thickest of ground cover and then freeze. It will squeeze into a woodchuck burrow, slip into a stone wall or the hollow of a stump. Stricken, the bird may announce its location with a spasmodic thumping of wings, but don't count on it.

If a grouse is easily seen at the moment a charge of shot goes home, some assessment is possible. A puff of downy feathers is no guarantee; sometimes pellets merely shave breast and rump without penetrating. The best indication of a direct hit is a combination of that feather puff and an inert form arcing downward. When a bird cartwheels, there is a better-than-even chance that it is winged and will run immediately after touchdown. Often one catches a momentary glimpse of a wing folded back and a gyrating, descending grouse carefully craning its head to evaluate a crash landing. This flier will be running a split second after contact, so get there fast and forget dignity.

Occasionally a bird, apparently hard-hit if one counts the smoke puff of feathers and a befuddled pause in flight, will seem to gain strength and bore away. If the legs are dropped, that pat will very likely be dead on arrival, so mark it carefully. Occasionally the final touchdown will be 100 yards from point of flush.

A "beaned" bird, one hit in the head, is likely to tower rapidly. This doomed flier seeks the zenith in a fast, spiraling climb. At the very apex of that wild zoom the pat will seem to be clawing for altitude, and then it will release all holds and plummet to earth. Again, mark it carefully, for wherever that bird lands, there it will be found.

Very often we snap off a shot at a grouse that is disappearing in fall foliage. Perhaps we have missed, but just possibly the aim was true. Without a dog it is extremely difficult to locate such a kill, and if the bird is wounded, it will of course scuttle into nearby

A longtime editor of Field & Stream, *"Tap" Tapply holds a council of war with his Brittany, Buck, during a midday break.*

cover and hide. Often, when you're working with a good retriever, shots you would have considered impossible will prove to have been right on target. This is more good argument for the use of a dog.

Even this can fail. For some curious reason, wounded grouse often seem to be almost scentless. Grand dogs have been known to lose them, whether through a natural loss of body odor or through competition from other aromas in a still-green woodland. In New Hampshire I tumbled a pat traveling almost overhead and saw the bird plummet into a jungle of juniper. "Tap" Tapply's Brittany spaniel came tearing in, but couldn't locate my trophy. Tap, as a matter of fact, hadn't seen the pat go down, and I think he wondered whether I had really hit it. Buck, the Brit, finally made contact—a day later—after I had repaired to my own digs in Massachusetts. The bird had a broken wing, but was still very much alive.

A similar thing happened when I was hunting a Bay State covert with Paul Belton, a local friend, and his astute Labrador retriever. My bird was hard-hit and went cartwheeling into a tremendous stand of juniper and brier. Characteristically, the dog watched that grouse from moment of flush to interception and was off in pursuit as it tumbled. He couldn't find it, and I wonder if the pungence of juniper may somehow overpower bird scent.

Very often the beaned birds seem to lack scent, and a lot of dogs will never find them although they are still alive and groggy. One must simply mark the touchdown point and search carefully. The grouse will be found precisely where it landed, usually with a drop of blood at the bill.

Grouse hunting is one sport in which a veteran is likely to outclass young athletes, and that is because it takes half a lifetime to learn the ground rules. Some men simply avoid pats, since they want the easy poke at a more obliging flier or cannot see spending years in trial-and-error gunning to master a difficult target. Much of it is psychological.

The average pat comes out of thick cover, and he screams out of there like a scrambling fighter plane. His wings thunder and he automatically places terrain features behind his line of retreat. If there is so much as a single tree, you can bet that he'll use it to screen his departure. For the one pat that travels straight away, five will curve right or left, dodging artfully. There will be a couple of seconds, at best three, to get on and direct a charge of shot. A gunner has to be alert and quick on the trigger. There is no time to think about it and calculate leads. Instant reflex action is the ticket, and accuracy must be taken for granted. There are shortcuts, practically all of them tied into experience and ice-cold determination at the moment of flush. The toughest thing for a beginner to master is cool execution in shaved seconds. Grouse can scare the hell out of you unless you are ready for them.

Logically, you go in with the sun at your back, like a fighter pilot stalking an enemy formation. Ideally, you will know all about the hot corners and be prepared when it is likely that a bird may go rocketing skyward. Your shotgun will be at port arms, never slung over a shoulder or held in the inept cross-armed Indian carry. At flush it will be necessary to move fast—indeed, to initiate action before any bird is seen. If you are to be successful, snap that safety catch off and point at the sound of wings before a target is visible. Aim at sound, and then wait for a visible target. Correction is almost automatic at this point, and you hose the mark. It all happens quickly, but there is a logical sequence.

The hunter at left has his shotgun ready for action, index finger on the safety catch. Over-the-shoulder and cross-armed carries lose you valuable time when the bird goes up.

Rightly, the infamous "sound shot" is scorned; it can be dangerous, and it is unlikely to collect game. You shoot at a mark, and that target should be evident. A hurtling ruffed grouse will first make itself known by sound, and that's the time to get on— roughly. Correct as the bird appears, curving left or right or perhaps towering. There won't be much time, but there'll be enough. The important thing is to take full advantage of all available time from the moment of lift-off to that swift departure in screening foliage.

Both strategy and tactics are involved. The deadliest of gunners know their coverts and plan every approach to a hot corner. With or without a canine companion, it becomes common knowledge that a specific grapevine sprawling over an ancient wall, or a wild apple tree huddling in the birches, is likely to host one or two birds. Certain runs are "sure things," meaning that birds have been there in the past and are almost certain to be back in residence.

It doesn't always work, but odds are better when a man can approach a great clump of barberries that have hosted pats for years on end, a sere little edge of swamp, a forgotten orchard slumbering in second growth, a birch knoll favored in sunny hours. Unless a covert is reverting to pole timber or has been radically altered by the destruction we call "progress in development," then it is reasonable to assume that pats will be where pats have been.

A working knowledge of the birds' habits is essential. One looks for the anemic gleam of poplars. Birch and alder edges bordering suburban orchards often resound to the thunder of wings. There are grand feeding grounds on beech ridges and in scrub oak thickets where acorns carpet the ground. In a dry autumn, swamp edges are profitable—and they will be more important after the first killing frosts, when birds seek warmth, shelter and an abundance of winter-over fruit.

In northern areas it is always wise to prospect old, huddled apple trees in brushy second growth. After autumn leaves have fallen, there are always a few green leaves left on these trees, and pats desire them. Apples are not so important on a southern range—say, in West Virginia—for there is an abundance of greenery available. A sagacious local gunner will evaluate the food esteemed by his quarry during any segment of a long shooting season and will expect hectic flushes at banquet tables.

There is no guarantee that an examination of crop contents will solve problems. One grouse may have dined on a variety of buds, a snip of mushroom, a few green leaves and an acorn that must have proved difficult to swallow. Others will be stuffed with barberries, apple pulp and maybe the toxic little gray berries of poison ivy. In a lavish season they all sample a smorgasbord. Early fall sees wide dispersal of summer's broods, and there is a grand array of foodstuffs—from blackberries, late-ripening, to fox grapes and apples and beechnuts and the green salad that always seems essential. I have studied crop contents and have reached no conclusions; the bird is indiscriminate until such time as the weather clamps down and variety is limited.

As temperatures plummet there is a gravitation to thick, and therefore warm, cover. Tangled swamp growth, smoldering in its self-generated heat, is a magnet. Conifer edges become loafing grounds, and juniper or laurel cuts the edge of an arctic wind. By that time woodlands have been stripped of foliage and the thickets offer shelter. Also, in this tag end of the year, resident grouse are wary and prone to flush well ahead of dog or man. Thus the unfortunate conclusion of game biologists that "you can't shoot them out" because survivors become hawk-wild.

Our grouse is a day bird. There is little sense in hunting at dawn, because pats are unlikely to leave their roosts until the sun is well up. They like warmth and fear half-light, when great horned owls are sweeping through the second growth. Very often these birds feed avidly in the late morning, loaf on sunny knolls during midday periods and forage again in afternoon hours. By the time those purple shadows of sunset are staining the woods, they'll be seeking the conifers to roost. It is then that last-minute gunners trigger futile charges at biddies rocketing down out of trees —the hardest of all shots to make good.

Many roost on the ground, perhaps more than take to the trees. In a blizzard they'll often burrow into a drift, hollow out a chamber and remain there, entombed until the storm is over. Legend holds that crust often victimizes such birds, but there is little evidence to support the supposition. Certainly foxes, bobcats and other predators take them there; the snow trails document such attrition.

Without any doubt it is most satisfactory to hunt grouse with a good pointing dog. At the very least, gunners will know a bird is there, concealed in thick underbrush, ready to take wing. Two men are best able to cover the exits, moving in from different angles and studying escape routes. Unlike the more simpleminded game birds, this flier will not seek an opening or climb into a clear sky; he will usually head for the thickest of cover and attempt to dodge around any terrain feature that is available.

If a dog is making game along an edge paralleled by a reasonably open field, it is very wise to throw a flanking gun ahead to intercept the bird that chooses to flush wild. Many do so, and in heavily hunted regions the pat has become a runner par excellence. He doesn't sprint like a pheasant, but he sure trickles away through the cover and goes boiling into the air long before an astute pointer or setter can jack up and say, "There he is!"

In jump shooting there is less deception, but more gunner savvy is needed in spotting hot corners. One moves into position with studied strategy and, ideally, second-guesses the bird. It is all stop-and-go, yet an expert will know just when to stop. This is a primary secret of success.

The deadliest of jump shooters know each covert the way they know the whims of wives and children. Each little bonanza is well remembered, and in a new area terrain is either "birdy" or not very promising. The great trick is cadence, followed by a sudden halt at that point which indicates a possible flush. If done well, the tactic is very efficient.

Grouse are tolerant of sound, so long as it is not stop-and-go. A majority of biddies will lie tight if an interloper goes crashing through the brush. They lose their cool when any cadenced sound terminates. This seems to indicate the crouch of a predator prior to attack, and birds go battering skyward within shooting range.

Therefore a smart jump shooter moves steadily, with studied cadence. He surveys the cover ahead and determines where a pat may be hiding. Once he has done this, it is wise to select a spot where footing will be ideal and to go there directly, without pause. A quick halt then destroys the nerves of a skulking grouse, and that bird thunders into the air. If a gunner is poised and ready, the advantage passes to him.

Known hot corners, like huddled apple trees, tangles of fox grapes or little islands of barberries, deserve the same treatment. After a few sorties you will also know where to pause and expect action in a dry swamp after first frost. It is, of course, abject stupidity to approach any stone wall or fence without halting at the obstacle, then shuffling one's feet and making another tentative step before clambering over. Legions of upland gunners have been caught not with their pants down, but draped over a wall or snagged by barbed wire, as a grouse went triumphantly over the horizon.

The pat truly simulates a rocket at takeoff, but he is not a very efficient long-distance flier. He comes out not very fast, but building speed with each wingbeat and attaining maximum velocity after nosing over and slanting down toward a chosen landing site.

In an open field no grouse would be an impossible target, but this bird is sagacious enough to take advantage of terrain features. Straightaway flight is unusual; the norm is a curving, hipper-dipper course which takes advantage of every rise of ground or tree between gun and mark.

It is worth noting that a grouse is a heavier-than-air machine, capable only of short flights. The average would be something like 150 yards, and the flight is frequently less, so it is often possible to see a shot-at bird curve into a landing site. Second flushes not only are feasible but—if a gunner's tactics are well executed—may be far more successful than a first poke. There are debits and credits.

This tiring rocket has been approximately located, so a shooter will not be plagued by surprise in any new flush. Naturally, touchdown can be deceptive, because a pat may remain precisely where it landed or it may run in any direction. A jump shooter must go directly to that point which seems most promising, and he must never hesitate until it is time to suddenly halt. Remember the lulling effect of cadence, and use the pause only when it is time to swing and shoot.

Almost always, grouse fly to the thickest of cover. Some say they'll always drive upslope, but that depends on canopy and terrain. Trust them to select concealing foliage, and be sure that any mature grouse will be an aerobat, highly capable of changing direction just when you think that your swing and lead are coordinated.

In many states the hen pheasant is protected, and this poses a problem for dedicated grouse hunters who are quick on the trigger. Normally, pheasant eschew true grouse cover for more open farmland, but occasionally gunning pressure will push them back into the edges, where they are mistaken for native birds. If it's clearly seen, there is no alibi for mistaking a hen pheasant for a pat—the silhouette is different, and there is a thin whistle laced through the burr of pheasant's wingbeats. Nonetheless, a brown bird seen dimly as it batters through the thick brush of a grouse's domain tempts fate. It must be admitted that a lot of us who hunt pats tumble the odd hen pheasant and then feel like criminals as we skulk off into the woodlands muttering about honest mistakes and laws that hold ignorance no excuse.

Too much has been written about the necessity to fire within "a half-second" of a pat's flush. It is virtually impossible to mount a gun and get off an accurately placed charge in that space of time, especially in rough going where one's feet are always misplaced, the cover is screening, perspiration is trickling into red-rimmed eyes and, quite possibly, the bird is not even seen for the first half-second or more. There is a vast difference between swift gun handling and the quick poke poorly directed.

Therefore, the usual admonition to shoot quickly is poor advice. Speed is relative, and in action, seconds are eternities. The bird may remain within killing range for a full three seconds, depending on hampering cover at flush. Some of the most lethal operators in the uplands school themselves to wait for a precise instant while they track first the sound of wings, then the shadow of a hurtling target. If this is done coolly, correction is infinitesimal and smoothly coordinated. A veteran isn't reduced to a trembling mental wreck by that initial, battering thunder of wings. Beginners get all discombobulated at the roar of a flush, swing wildly and press a trigger in some forlorn hope that "pattern" will compensate for inept gun pointing. It rarely does.

Others, often youthful athletes with keen reflexes, simply stand there, mesmerized, while a perfectly beautiful sucker shot disappears into screening foliage. They mutter, "Boy, he scared the hell out of me!" and privately wonder how any marksman on earth can bring down this swift spirit of the brush. Old-timers smile, because they've long since experienced this stage of education.

It may be well, at this point, to discuss the so-called "snap shot." Observers, always folk attuned to slower birds in an open sky, think that the expert grouse hunter simply mounts his gun and fires within a split second, automatically placing a charge of small shot at the right place to intercept a speeding, elusive target. Kills are spectacular, so some legerdemain must be employed. There is none.

Snap shooting is nothing more than a speeded-up version of orthodox swing and lead. Nobody has repealed the laws of physics, so it is always necessary to place a shot string far enough ahead of a flying target to intercept it in space and time. Granted, the lightning-fast gunner has to do this almost instinctively, schooled by long years of poking at speeding marks, but he leads or he misses. It's as simple as that.

A majority of snap shooters use the swing-through technique; that is, they forget about formal lead and sweep the gun barrel through the hurtling target, pressing the trigger at that moment when some brain cell tells the index finger, *Now!* It takes practice, and it is a hosing operation, accomplished so rapidly that a witness sees no conscious lead.

Nonetheless, lead is there, and each bird is a different proposition. It is relatively easy to aim directly at the straightaway target, neither rising nor descending. (Many of the great scattergunners miss this one, because they overcorrect.) On a grouse curving to right or left, as the birds usually do, often towering as well, lead is essential or a clean miss will result. Toughest of all is a pat diving out of a tree. It somehow goes against the grain to shoot *under,* since most of our birds are ascending. Similarly, but to a lesser extent, the sharply towering mark can be difficult. For a seasoned sportsman the easiest is a gradual right or left deflection shot, angling shallowly upward. Speed is less important than direction and slant.

The gun must never stop swinging! Follow-through is vitally important, and you can prove this on any skeet field with the midcircle clays. It is always better to allow too much, rather than too little, lead. With the former, there is an outside chance that some part of the pellet sausage will connect; with the latter, every bit of flak is well behind and useless.

Taking all of these things into account, the major reasons for misses on ruffed grouse are gunner panic induced by that roaring flush; improper gun carry, which ensures the loss of vital seconds in getting onto the target, and an almost psychotic belief that it's necessary to shoot the moment a butt plate touches a shoulder.

How well should you do? There are no cold statistics, but veterans offer educated guesses about the won–lost column. It figures this way:

A very small percentage of hawk-eyed specialists can rack up 50 percent—that is, one out of every two birds shot at. This is superb shooting, rarely achieved; indeed, it is freely admitted that one out of three is excellent, truly big-league. Anything approaching 50 percent or better is phenomenal in coverts where grouse are wild and the sportsman doesn't wait for a sucker shot. Early gunning, in which dense foliage is a factor, ruins seasonal averages, while late-fall success builds reputations.

In the green and gold of an early covert, before the foliage has been destroyed by killing frosts, birds lie closer—but are soon swallowed by the screening brush after flush. All hands attempt line-of-sight shots—perfectly feasible where the target is well identified and tracked. There are glorious successes, and abject failures. One requires a good dog to retrieve or point dead. Averages decline unless the gunner is an ice-cold type who is unwilling to bet on anything other than a sure thing. But the hunter who will not attempt a difficult flying poke, within range, is counted contemptible. The sure-thing characters are not, and never will be, wing shooters. They are ranked with the old market hunters who collected birds with horsehair or wire snares.

A double on grouse is something to brag about, and although one constantly meets citizens who say they "do it all the time," the feat is not very commonplace. Great scattergunners will admit to four, five or a half-dozen in a lifetime. Each is a glorious triumph. I boast three true doubles, and still cry about a possible fourth that was defeated by an erring gun.

For a double, both birds must be in the air simultaneously. It is not enough to knock one down and have another flush immediately afterward. That produces back-to-back singles—well remembered, but not true doubles. It takes a measure of luck and skill to swing from one to another on a simultaneous flush, to powder one and then swing back on a second to score as solidly. Both will be traveling at full bore, often in different directions.

The last time I did it, two pats flushed in thick birch growth and towered toward a blue October sky. It was really an easy brace, and it happened so quickly that there was no time to get psyched. One came down in a smoke puff of feathers, and instinctively, I shifted to the other, still battering out of the birches. That one also collapsed at the shot. I'll remember them until doomsday.

I'll also remember the possible double that backfired. Late in November, toward the end of our northern New England season, I'd stepped into a little island of juniper—and two birds came out.

One towered left, and I took that one at the apex. Then, swinging quickly, I had the other dead to rights with an almost straightaway shot in light pole timber. The autoloader jammed, thanks to a twig that had worked its way into the receiver and blocked the sear. (Is this another argument for the side-by-side or over/under?)

A ruffed grouse is a native American, a bird of the fringe wilderness. No game farm put-and-take release has proved feasible, both because the bird is difficult to propagate under artificial conditions and because it becomes too thoroughly domesticated when ordinary rearing problems are solved. *Bonasa* can be raised by man—but forthwith loses a measure of wildness.

Fortunately, the native endures and seems to become even wilder as civilization makes inroads. Biologists seem convinced that it is "impossible to shoot them out." I do not agree, even though it is obvious that hard-hunted birds become ever warier. It still appears reasonable to take into consideration that a creature you kill is no longer there. In some cases I have the sinking feeling that politically oriented game biologists may use the pat as a buffer when they lack game-farm pheasants and quail to please an increasing army of license holders, and I hope I am wrong.

Actually, the hunters of grouse are their most dedicated champions. All desire a safe harvest, a renewable resource. Practically all zealous upland shooters scorn the "can't shoot 'em out" belief and favor seasons based on abundance or scarcity determined by spring drumming counts. There is a general dislike of the spring shooting season advocated by some management people. Spring is a time of renewal, not of harvest.

There is, fortunately for ruffed grouse, a burgeoning of interest in management. Most of the northern states employ crack teams of game biologists who are studying our grand flier and adding much to knowledge about the bird. Only a few commissions are motivated solely by political expediency.

Two citizen organizations are laboring to improve the lot of ruffed grouse. They are The Ruffed Grouse Society of America and Grouse Cover. The former has set up chapters in many states and is exploring the possibility of improving coverts by a process of cutting, gridding and planting of natural foodstuffs. Grouse

Cover offers no physical management projects, but keeps its members informed about worthy endeavors. Serious upland hunters profit by membership in either or both of these organizations, since they fight for the conservation and safe harvest of a bird that is the American wilderness epitomized. Can they win?

In an age of breast-beating about the rape of an environment, it may be unpopular to answer in the affirmative. But one must recall that the ruffed grouse is not easily defeated. *Bonasa* is a master of adversity, an atom of life that prospers in spite of constant attrition, an old native of a new world, fully capable of rolling with the punch and staging a comeback against all odds.

Grouse may be around long after all of the imported pheasant are pushed into city limits or the wire-enclosed acres of sophisticated game preserves. They'll be around—with quail and woodcock—because they cannot be domesticated and stocked to the gun. When cement and steel devour his coverts, *Bonasa* will simply move to the next hill. Characteristically, he will return to take possession of any ground that reverts to wilderness. There will be no compromise with humanity, no abject surrender. Our grouse will remain a supreme challenge, a flickering rocket in the shadow and shine of autumn foliage, a prize par excellence and a gourmet's delight at the last. Would you have it otherwise?

Great game birds earn reputations according to difficulty in flushing and the degree of skill necessary to bring them down. It is fatuous to place one over another, because the greatest is always the one that is over the guns at any moment in time. Who is to say whether a wild turkey is not most important in the dim dawn of a Carolina morning? Who challenges a white-winged dove darting through Texas skies? It would be futile to bad-mouth coveys of quail on a frosty-smoky morning in the Deep South, or pheasant clattering out of a golden Nebraska cornfield. Are there any to argue against timberdoodles, whistling through a screen of New Brunswick alders, or ducks cupping their wings against a screaming Chesapeake wind? I love them all.

But personally—and with a bow to colleagues who do not agree —I opt for ruffed grouse, the wild, educated type who batter out of thick ground cover and screening canopy in October and November. At that time, when the red maples are flaming and a fall woodland is stricken by frost, no other game bird seems quite so satisfactory, so absolutely challenging.

If this is a personal opinion, make the most of it. In any event, agree that ruffed grouse deserve loving care and careful management. We should never harry them in the spring; we should harvest carefully in the fall so that there is no possibility of depletion. Take no chances with an All-American game bird: always give *Bonasa* a fair shake, and scorn the opportunists who would gamble.

This may, or may not, be the greatest of all flying targets on earth; certainly it is among the greatest. For the little time we have left on this spinning sphere, it is only right to protect and to utilize properly one of the finest of them all.

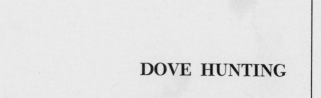

DOVE HUNTING

BY BOB BRISTER

THE SUN was a bronze ball of fire in the September sky, parching the field of freshly cut maize and sending up shimmering heat waves between the two groups of hunters huddled in the shade of mesquite brush along an irrigation levee.

The hunters were perhaps typical of the thousands of out-of-state sportsmen who in recent years have descended upon the Texas and Arizona "border country" for the white-winged dove season and then stayed around a few days to have as much or more sport with the surprisingly great concentrations of mourning doves.

One group was from the Deep South, to judge by their accents and double-barreled Parkers, and the other was from the Midwest. I chatted briefly with both groups in walking up and down the edge of the field looking for a good shooting spot where downed birds would be easy to find once the afternoon feeding flight started.

One of the midwestern group, a somewhat cocky youngster of perhaps eighteen, had distinguished himself by downing as many as ten whitewings with eleven shots, I was proudly told by his father. If I wanted to get some good action pictures of birds falling, he would be the one to stand behind.

I sized the boy up and decided otherwise. For one thing, he was suffering from the heat in heavy mustard-colored canvas hunting pants tucked into oiled lace-up boots, and at least one big red ant from a sizable mound in the sandy soil had infiltrated the boots, along with probably countless grass burrs and weed seeds. The boy was suffering more from heat than from the ant sting; the rows of colorful shooting patches proclaiming his prowess at breaking skeet targets only added thickness to his sweat-darkened shooting jacket—which happened to be black, the hottest color a man can wear in the southwestern sun.

Quite possibly because of the camera around my neck, or maybe the ant in his pants, the boy couldn't keep still. He walked along the edge of the brush with me, watching the sky and making imaginary fast points with the gun—"limbering up," as his father pointed out with obvious pride.

As we neared the other group of hunters, the boy cradled his 28-gauge autoloader and walked up to the first hunter, a white-haired and slightly portly gentleman with a worn 12-gauge double across his knees.

"Ah didn' know you needed a twelve-gauge for lil ol' mournin' doves," the boy remarked mockingly in a contrived Southern accent. "What do you shoot ducks with, a cannon?"

The white-haired man chuckled something to the man next to him.

"What was that?" the youngster asked belligerently, obviously smarting from his various discomforts as well as the stranger's distinctly unimpressed attitude.

"I said," the older man drawled, "that in a while these li'l ol' doves may make you wish you'd left that scare jacket at home."

The boy looked down, suddenly embarrassed by the shooting jacket and its patches, and then sized up his adversary. The man was probably sixty and well past his prime with a shotgun. The rolled western straw hat meant he was probably a local yokel; he seemed too cool and comfortable sitting there in the heat in loose-fitting khakis and Wellington boots—not at all the sort of clothing the boy had seen in the hunting magazines.

Bob Brister shows how to dress for most dove shooting—cool and camouflaged. Laceless boots, a light shirt and a straw hat all help to ward off the heat, and a belt-type shell-and-bird sack is more comfortable than a regular game bag, worn at the shoulder.

The boy's father had heard the exchange and reached his son's side, whipping out a billfold.

"How much would you like to bet against my boy's shooting now that you've insulted him?"

The old man smiled. "Suh," he said softly, "your boy walked over here and made remarks about my ol' gun, and where I come from we don't talk about a man's gun nor his dog. Now we can shoot for a hundred a bird or just whatever you think is right."

"You wouldn't want to make it a thousand, would you?"

"No, sir," the old man said. "I wouldn't want to have to take a check."

About that time the first flight of birds came whipping in—low, twisting with the wind in their tails, flying the course of an irrigation canal and its jungle of waist-high sunflowers and mesquite.

Guns began cracking up and down the canal, and as a string of swift dots appeared from behind him the boy picked one going away overhead and the bird slumped dead in the air.

"High house one!" he yelled back at his dad, trotting out into the open field to get a better look at the incoming flight.

Another swarm of gray shapes appeared over the brush, dipping, darting, wings whistling.

The boy tried an overhead incomer and got tail feathers, instantly realizing the birds were flying faster than they appeared to be. He pulled out farther ahead and killed one clean, then missed as the second bird dived and picked up speed. In fifteen minutes the 28-gauge had missed three, killed three cleanly and crippled four, two of which could not be found in the levee jungle of brush.

The man with the double had not fired a shot.

"That's not fair," the father bellowed down the line. "My boy took 'em as they came and you're going to wait and pick your shots."

"That's right, I was," the old-timer drawled, "but I don't reckon I'll have to now."

Down the row of mesquites came a single, and in one motion the old double picked up the darting dot, hesitated a split second as the bird cleared the brush over the open field, then swung past as the bird burst into a puff of feathers.

In the "swing-through" method of pass shooting, the gun barrel is swung past the bird, and just as it clears, the shot is fired. The momentum of the swing creates the necessary lead.

The next six consecutive birds in range folded as if poleaxed; the seventh was a high and wildly darting gray streak which made a down swoop just as the double fired. After that, the old gun did not falter.

The boy's father walked over, red-faced and peeling off bills, and when he had finished the old man handed them back to him.

"You go tell your boy he's had a good lesson," he grinned. "Just tell him to never hustle a hustler, particularly when he doesn't know the game."

All of which is a true story with several morals, the most significant one being that there is a distinct difference between shooting and hunting and another that neither youth, reflexes, skeet nor trap fully substitutes for judgment and experience in the more difficult tests of shotgun handling—of which mourning dove shooting is one of the toughest.

Another moral may be that dove shooting is a skill in which the hunter with proper clothing and equipment and with knowledge of the game and its flight characteristics has a tremendous advantage. Some of this can be learned from books, but the fine honing comes with experience.

In taking on an old-timer with a lifetime of experience shooting over southern millet fields and pea patches, the youngster had made his worst mistake. But the next-most-serious was attempting to compete with a 28-gauge skeet gun against the longer-range pattern of a tightly bored 12 on high-crossing doves. Some of the others were in not being properly dressed for the hunt (no one shoots very well when uncomfortable) and failure to pick the right shooting spot. In dressing for looks rather than camouflage, the boy had given away a percentage of easy shots. Doves may not flare as wildly as ducks, but they have a way of staying wide of hunters who stand up with shiny-stocked fire sticks in the middle of open fields. The distance differential between shots taken from camouflaged concealment and those standing in the open is usually several yards. Also, shots will be at more erratic targets once the hunter has been spotted.

Firing at birds traveling in such a direction that if killed they'll fall in heavy cover is not only poor betting form but poor sportsmanship. Picking the right spot for a stand is the first step a real dove expert takes in ensuring that his birds can be retrieved.

By actual sales of hunting licenses and ammunition and by state and national hunter surveys, the little gray streak is the most popular game bird in America. He's also the most populous, nesting in virtually every state and so prolific that his numbers seem to be holding up (and in some areas increasing) in the face of intensive hunting pressure. And the dove is, in this writer's opinion, the best-eating game bird of them all. I'd gladly swap pheasant under glass or quail and gravy for deep-fat-fried doves with a little cumin-seed seasoning.

To be a little more specific, dove hunting in the United States includes two species, the mourning dove and the whitewing. The first, as I mentioned, is found in every state of the Union except Alaska and Hawaii, while the whitewing resides in the South, extending from Texas to Florida in the southernmost tier of states.

Both the male and the female mourning doves are between 11 and 13 inches long and weigh in the neighborhood of 4 ounces. Overall, the body plumage is a grayish-brown with olive-colored highlights. The belly feathers are buff, the tails are bluish-gray and the wings are brown with white spots.

Whitewings are somewhat shorter than mourning doves and slightly heavier, and the females are a bit smaller than the males. Both sexes lack the color variations of the mourning dove, tending to an overall brownish gray with a bluish-black patch on the side of the head. Each wing has the large white patch that gives the bird its name.

The two species are quite similar in feeding habits, preferring grains and cereals to other foods and invariably dining in flocks. As a rule, whitewings are spookier than mourning doves and lack the trusting attitude that the latter develop in the off-season.

But then, the first step in preparing dove fricassee is finding the doves. And that varies widely in different parts of the country. The principal problem is finding birds sufficiently concentrated for a shoot. Just a few doves here and there likely won't mean many in the sack. Once you start shooting, they'll just move out.

Finding a huntable concentration (at least in most parts of America) means finding some agriculture, preferably small grain. Since mourning doves are ground feeders and do not like to feed on grain while it is standing, it does little good to find just any grainfield. But it can do plenty of good to make friends with farm-

The prime dove food throughout much of the Southwest is croton, or "goatweed." The birds concentrate in such fields after large black seeds begin to drop to the ground in September and October.

Having spotted doves on the telephone wires at left, a hunter moves into the area, expecting action. He got it; for every bird on the wires, there were several dozen feeding on the ground. This is one of the best ways to spot a feeding concentration early enough in the afternoon for a good shoot.

ers in some likely area and try and get tipped off when a grain-field is to be harvested. The doves will usually find their new banquet in a day or so, and every bird in that part of the country will try to get in on the feast.

Doves will also zero in on a natural grass or weed field if the food there happens to be ripened to the exact state they prefer. In the Southwest, where the largest populations of doves (and hunters) congregate every fall, one of the most important dove-drawing foods is croton, sometimes called snow-on-the-mountain or goatweed. It has a round, rather large black seed which usually drops to the ground after dry weather or a frost. Once the seeds begin dropping, doves may congregate by the hundreds in one field that is more mature than others nearby. Frequently this will be a pasture or laid-out field at a higher elevation or of sandier soil than the surrounding countryside.

The trick is to find a field with birds visible on wires, in dead trees, etc. Some of the time an investigation will prove those "sentinel" doves were the only ones around; other times the whole field may erupt in feeding doves. As a rule, when there are quite a few doves visible on wires and trees during the main feeding periods of early morning and midafternoon, there will be others feeding on the ground. I don't believe those doves sitting on the high spots are actually sentinels in the sense in which some other species, notably geese, seem to post "watchbirds." It's more likely that the doves sitting around have fed and are preening themselves and resting, waiting to have another go at the grain or weed seeds.

Interestingly enough, I believe these birds in conspicuous spots (they'll almost always pick a dead tree rather than one with thick vegetation) guide other doves to the feast. In other words, birds use the same system as hunters to find the best spots.

This means that doves are extremely susceptible to decoys, and why decoy hunting has not become more popular is difficult to understand. Doves seem to like company as much as ducks or more, yet whereas almost everyone hunts ducks with decoys, few dove hunters bother.

There are several types and brands of dove decoys on the market, and the only difficult thing about using them is getting them into place in a tall tree. If the country permits access by vehicle,

In picking a likely waterhole for doves, one of the prime considerations is a clean, flat shoreline with brush some distance away from the water. Doves are cautious when too much brush is too close. Look carefully and you'll see about twenty-five birds watering here; they blend in perfectly with the ground.

a stepladder is most convenient; the higher you can get the decoys, the farther away they'll attract doves. Just make sure it's a natural spot; if nothing else is taller, a barbed-wire fence will work. A half-dozen decoys will do; a dozen will do much better. Doves instinctively know that a real concentration of resting birds means there's likely to be something really good to eat nearby.

Another cause for a concentration of doves is the right sort of waterhole, which is not to be confused with just any sort of waterhole. I've seen concentrations of hundreds of birds waiting their turn to get a drink at one "tank" when dozens of other waterholes in the immediate area went completely without customers.

One of the most important considerations seems to be a flat, vegetation-clean shoreline, preferably one with some dust back away from the water. Steep or brushy banks are much less desirable, and smart old doves are wary of waterholes with dense timber almost to the water, presumably because of the predators (including man) that could be hiding there. A little flat pond in the middle of an open field with a couple of trees nearby is just about perfect. Early-arriving doves from the afternoon watering flight will usually go first to the trees, sit there awhile to case the countryside and then flutter down to drink. Later in the afternoon, usually from sundown to dark, the flights will whip in with less caution, often buzzing around the water like bees.

Doves tend to be creatures of habit, and if they have been accustomed to watering at a certain spot they will usually continue to come to it even after they are hunted there a time or two. But the more the hunting, the later they will come, and usually fewer of the original numbers will show up.

Rains that fill up every cow track and pothole will naturally scatter the birds to some extent, because they can water almost anywhere. But even after such rains I've seen birds piling into the same tank they were using before; they'll tend to follow that pattern by habit until the guns start booming.

Waterhole hunting is probably the easiest form of dove shooting, because the birds tend to slow up as they arrive, and also perhaps because in the late-afternoon light hunters are more difficult for the birds to see. But that doesn't mean it is best to stand out in the open blasting away. A shooting spot with some concealment, well back from the water, will get the most doves.

River sandbars are often excellent dove-watering locations, especially if there is some grain farming in the area. This particular spot is on the Red River on the Texas-Oklahoma border, a red-hot dove-hunting area in September.

Often downed birds will land in the water, and most hunters without dogs just wait until they drift to shore. But small lakes frequently are infested with hungry turtles, and many a hunter has seen his downed dove bobbing like a crappie cork suddenly disappear. A rod and reel tied with a sort of "bridle" to a stick or some other floating object can be used to retrieve doves that refuse to drift ashore. But the best bet is to try and dump 'em where they'll fall on land.

Roost shooting tends to be a rather hazardous procedure, in that doves normally come to roost just about at the end of legal hours, particularly after they've been hunted a bit, and game wardens rarely have slow watches. However, learning where roosts are can provide some good late-afternoon hunting if major flyways to a roost are scouted in advance. Again, doves tend to be creatures of habit and they'll usually go the most direct route.

The Greater Houston Gun Club, where I do much of my shotgun patterning and shooting, happens to be smack in the middle

Locating a heavy line of birds flying from feeding field to roost usually means a hot and heavy shoot. The hunter is using a shoulder bag which can be removed when the action starts.

Close shots at flights of doves are usually possible only if the hunter wears camouflage clothing and conceals himself in the background. These are whitewings in the Rio Grande Valley of Texas—large, swift birds almost one-third larger than mourning doves, and excellent eating.

of a dove-roost flyway, and since birds pass over it all year without associating much danger with the banging of guns below, it would be possible at the start of the season to get a limit off the trap or skeet range. But after hunting has been going on a couple of days, it is interesting to see just how wild and smart those same birds become.

Doves prefer dense thickets of young trees for roosting, and often a tree nursery is a great spot, except that the owner probably won't let you shoot within range of his plants. One roost I used to hunt finally was closed to the public because the nursery owner had trouble selling his trees; they had so many shot holes in 'em his customers thought they were full of worms. Perhaps the toughest shot in dove hunting, by the way, is at birds jumping out of a tree. A dove usually jumps, loses altitude to gain speed and thus is often shot over by hunters who can't figure out why they missed.

But say you've located your birds and bothered to take a friendly farmer the jug of his choice or some such favor, and you're in business. Next step is getting within range.

Doves are not mental giants. They may fly over a hunter standing in an open field wearing a red-and-yellow polka-dotted shirt. But the hunter who hides from them as he would from ducks will usually have more birds at the end of the day.

Those birds which fly over unconcealed hunters are often young of the year, and they aren't around long if they're that stupid. After the hunting starts, a large percentage of them learn to look for fire sticks on the ground. They may not visibly flare away, but they keep their distance, and the hunter deduces that they just happened to be passing out of range. Chances are they saw him.

Camouflage clothing can be a big help. If you get caught in an opening with doves coming, stand perfectly still and make like a dead tree or fence post. Doves apparently do not see objects very well, but like all wildlife they react immediately to movement. If they are close, it doesn't pay to drop down and try to hide. If

This young man was perfectly prepared for a warm-weather hunt—no shirt and a nylon-mesh camouflage vest. The Lab will prevent him from losing birds in the high grass.

These young hunters have been taught well. They're perfectly still as a dove passes, waiting until the bird clears heavy cover and can be killed over relatively open ground beyond the photo at the left.

they're still just dots in the distance, it does help to get down into the weeds, grain or whatever cover is available.

Next comes the most difficult part of dove hunting—which is not looking like an idiot who is shooting blanks.

Many reams have been written about how difficult the mourning dove is to hit. Other reams have been written to the effect that he isn't difficult at all if you know how.

I say it depends entirely upon hunting conditions. I've never seen the man who couldn't miss doves in a high wind over a feeding field.

On a still day, early in the season, with birds flying some route they're accustomed to using, it can be almost too easy. There will be a great many young birds, and they will come close and probably not flare with the shooting.

But any hotshot who's convinced he's figured out the game should try going back at the end of the season, or maybe to Texas or Arizona or Louisiana late in the fall when the big northern birds that have been hunted all the way south on their migration finally arrive on their wintering grounds. I can assure you that any hunter who tries them, particularly with a good wind blowing, is going to witness some tail feathers floating on the breeze.

Most shooters will kill more game with high-velocity loads, because of the slightly reduced lead involved, unless they are bothered by the additional recoil. There will be, at 40 yards or beyond, very little difference in retained velocity or striking energy between the high-velocity and the standard load (provided shot sizes and all other factors are equal). In general, the lighter loads will pattern more evenly than the high-velocity loads, but they take just a tiny bit more time getting there.

Increasingly popular as a dove gun is the 28-gauge, which is light and fast and has ballistic advantages over the .410 in that it deforms less shot and gets more pellets to the target in the same time because of a shorter shot string. Of course, you must be aware of its range limitations and not expect it to do the work of a 12.

But the main reason the 28 seems to "puff" birds so soundly is that it is fast, and the average shooter can get by better with a little less lead than with slower field loads in the other gauges. The only factory-loaded 28-gauge ammunition available happens to be high-brass, high-velocity, and the same hunter who scoffs at the "need" for high-velocity 20-gauge ammo for doves often praises the 28 for the very fact that it does employ high-velocity shells. This is simply speed of load, and contrary to what anyone says or how little feet-per-second difference there may be, I'm convinced the difference is very often a hit in the front end of a bird rather than shot in his tail feathers. Since doves have a propensity for flying quite well with their tail feathers dusted, this can be equated with the difference between dove and cheese that evening.

If you like "dove hamburger," then subscribe to the school of thought which suggests very tight chokes from a 12-gauge gun and at least 1¼ ounces of shot, on the theory that the bird is so small it can otherwise escape through holes in the pattern.

It is readily admitted that at 40 yards on a patterning board, even from a 12-gauge bored modified, there may be holes a dove might get through safely. Yet improved-cylinder in either 12- or 20-gauge is one of the deadliest dove chokes going.

How can this be? Well, the sages of patterning boards possibly do more patterning than dove shooting, and they may fail to consider that most doves offer crossing or high incoming shots. Very rarely are they going directly away or coming perfectly head-on to the hunter.

The patterning board shows what would happen to a straight-away. The more significant thing seems to be that crossing birds connecting with an elongated string of shot seem to get hit by several more pellets than they would be if they were going straight away. It may be that the bird is slowed or stopped by the front of the shot column and the trailing shot then piles in.

Certainly I did not arrive at this idea alone, although I've learned in years of live-bird competition and field shooting that it is easier to down a bird with an open choke if he's going at an angle to the gun—the more acute the angle, the more open the choke that will kill cleanly.

At the Perazzi factory in Italy, designing genius Ennio Matterelli showed me a complicated, computerized clay-target-launching device regulated to throw targets at various angles in front of a machine from which Perazzi guns are patterned. The gun is pre-set in its mount to ensure a well-centered hit on a target at any angle.

The purpose of this machine at Perazzi is to determine the minimum choke that is "safe" for International trap guns, which are bored to perform on the safe side for the hardest target in that game, the dead straightaway. Matterelli found that even an improved-cylinder would "smoke" targets crossing at right angles, yet would occasionally let them get by unbroken if they were thrown directly away and shot at the identical yardage.

Thus, the patterning board tells only part of the story, and the use of very tight chokes on doves at the ranges at which most hunters know where to hit a fast-crossing dove often translates into doveburger.

My own observations are that modified is a fine all-around 12-gauge choke for modern ammunition, and that on any but the windiest days No. 8 shot in an improved-cylinder barrel is murder. However, if the birds are extremely high and/or wild, a modified or full choke and 7½s may be indicated.

Most of the time a 20-gauge loaded with 8s or a 28-gauge loaded with 9s will do the job beautifully. Some shooters prefer 7½s because each pellet has more "authority" and because too dense a pattern of 9s tends to put too many shot into the bird. I agree with this theory personally, even though it tends to look patchy on paper. I've learned that hits by a couple of 7½s may mean more than multiple hits with 9s, but more important from the eating standpoint is that the heavier 7½s usually will penetrate the breast and lodge against the breastbone, where they're out of the way. Lighter shot often lodge in the breast muscle, and these are the ones that can send the consumer to the dentist.

There are many theories as to how best to hit doves in flight, ranging from the long, sustained leads taught by some skeet coaches to the "point directly at the bird and swing" theory of the late Robert Churchill.

Most of the best field shots and live-bird competitors I know in this country use the "swing-ahead" system—or to put it into dove terms, they "paint a gray streak" right through the dove and touch off when they see sufficient daylight between barrel and bird.

This "paint 'em out of the sky" approach is particularly important on doves because the birds are erratic fliers, constantly making sudden changes in angle of flight even when nobody is shooting at them. And they *really* cut some didoes when someone is. The swing-through shooter who starts his gun *behind* the bird and uses it as a "paintbrush" in sweeping through the target naturally reacts to sudden changes in direction or angle more easily than the shooter who is trying to hold a sustained lead far ahead of the bird, watching the target out of the corner of his eye. The swing-through shooter may start his move just as the bird makes one, and the "paintbrush barrel" just does whatever the bird does and then goes on past.

How far past is another matter, but to some extent the system is self-regulating. For most shots well within range about two to three bird lengths would be a pretty good average, because what appears to be two bird lengths at 30 yards may be considerably longer than that at 40 yards. On really close birds, one length usually does it. To be on the safe side it is better to lead a bit more on the long shots than seems necessary, particularly if you realize you've been dusting the previous birds in the behind.

For the low incomer at close range, almost no visible lead is required. Just blot out the bird with the muzzle, keep swinging and pull the trigger. If the bird is some distance out—say, 35 yards—start under the bird; come up through him, precisely through his head, and touch off when the barrel passes his head by about one bird length. These "bird lengths" are admittedly pretty rough indicators (they're to be figured for the whole bird, tail and all), but they're better than nothing for a beginner. It is all but impossible to estimate leads in terms of feet at anything but very short range. If you doubt that, pick out a spot you think is 40 yards away; then, while looking over a gun, pick out a couple of clumps of weeds which to you appear about a foot apart. Then have a friend measure. I think he'll find that the spaces are nearer two feet.

Most wing shooting is learned through experience, but the swing-through system with a fast-moving gun can definitely cut down the required forward allowance because of the lag in human-reaction and gun-ignition time between the mental order to

Here's one of the most common, and best, shots in dove hunting. An incomer taken at this instant will fall almost at the hunter's feet, and other birds will pass even closer for an easy second shot. Waiting until the birds are overhead will make subsequent shots more difficult.

"pull" and the gun's answering bang. This combination of the gun's lock time, ammunition-ignition time and mind-to-trigger-finger time takes only milliseconds, but it matters plenty when the target is zipping along in excess of 50 miles per hour and the gun barrel (in order to catch and pass it) must be moving even faster.

Years ago, as a youngster, I really fouled up my field shooting one fall by reading some of the expert treatises published in those days relating to 5- and 6-foot leads ahead of crossing birds. I found myself trying to slow down and measure 5 or 6 feet, and I was still hitting birds in the tail. On downwind doves at maximum range I found it almost impossible; I'd have the barrel so far out in front I could barely see the bird out of the corner of my eye, and I'd still be cutting tail feathers. So I went back to the old instinctive way—coming from behind, seeing those several bird lengths in front and touching off at that instant. I could see the target better; I could get a better last-minute "readout" on angle and distance—but more important, the doves started falling again.

Actually, the trick of hitting doves solidly and cleanly is only collegiate level in the fine art of serious dove shooting; the master's degree comes when you learn *when* to hit 'em in order to make 'em fall where they can be retrieved. This is actually not as difficult as it sounds, particularly if the hunter sets up his shooting location with preplanned spots of open ground, a road or low cover in mind.

One of the easiest shots to make on a dove (and certainly the easiest for a retrieve if you hit him) is the incomer taken when he's well out in front of you, just as soon as he's within, say, 30 yards.

Instructions for this relatively easy shot bear repeating. A gunner can make it by starting out under the bird, coming straight up through him and, when he's blotted out by the gun, just swinging past and pulling the trigger. Taken in this manner, the incoming bird will usually fall almost at the hunter's feet. Most of the time, other doves in the flight (rather than flaring and climbing as ducks or geese would do) will just speed up and come barreling past, providing a good crossing or overhead shot well within range.

Most hunters I've observed in action, however, will watch a flight come within range, wait until the birds are directly over-

The versatility of a two-barreled gun is an asset, but just about anything works. Here, pumps, autos and over/unders all collected equal numbers of birds.

head and then shoot—which means any bird hit will fall some distance past them, and any second or third shot will be at a distant, much more difficult, bird to hit or to find afterward.

One of the reasons I personally prefer an over/under or side-by-side with selective chokes to an automatic or pump shotgun is the opportunity to kill the incomers some distance out (with the tight barrel) and save the open choke to "mop up" as they come on past. In other words, the barrels are fired in just the opposite of the "open-barrel-first" manner in which doubles and over/unders are customarily used.

Choice of gun type or gauge is purely a personal matter, and I know quite a few old pros who get their limits with a .410. But that doesn't mean a good little gun is as deadly as a good big gun. My personal favorites for doves are the 28-gauge and the 12. If the birds can be shot within 35 yards, I like the light, sporty feel and extremely fast load of the 28. If the doves are wild, I usually shoot a 3¼ x 1¼ 12-gauge load. Shot sizes depend upon gun and chokes: the tighter the choke and the larger the gun, the larger the shot it can effectively handle. Smaller guns and open chokes need the additional density of lighter shot to avoid holes in the pattern. I see no advantage in using shot larger than 7½s on doves.

The "harder-hitting" aspects of fast loads are to a great extent myth. This is because of a principle of physics which says that the faster something starts out against the resistance of air, the faster it will be slowed down by it. Shotgun pellets have poor ballistic qualities to begin with, and tests I've made have shown that a 3¼-dram load with 1¼ ounces of shot fired from a 12-gauge gun will penetrate as well (and thus hit as hard) as the high-velocity 3¾-dram load at 45 yards. The slower load is proportionately less affected by air resistance, and it also patterns better for that reason.

For the shooter firing behind birds, the fastest load he can get will help. This doesn't necessarily mean high-base loads. One of my favorite fast but light loads is now the official ISU-Olympic Clay Pigeon load, 3¼ drams equivalent with 1⅛ ounces of shot. A lighter fast one (for relatively short range) is the 3-dram, 1-ounce 12-gauge load. It has surprisingly light recoil for the powder charge and whistles out to its target at almost the same speed as a high-velocity duck load. For really pleasant shooting and loads that pack authority but don't disintegrate doves when they're close over a waterhole, I often handload 2¾-dram, 1-ounce 12-gauge loads, and they are a particular pleasure in fine, lightweight doubles which really don't deserve heavy "American" loads. I have a friend who shoots an English-made Boss over/ under; he wouldn't consider putting as much as 3 drams of powder through it. Yet he certainly kills his share of doves when they're within the range where most hunters can hit 'em.

That range, by the way, is not very far if consistency of kills is a part of the equation. I read someplace that a dove for five shells is considered pretty good shooting. And from observing a great many hunters in the field I'd believe that, along with the idea that about 90 percent of the birds killed are downed at ranges inside 35 yards (which is probably just as well, because the nearer a dove falls the easier he is to find).

On some hunts I've witnessed losses of dead birds that were sickening—hunters continuing to shoot bird after bird while knowing they would never find even a small percentage of them.

Certainly the loss of some doves is inevitable in heavy cover when the gunner is hunting without a dog. The birds blend so per-

fectly with the ground that they can be difficult to see even against
bare dirt—much more so if they fall into dense weeds or grain. But
they're not impossible to find if the looking is combined with common sense.

If there is a road through a grainfield or pea patch, perhaps the
obvious place for hunters to shoot would be along that road. But
if the birds tend to be coming mostly from one direction (as they
so often will be), the hunter may find that by backing off the road
and hiding in the field he can drop a good percentage of his incoming birds into the road clearing or near enough to it so that
they are easy to mark and find.

For some reason, most hunters just won't do this. Last fall I
watched one group standing along a road in the Rio Grande Valley of Texas dropping dove after dove into the same tiny patch of
mesquite brush and cactus. They could have moved almost any-
place and eliminated that loss, but they continued shooting at the
same spot in the same way until a warden walked over and

*Here is a dove about to be lost forever. Shooting over such thick cover
inevitably results in very few retrieves. The hunter should have backed
off the road and shot sooner.*

pinched the whole bunch for failure to make "reasonable effort" to retrieve their limits.

That particular tidbit is passed on for future reference; the mere fact that you do not have the limit in your hunting sack doesn't mean you can't be in trouble for shooting bird after bird that you don't find. Wardens are usually reasonable about such things, but they also expect a reasonable effort on your part.

The best way to eliminate lost doves is to shoot 'em one at a time, watch exactly where they fall, mark the spot in line with some distant tree or landmark and, most important, never take your eyes off that spot and go straight to it.

If there is nothing to mark it by, try to estimate the range at which the shot was made, get on a line directly to where the bird fell and count steps. If the shot was approximately 30 yards, you'll at least know by counting when you're getting close.

I've found it best to stop a few yards short of where the bird fell, look carefully, then take another step or two and stop again. This is because the human eye sees things better standing still than when the landscape is moving past as you walk. To see a dead dove often requires the sharpest vision you can possibly muster. Look for feathers, because the lighter underfeathers often show up against grass or soil that may blend perfectly with the darker gray outer feathers of the bird. A great deal of the time you'll find feathers first, then track down the bird.

If you're looking for a bird in some vast open field and you're close (perhaps having found a few feathers or counted steps to the spot), mark the area with a handkerchief on a grain stalk or weed so that it can be seen from some distance. Then work around that spot in ever-widening circles. You'll usually find your dove, although it may be because you stepped on it. Failure to mark the spot may mean you'll lose your point of reference and give up too easily.

The big problem in dove shooting is that it so often happens all at once. The flight starts, you knock down a bird and about that time two more come zipping past. There is terrible temptation to try for that double and to go ahead shooting without retrieving. But once several doves are down, the odds of finding them diminish drastically.

All of which is written in the knowledge that most dove hunters

Given the command to retrieve, a young Lab goes at it with gusto. The bird is in the foreground, in the dog's shadow.

do not use retrievers, and this is perhaps the saddest part of the story, because the loss of a fine little game bird can be cut to almost nothing by the use of almost any dog.

Once I took my old Labrador, King, through a cornfield where a party of hunters had just passed, and I never fired a shot. King brought me my limit of dead birds and cripples that the other group, which had no dog, had simply been unable to find in the heavy cover.

Although a retrieving breed is great for doves, a lot of other dogs will at least find birds for you. My wife had a little Cairn terrier, Hoot Mon, who, until he died at the age of fifteen, brought back many a dove that otherwise would surely have been lost. My two Brittany spaniels will both retrieve doves, although the older dog persists in pointing each dead bird rather than bringing it back. I don't mind; so long as he finds 'em, I'll go get 'em.

The old idea that a "good dog" won't pick up a dove because of the loose feathers he'll get in his mouth is, I've found, mostly a matter of talk. A good dog will do what you tell him to do. Dogs don't like those loose feathers, sure, but most hunting dogs would

rather go hunting, any kind of hunting, than stay home in the kennel. My dogs like dove hunting because they like to go hunting,
period.

One thing to remember, particularly with Labradors or other
heavy-coated water breeds, is that dove hunting in most parts of
the country is often done in quite warm weather and the dog suffers because of the heat. Make sure you carry plenty of water. I
usually take along a canteen, and I've shared it with many different dogs; they soon learn to drink from a stream of water poured
out of a canteen—that is, they'll learn if they're thirsty enough.

Mourning doves like warm weather, and they also like dry
weather if they can find it. I've seen whole populations shift across
country just because of a local rain. In the Southwest during September and October, temperatures often hover around 100 degrees, and this means the hunter should dress accordingly and also

*Almost any dog, even a cairn terrier (right), can retrieve doves if well
trained.*

make sure his birds don't spoil in a poorly ventilated hunting sack.

Actually, doves can take a great deal of heat without tainting, but it is a good idea anytime shooting slows up to field-dress the birds in hand, because it permits them to cool out a bit sooner and eliminates the possibility of a "wild taste." Doves are very easy birds to clean; you really don't even need a knife. Grasp the bird at the bottom of the breastbone with one hand and hold the back firmly with the other. Then just pull the breast loose from the body. The entrails will be right under the base of the breast and can be removed with little muss and without picking of feathers until later.

Many hunters do it the other way around—plucking feathers while they wait for more birds to come, but rarely gutting out the ones they've plucked. This saves cleaning time afterward, but does little to improve the quality of the meat on a hot day.

To tell the honest truth, it is very difficult to foul up the flavor of a dove. I've carried doves all afternoon in 100-plus temperatures and cleaned them hours afterward, and they were still great eating. In fact, in our part of the Southwest an increasing number of hunters will quickly swap a quail for a dove—and that's testimony enough to the dove as table fare.

| TURKEY HUNTING |

BY JIM BRADY

I'M NOT altogether sure that a chapter on hunting the wild turkey rightly belongs in a book devoted to shooting of upland game and waterfowl. It's not because of any reservations about the wild turkey's place in the hierarchy of game birds that I voice this doubt, but rather for the reason that the successful hunting of this great American bird requires skills, knowledge and attitudes that are totally different from those employed in the pursuit of all its avian brothers.

Hunting the wild turkey is more akin to big-game hunting than to the pursuit of any other feathered game. In fact, the turkey is classified as big game in some states, and others are contemplating placing the turkey in this category. To all such moves I say—amen!

When I started my hunting career at the age of twelve, no man I knew had ever hunted wild turkeys or had any hope of ever doing so. They were a game species of the distant past, gone like the buffalo and the passenger pigeon, never to return. Like the buffalo, the wild turkey had retreated before the habitat-destroying advance of civilization.

The turkey's greatest enemy was the woodsman's ax which decimated the mature and open hardwood forests that provided prime turkey habitat over most of the bird's range. Coupled with heavy hunting in all seasons of the year, this destruction of its range resulted in the retreat of the wild turkey to seldom-penetrated pockets of wilderness in Pennsylvania, West Virginia, South Carolina, Florida and a few other states. How fortunate for all of us, hunter and nonhunter alike, that this seed stock was able to survive.

The turkey is a native of the northern part of the Western Hemisphere, and there is no evidence that this bird existed anywhere but in its original range, which stretched from Quebec and Ontario southward to Florida and west to Mexico and the Rockies.

When the devastated forests had reseeded themselves, there occurred an era when most of our woodlands consisted of brushy forests in early stages of growth that provided ideal habitat for deer and grouse, and these two grand game species proceeded to multiply abundantly and to supply magnificent sport for generations of hunters. During these years, wild-turkey hunting was a sport enjoyed by a tiny minority of men who lived in the Deep South and were privileged to hunt on some of the great private hunting clubs that existed on the remnants of the old cotton and rice plantations of this region. These southern hunters kept alive a reservoir of turkey-hunting know-how and tradition that have now spread into the vastly expanded turkey ranges that exist today.

The turkey is by far the largest of our upland game birds, and hunting it is much like hunting a big-game animal.

As the woodlands of the continent slowly recovered from the ravages visited upon them and mature tree growth gradually shaded out the brushy understory, the remnant turkey population began a slow migration into this newly available habitat. Ideal turkey habitat consists of open woodlands with little undergrowth, so that the bird can use its first line of defense against its enemies —its piercing eyesight. Mature woodlands also provide the roosting trees so necessary to the turkey and the mast crops that make up a large part of its diet.

This natural spread of the wild turkey into suitable habitat proceeded with all the deliberate speed of an advancing glacier, and if turkey-hunting opportunities depended upon it today, the sportsmen of the present would have little more opportunity to hunt turkeys than those who lived forty or more years ago.

The habitat required by the wild turkey existed, but how to fill this great void? This was the problem that faced wildlife biologists and game managers. To their great credit, and after many trials and tribulations, it was finally solved. First, turkeys raised on game farms were tried and found wanting. These birds just could not make it in the wild. So box and pen traps were used to capture wild stock, and plantings of birds so obtained into suitable habitat showed great promise. But not enough birds could be captured by such methods to permit large-scale transplants of these true wild turkeys.

At this point, some genius thought to try the cannon-projected net that was being used to capture waterfowl for banding and study, and the return of the wild turkey was under way. By the use of this equipment, turkeys could be captured in sufficient numbers to permit the eventual stocking of all available range. Within a very few years after the successful establishment of a new population, turkeys can be trapped from it for transplanting to still other locations. By reason of this wildlife-management breakthrough, wild-turkey hunting is available in forty of our fifty states—even in areas far beyond the original range of this bird, such as west of the Rocky Mountains.

In the hunting of no other game is a knowledge of the habits of his quarry throughout the year so necessary to the hunter's success. With this in mind, let's pry into the home life of the wild turkey.

At daybreak, the spring woods echo with the mating gobble of the tom turkey.

As the hours of daylight lengthen with the coming of spring, the procreative impulse is triggered in our wild-turkey populations. This may take place as early in the year as March in some areas. Wildlife biologists are not yet certain as to whether the causative factor is temperature, increasing daylight or perhaps the changing angle of light as the sun reaches and passes the vernal equinox.

Whatever the reason, the spring woods in turkey country begin to ring with the gobbling of the males. Gobbling is the mating call of the male bird and is frequently sounded just at daybreak, while the tom is still in his roosting tree. It is sounded more frequently after he has descended from the roost and alighted on the ground. It is a signal to the hens that he is ready, willing and able; for the male turkey leads the good life in that the hens will usually come to him for mating when His Highness sends his message belling through the forest.

Polygamy is the rule among turkeys, and the gobbler will mate with a number of hens which form his harem. The gobbler will answer the mating yelp of the hen by gobbling in response to it, and if the hen does not put in an appearance in short order, he will advance toward the source of the yelping in an effort to find her. This last bit of behavior is the cornerstone upon which the whole technique of spring gobbler hunting depends.

When hens are in his presence during the mating season, the gobbler will "strut" by fluffing out his feathers and erecting his tail feathers in the shape of a great fan. The head and neck will be drawn back, assuming an "S" shape, and the wing tips are dropped to the ground so as to drag upon it. I recently examined the wing tips of a big gobbler that had been shot by my hunting partner and found them to be broken and frayed—certain evidence of recent strutting. This was a mature gobbler weighing 21 pounds that carried a beard 10 inches in length.

As the gobbler struts, he will at times make a booming sound from within his chest. Some grouse hunters turned turkey hunters refer to this as drumming, while others call it booming. While he is strutting or excited by the presence or expected presence of hens, the gobbler's head, which is normally of a pale bluish color mixed with white, will become suffused with an almost glowing shade of bright red.

Gobblers do little feeding during the mating season, subsisting in large part on the stored nutritional value of the breast sponge, a rich layer of oily fat lying immediately over the breast. New hunters sometimes look with suspicion on the breast sponge when they come across it while dressing their birds, thinking that something is radically wrong that has rendered their turkey inedible. Just this past spring I was hunting with a partner who is a surgeon and had bagged his first spring gobbler. When Doc spied the breast sponge while dressing his bird, I thought for a moment that he would call for the services of a pathologist, until I assured him that it indicated a gobbler in prime spring condition.

During the months of winter, the male turkeys have kept to themselves in their own all-male flocks. They have very little if any contact with the hens and their family flocks, consisting of the previous spring's brood. By midwinter, even the young gobblers born the previous spring will have left the family groups and gathered into their own flocks. This flocking together of gobblers is according to age classes, and the flocks will consist of birds hatched during the same spring. The older birds will usually repel any attempts by younger males to join their club.

With the arrival of spring, these all-male flocks will break up into trios, pairs or individual birds, which will establish and lay claim to breeding and strutting territories. The boundaries of these breeding territories are somewhat flexible, but the individual birds or groups will defend them against invasion by other gobblers. All is now set for the great show, and gobbling begins.

Gobbling is most intense just at daybreak and tapers off in frequency and intensity as the morning sun climbs higher. This lessening of gobbling frequency is due in part to the gobblers' having made contact with the hens. Once this contact has been made, there is, of course, no compelling reason for the males to continue gobbling. Intermittent gobbling, however, will be heard throughout the day, and the man who knows what it's all about can sometimes turn this knowledge to his advantage in those states where spring hunting is allowed all through the hours of daylight. This midmorning and afternoon gobbling may be by males that have not succeeded in gathering a harem of hens, or by gobblers that have recovered their vigor after mating in the early hours of the day and are now of a mind to seek further female companionship. These birds can be called in to the gun.

The toms will also gobble in the evening, just before or after ascending to their roosts. This evening gobbling probably serves two purposes: it lets the hens know where their lord and master is roosting and is also a declaration of territorial rights addressed to other gobblers, letting them know that this area and the hens in it are private property. The stage is now set for the entrance of the second most important character in this script: you, the hunter.

Locating a general area for hunting the wild turkey is the first—and easiest—step that must be taken on the road to success in bagging our largest and wiliest game bird. Very few turkeys will be killed if the hunter relies on vague reports which allege that turkeys are present or have been seen in some general area of a state. More specific information is required, and in my experience the wildlife agencies of the various states are the best and most reliable sources of this kind of information. These organizations are interested in your success. It is one of the main reasons for their existence, and I've invariably found them to be helpful and courteous.

When information has been received as to the location of a good turkey-hunting region, local agents of the wildlife departments can usually be relied upon to supply explicit information as to where turkeys can be found at the particular season of the year. Even with this assistance, pinpointing the location of turkeys on a proposed hunting ground is a do-it-yourself project that the hunter must be willing to tackle. If he is not disposed to do so, he might just as well leave his gun in the rack and forget about turkey hunting.

In both spring and fall seasons, it will pay off in birds brought to the gun if the hunter can be in the area several days before the opening of the season in order to locate the birds and become familiar with the country. In the spring, turkeys are likely to be in mature timber adjacent to brushy openings and forest edges. These open, brushy areas provide the type of cover preferred by the hen turkey for nesting.

The incubating hen will leave the nest for short periods each day in order to feed, water and use the dusting spots of which all turkeys are so fond. These dusting spots are one of the best indications of the presence of turkeys. They are shallow, oval depressions in dry or sandy soil, and turkey body feathers are frequently found in them. These depressions are about 2 feet in length and 10 to 12 inches wide.

Turkeys are so fond of these dust baths that personnel of the West Virginia Department of Natural Resources have trapped turkeys for transplanting by loosening the soil and providing ready-made dusting spots. A cannon-projected net was set after turkeys began using the area. Look for these dust baths and for droppings, feathers and turkey tracks in moist ground such as the edges of ponds, streams and waterholes.

Turkey droppings are a prime source of information for the hunter. In addition to their value as an indication that turkeys are present in a given area, the hunter can determine the sex of the bird that left the dropping. Gobbler droppings are straight for the greater part of their length, with a hook or curve at one end so that they roughly resemble the letter "J." Hen droppings are deposited in a small flattened pile. Fresh droppings look like just that, and the hunter should take into account the effects of weather conditions when assessing the age of turkey droppings.

Scratchings, which are the bare spots on the forest floor made by feeding turkeys, are of more interest to the fall hunter than to the spring gobbler hunter, since most feeding by this method occurs during fall and winter. Occasional scratchings will be found in the spring, but these are probably due more to behavioral reflexes than to any extensive feeding.

Hunting any game in the springtime is an entirely new notion to most gunners. All the customs and traditions of generations of sportsmen have been built on the idea that fall is the time for hunting, and that those crazy turkey hunters are probably ruining their own sport by killing gobblers in the spring. The statement that the hunting of toms in the spring is, from a game-management standpoint, a sounder procedure with regard to its effect on total turkey populations than fall hunting (when any turkey may be taken) is at first viewed with suspicion.

Wildlife biologists who specialize in the management of turkeys are unanimous in their opinion that spring hunting is the preferred method of harvest in those areas where turkey populations have been newly established or where a low population must be built up in numbers. This opinion arises from study and research, which have revealed the following facts regarding the effects of spring hunting:

The standard method of spring hunting is to call in a gobbling bird, and only males are taken. Since turkeys are polygamous, most males are in excess of reproductive requirements. A percentage of males have no opportunity to breed in a particular season, and their removal has no effect on the total turkey population the following year. Spring hunting, when the gobblers are at their greatest weight and in their finest plumage, begins after the mating season has passed its peak, when it is reasonable to assume that all hens capable of reproduction have been mated.

Marginal turkey areas where populations could be seriously depleted during fall seasons, when any turkey may be taken, have the capability of providing high-quality spring gobbler hunting. Some southern states with high turkey populations have traditionally held spring seasons only. No real gentleman in these states would even *think* of hunting turkeys in the fall. Fall hunting in these states is regarded as a game for poachers, game hogs and other such trash.

When the all-male flocks break up for the mating season, individual gobbling and strutting territories may be separated by some distance, and the most successful method of hunting at this time is for the hunter to locate individual gobbling birds. In the hunter's favor is the fact that the spring gobbler believes in advertising and loudly announces his whereabouts to the world.

Just at break of day, the gobbler will sound off while still on his roosting tree. He may do this several times before descending to the ground. This gobbling while still on the roost is probably done to let the hens know of his whereabouts. When he has left the roost and is on the ground, he will send his summons reverberating through the forest again at frequent intervals. To the dyed-in-the-wool turkey hunter, there is no greater sound in nature. Not without reason has the spring turkey gobbler been dubbed "The Mountain Shaker."

The most successful turkey hunters spend considerable time in efforts to locate gobbling turkeys prior to the opening of the season. I can think of no finer way to spend a beautiful spring morning than scouting for gobblers. It is almost as much sport as the actual hunting. If your territory is traversed by a network of roads, be out well before dawn and drive through the area, stopping every quarter of a mile or so to listen for gobbling. Each gobbler has established his own territory, and if you hear him sound off, you can be fairly certain that he will be in this general area on subsequent mornings. If there are no roads through your hunting ground—the usual thing, since high turkey populations and navigable roads are mutually exclusive—travel through the area on foot along trails and ridgetops.

While engaged in this preseason scouting, keep your eyes open for such turkey sign as tracks, droppings, feathers and dust baths. Keep your ears attuned to catch the sound of gobbling toms. Once you have heard the gobble of a wild turkey, you are not apt to confuse it with any other sound in the wilderness. It is usually much louder and clearer than the gobbling of a barnyard bird, and on a still morning in mountainous country it can be heard for at least a mile.

The three most popular types of call are, from left: the lidded box, the diaphragm and the slate-and-peg call.

A turkey call is a valuable adjunct to these preseason jaunts. Sound the mating yelp of the hen at each stop you make. Any male turkey within hearing will very likely gobble in response to your calling, and you will have his position pinpointed. If you are using a topographic map—an excellent idea indeed—mark down his approximate position for future reference.

In the late afternoon or evening, right up to full dark, you can locate toms on their roosts by inducing them to gobble. You can do this by sounding the gobble on the type of turkey call known as a gobbling box. This is a typical two-sided box call with the lid attached to the box by rubber bands inserted into small screw eyes. Shaking the box produces a fair imitation of the gobble as the lid slides back and forth across the two edges of the box. A tom on the roost will answer by gobbling in reply, and you have another one located.

Roosting toms will at times sound off with a gobble on hearing any sudden and sharp sound. They have been known to gobble in answer to such sounds as shots, the clapping together of two pieces of wood, automobile horns and—believe it or not—the notes of a bugle. But I stick to the gobble when attempting to locate roosting toms; it is a natural sound and the one most likely to bring a response.

An experienced spring gobbler hunter will make every effort to locate as many birds as he can before the season opens. If the success of your hunt should depend on your having located one bird, you might run into the problem of competition from some other hunter who has a fix on the same turkey. Competition is *not* the spice of life when you're hunting the wild turkey.

Most of the action when you're hunting gobblers in spring will occur during the first few hours of daylight, from daybreak to about 8 o'clock. The first hour is by far the most productive, and it will pay off in birds bagged to arrive on the scene as early as possible. Try to be onstage well before daylight. Assuming that you have the roosting area of a gobbler located, carefully work your way to within 150 to 200 yards of him. You will have used your flashlight up to this point while working your way through the woods, but now it is time to put it away.

It is impossible to travel through the forest at night without making some noise, but the slight sounds of breaking twigs under-

foot and the soft swish of brush and branches against your clothing are normal night noises made by many nocturnal animals and
are not likely to disturb the turkey. During the last 100 yards or so
to your calling position, you must move without light, but you'll
soon become skilled in moving short distances through the woods
in total darkness. If you have started your hunt at an early enough
hour, you will have plenty of time to execute this maneuver.

Now the magic hour for the spring gobbler hunter approaches.
The sky begins to lighten in the east, and the first faint notes of
small birds are heard. The slight morning breeze that always
seems to arise with the dawn brings with it a faint chill, and you
turn up the collar of your camouflage jacket in response to it. As
the eastern sky grows still lighter, your gobbler may sound off
from his roost. If he does not, do nothing. Stay put and be patient.
The skilled turkey hunter is a past master of the waiting game.

If you are good at it, you may at this point sound the hoot of the
barred owl, and this may cause the turkey to gobble. Don't use the
hoot of the horned owl, as this bird is no friend of the wild turkey
and the sound may silence a tom that was about to gobble. You
should not sound the hen yelp on your call while the gobbler is

*Just at daybreak, the spring gob-
bler hunter uses his call to send a
series of searching yelps through
the forest. The productive hours
last from first light until about
8 A.M.*

still on his roost. Since the hens normally come to the gobbler for mating, the sound of a hen yelping at this time may cause him to stay on his roost, expecting to see one approaching. The greatest value to the hunter in hearing the tom gobble on the roost is that his location is now known.

On a quiet morning, you will usually be able to hear the turkey leave his roost and alight on the ground. He will accomplish this by flying down to a small opening some 50 to 80 yards from his tree. If you had approached closer than 150 yards or so, he might well fly right over you or land so close to your position as to make things extremely interesting, to say the least. There is also some danger of spooking the gobbler if his roost is approached too closely.

When you hear the gobbler leave the roost, or if enough time has passed since daybreak so that, in all likelihood, he is on the ground, get ready to call. Don your camouflage gloves and drop the face mask into position if you will be wearing these items. Sound a soft and low series of three or four hen yelps on your call. *Keouk! Keouk! Keouk!* In most instances, your calling will bring forth a nerve-shattering gobble from the turkey. Answer immediately with another series of hen yelps. The turkey will probably continue to gobble for some minutes in an attempt to bring the hen to him. There will now ensue a contest of wills between you and the tom. Thinking he has heard a hen, the gobbler will try to lure the lady to him by gobbling and strutting. You must play the part of a hen who does not appear overanxious to rush onto the scene with unseemly haste. By so doing, you'll force the tom to come to you.

Sound the hen yelp in reply to the turkey's gobbling by answering about every third gobble. Some hunters advise that all calling should cease once the tom has gobbled a few times in reply. It has been my experience that if you stop calling altogether, the gobbler is likely to think that the hen has departed the scene, and he will go off in search of another partner. If you must choose between calling too much and calling too little, I advise frequent calling. I've never had a gobbler depart because of too much calling, but on several occasions I'm sure that I've had one wander off when I was stingy with my replies.

Some extremely successful gobbler hunters of my acquaintance call almost constantly once a gobbler has become interested. When a turkey that has been gobbling in fine style suddenly stops, be on your guard. He may be coming straight on to where he supposes the hen to be, or he may be circling so as to come in from the side or rear. You must keep your eyes and ears sharply attuned at this moment so as to catch the slightest sound or movement. This is one of those times when eyes in the back of your head would really help.

If a turkey gobbles from a position on higher ground than your own, move quickly where possible so that you are about 50 yards above him or on the same level. It seems to be much easier to bring a turkey uphill or in on the same level. It is also difficult to bring a gobbling bird across a brushy hollow or a stream, and such features of the terrain should be taken into account when you're selecting a calling position. Turkeys will not enter brushy thickets, so you must use whatever cover is available on fairly open ground when calling.

When you are sure that the gobbler is advancing toward you, a quick check of your cover and equipment should be made. Bring your gun up to where it can be brought to bear with the least movement. Because of their magnificent eyesight, turkeys will spot the slightest movement when they are in close range. Sunlight reflecting off a moving gun barrel has saved the life of many a gobbler.

As you turn your head slowly from side to side in an effort to see the oncoming turkey, you are suddenly aware of a slight movement through the sparse vegetation in front of you. Suddenly, the turkey's head and neck dart forward like a striking snake, and you almost drop your gun as a thundering gobble rings through the aisles of the forest. Recovering your composure, you see the turkey go into full strut—wing tips dragging on the ground, tail feathers spread into a gigantic fan, head and neck drawn back tightly against his chest. You almost forget what brought you to this mountainside as you stare with fascination at this marvelous display.

As the gobbler continues to advance, you can see the full beard dangling from his chest. This beard, a coarse and hairy growth, is the proud badge of the male turkey. At this moment you may hear a deep *vrooomm!* coming from deep within the turkey's chest.

The "beard" protruding from this bird's chest is the badge of the gobbler.

This is the "pulmonic puff" often sounded by a strutting gobbler.

This is the moment when you must impose upon yourself the utmost restraint. You will be tempted to shoot while the gobbler is still a good 50 yards or more from you. Hold it! This is much too long a range for delivery of the turkey-killing head-and-neck shot favored by almost all experts. Keep a tight rein on yourself. Hold your shot until the turkey is within 25 to 30 yards of you. I killed a spring gobbler this year at 27 steps, or about 16 yards. On the morning before, I had called a gobbler to within 20 feet of my hiding place but was unable to shoot because this bird came in on my off side—I shoot from the left shoulder—and the small motion I made in order to bring my gun to bear sent him streaking through the brush.

When your gobbler is well within range, aim just below the junction of head and neck and press the trigger. If your hold is good, this shot will usually anchor the turkey right on the spot. Move swiftly to where your turkey is beating his wings on the ground and take hold of him. Watch out for those sharp spurs on the gobbler's legs, as they can inflict painful wounds. Failure to get to your turkey immediately may result in the loss of a bird that is mortally wounded. Such birds may run off and hide in some brushy hollow or log pile where they will eventually die.

At times, a gobbler will come in to your calling without a sound, and you will not be aware of his presence until it is too late. Wise old gobblers who have had previous contact with hunters may cir-

*The open character of the woodlands inhabited by the wild turkey re-
quires that the hunter become adept at using whatever sparse cover is
available. This man has chosen a root hole, the only concealment in
the area.*

cle around your calling position and come in from the rear. This
very thing has happened to me more than once, and by the time I
became aware of the turkey's presence and tried to turn and fire,
my target was a mere dark streak through the brush. I personally
will not take such shots, for fear of merely wounding the bird. I
would far rather not even see or hear a bird all day than have this
happen. One trick used by some experienced hunters is to wait
until the turkey's head is behind a tree or other solid object before
snapping the gun to the shoulder preparatory to shooting.

While calling to a previously located gobbler is perhaps the
easiest and most satisfying method of spring hunting, thousands
of toms are bagged each spring by hunters who, having located
good turkey range, enter the woods early and by combined listen-
ing and calling manage to ring up a fine gobbler. Travel slowly
through the spring woods and call every 300 or 400 yards. Sit
down on a log or rock and listen intently. Many times you will be
rewarded by hearing a gobbler's call ringing through the morning
air. Advance toward the source of the gobbling, and when you estimate that you are close enough, conceal yourself and proceed

just as though you had known the turkey was there when you entered the woods.

For me, the hunting of turkey gobblers in the spring is the cream of all gunning sports. Not all turkey hunters will agree, and many hold fall hunting in higher esteem. Turkeys are more abundant in the fall, but they are more difficult to locate. The toms no longer let the world know where they are by gobbling, and the mating yelps of the hens have not been heard since late spring. The larger part of fall turkey populations consists of family groups containing the mother hen and her now almost full-grown brood of the year. The flock may also have among its members some unbred yearling hens and adult hens that have lost their broods. At times, several of these family groups will gather into one large flock which may contain upward of fifty birds. The toms will also have flocked together, but their all-male flocks will be smaller than the family groups and will contain only birds of the same age class.

In contrast to the location of spring gobbler territory, the fall hunter will use his eyes to a greater extent than his sense of hearing, choosing his hunting ground by the sign that the turkeys leave during their feeding and traveling throughout the day. A single flock will range over an area up to 8,000 acres, with 3,000 acres being about average. The flock will cover this area on a rather regular feeding circuit in about a week's time. A single flock will range over about 500 acres of this territory each day. This extreme mobility of turkeys during the fall makes their location by the hunter no easy undertaking.

While feeding, turkeys in the fall use their feet to scratch the ground bare of leaves, twigs and forest litter in order to uncover acorns, seeds, nuts and other items upon which they feed. The fall hunter should be always on the lookout for their scratchings, since this is the time of year when turkeys feed almost exclusively by this method. When scratching, turkeys throw leaves and other ground litter to the rear. The scratchings are roughly triangular, and to the hunter they are like an arrow, with the apex of the triangle pointing out the direction of the flock's line of travel. Fresh scratchings are evidenced by moist, dark earth—the last material uncovered and thrown to the rear—lying atop the leaves or undisturbed surface of the ground. Leaves piled to the rear of fresh scratchings will, because of their higher moisture content, be of slightly darker hue than those on undisturbed ground.

Close observation of these scratchings will often reveal the rake-like marks of the turkey's toes. These marks and the presence of typical turkey droppings and an occasional body feather will enable the hunter to distinguish between turkey scratchings and the work of deer and squirrels. When the ground is covered by dry leaves, turkeys will make an unholy racket while scratching, and the sound will carry for quite a distance on a still fall day. On hearing this noise, the hunter can estimate the flock's direction of travel by the sound. He may then be able to set up an ambush somewhere along the route.

The most widely used and successful method of hunting turkeys in the fall and winter seasons is that wherein the hunter locates and scatters an intact flock and then endeavors to call in individual birds. Because of their strong flocking instinct, the turkeys will attempt to reassemble by calling to each other. When breaking up the flock—by shooting into the air, running toward the birds, shouting and raising all kinds of hell—the hunter must make every effort to get the individual birds scattered to the four winds. If all of the turkeys should fly or run off in the same direction, they will soon contact each other and reassemble at some distant point, and the most artful calling by the hunter will be to no avail.

Having gotten the flock well scattered, conceal yourself in the *immediate vicinity* of the point of breakup. This is the spot where the birds will almost invariably attempt to reassemble. Wandering away from this area for 100 yards or so in an attempt to find concealment more to your liking is an almost sure guarantee that you will not get a shot. Use all your ingenuity in concealing yourself at the point where the birds were scattered, and prepare to call.

The scattered birds may begin calling to each other immediately, even before you have uttered a note on your own call. Listen to this calling and try to imitate it—note for note, cadence for cadence. You are receiving the world's best lesson in the art of turkey calling. You will sometimes know when a bird is getting close to your hiding place in the fall even though you can't see it. Turkeys walking in dry leaves make almost as much noise at each step as a man does, and the sound is somewhat similar.

When an answering bird is in close, answer its call by occasionally sounding the *cluck!* on your call. Use this *cluck!* only if you
are certain that you can do it properly. The somewhat similar-
sounding alarm *pert!* will send the turkey off in a panic and will
alarm any other bird within hearing. Anyone who hunts turkeys
for any time at all will become all too familiar with this alarm
note. I'll later describe all the calls necessary for hunting turkeys
in both spring and fall, but the *pert!* should be avoided like the
plague.

When you are aware that one or more turkeys are approaching
your hiding place near where the birds were scattered, be on the
alert and exercise the greatest caution. Your heart will be pound-
ing, and you will be tempted to bob your head up and peer over
the cover in an attempt to see the approaching birds. Don't! Remember that many pairs of the sharpest eyes in nature will be
seeking you out.

As in hunting gobblers in the spring, have your gun ready to deliver the shot with the least possible movement. If you can see the
approaching turkey, you can wait until its head is behind a tree or
other object and snap your gun to your shoulder. In choosing your
cover, make sure that you have a clear field of fire in the widest
possible arc.

In the early part of a fall season, young turkeys will start to call
and move toward the assembly point within a short time after the
breakup of the flock. As the season progresses and they have been
exposed to hunters a few times, they will be much more cautious
and will call at less frequent intervals. Again, as in spring hunting,
be on the alert for birds that may come silently to your call,
making no calls in reply to yours. If you receive no answers to
your calling, and the turkeys fail to come into the assembly area
after thirty or forty minutes have passed since the flock was
broken up, try to find another flock. However, if you will be passing through this same area again on your way out of the woods,
it might pay you to stop and sound a few calls on the off chance
that the birds are nearby.

While the location, breakup and subsequent calling in of birds
from a scattered flock is the easiest method of hunting turkeys in
the fall, failure to do so is not fatal to success. Turkeys are endowed with great curiosity, and because of this trait they will

From left to right, at front, are the two halves of a slate-and-peg call, a diaphragm call and an owl hooter. In the middle is a suction-type yelper. At the rear are two lidded-box calls. The one at the right with rubber bands can be used to sound the gobble.

many times answer and come in to your calling even though undisturbed. Then too, a flock may have been scattered by other hunters, predators or other causes.

When traveling through the fall woods in search of turkeys, stop and call every 300 to 400 yards. Sometimes the birds in an intact flock will answer, and you will have succeeded in locating a flock for subsequent breakup. At times, this random calling will bring a response from a lone turkey that has been separated from the flock for some time. Such birds are usually easy to call in.

Fall hunting in all states is a daylong activity—unlike spring hunting in most states, in which the gunner must stop hunting at noon or before. One feature of fall hunting that appeals to many sportsmen is that there is no compelling necessity to rise at an ungodly hour in order to enjoy success. Even so, the dyed-in-the-wool turkey hunter is willing to spend from dawn to dusk in pursuit of his favorite game.

The subject of turkey calling has always been surrounded with a great deal of blather about its supposed difficulty. I've been told by some men that they would like to take up turkey hunting were it not for the "fact" that calling the wild turkey is a skill reserved for a gifted minority. This is absolute nonsense. Turkey calling can be learned by anyone willing to spend the time and engage in the practice needed to acquire its rudiments. The newcomer may not be able to perform like an old hand at the game, but he will, with good instruction and the necessary practice, be able to call well enough to bring quite a few turkeys under his gun.

The best way to learn to talk turkey is by receiving instruction from a skilled caller. If the teacher is good—and the student does his homework—he will be calling well in a very short time. The second-best way to acquire skill in calling is through the use of some fine recordings that are available from several sources. It will take a little longer this way, but turkey calling can certainly be learned from these recordings, which have been made by some of the world's most expert callers.

There are only three essential calls that must be learned—one for hunting the gobbler in the spring and the other two for fall hunting. These are the mating yelp of the hen, the absolutely essential call for bringing in a spring gobbler, and the *kee-kee* call and the "lost" call for use in the fall. All three are easy to produce with good turkey calls and plenty of practice.

Those about to try turkey hunting for the first time are faced with the question of what type of calling device they should acquire. Let's examine the different types of turkey calls, in addition to the gobbling box, and their methods of operation.

The most difficult call to use is the suction-type yelper derived from the old-time turkey-wing-bone call. The beginning caller would do well to pass up this type until he has mastered those calls which are easier to use, such as the lidded-box call. This box call consists of a hollow wooden box with a pivoted lid fastened to one end with a loose-fitting pin or screw. The opposite end of the lid extends past the end of the box and is shaped into a handle. To operate the box call, the hunter strokes the thin edges of the box with the lid. Both lid and box edges are coated with soft chalk in order to bring out the proper tones. The box is probably the most popular of all calling devices and will make all the necessary calls except the *kee-kee*.

The slate-and-peg call is one of my favorites. It consists of a small hollow box, the top of which is covered with a piece of slate, and a wooden peg about an inch in length which is fitted into a hollow knob. This is a two-piece call, which the hunter operates by rubbing the peg over the slate in a circular motion. The slate-and-peg call will produce excellent hen yelps, "lost" calls and *kee-kee* calls. It is a fairly easy call to master.

The diaphragm call is a small, "U"-shaped piece of metal which is covered by a thin membrane. It will make the most realistic of turkey notes, including the yelp, *kee-kee* call and "lost" call. Some expert users of the diaphragm call can produce a fairly good imitation of the gobble from it. The hunter uses it by placing the entire call inside his mouth with the open end of the "U" to the front, holding it in place against the roof of his mouth by tongue pressure. Air expelled from his lungs causes the diaphragm to vibrate and produce the desired notes.

If I have a favorite among turkey calls, it is the diaphragm. In addition to the realistic notes produced by this call, it requires no movement of the hunter's hands which might spook a wary turkey. In addition to these virtues, this call leaves the hands free for the ready gun handling required when a turkey is in close.

The snuffbox call, as its name implies, is made from the cylindrical type of box in which some brands of snuff are packaged. It too is a diaphragm-type call, but operates on a different principle. The diaphragm is stretched across the open end of the box with the lid removed, and the lid, with a semicircle of metal removed from it, is replaced on the box. The hunter operates the call by placing his lower lip on the exposed diaphragm (which has a small horizontal slit cut into it) and blowing into the call. This call produces excellent turkey notes, and a commercial version, the E-Z Call, is now on the market.

My recommendation to the newcomer to turkey hunting is to purchase a good-quality lidded-box call and a slate-and-peg type. These are the easiest types to master and will, between them, make all the calls needed for hunting the wild turkey. All of these calls are accompanied by instructions for their use. Printed instructions and recordings intended to teach turkey calling will contain a great number of calls other than the mating-hen yelp, *kee-kee* call and "lost" call. These other calls are nice to know, but if the hunter never learned to make any calls other than these three, and perhaps the *cluck*, he would be able to call in turkeys anywhere in the country in any season.

The mating yelp of the hen is a staccato *keouk! keouk! keouk!*

The call is sounded with an interval of about one-half second between notes. The number of notes is of no importance—contrary to some instructions. I've heard hen turkeys sound anywhere from three to twelve notes in a series. When I'm prospecting for gobblers in the spring by random calling, I sound from five to ten loud yelps. When a gobbler answers and is coming in to my calling I sound somewhat softer yelps in series of five to six notes. When a gobbler is close enough so that I can see him, I call very softly and switch to the diaphragm call if I have been using some other type up to this point (all calls can make more than one sound), so as to make no hand movements that might catch the turkey's eye.

The *kee-kee* call of the young turkey is one call that every fall turkey hunter should master. It is a high-pitched, whistlelike series of notes that will be heard when the young turkeys in a scattered flock try to contact each other and reassemble. It may start out with several yelps at the beginning and end up with the whistling notes: *keouk! keouk! kee! kee! kee! kee! kee!* This call can be sounded by use of the diaphragm, slate-and-peg and snuffbox calls.

The "lost" call of the young turkey will be heard most often in the late fall season, when the young birds' voices have become more mature. It is similar to the hen yelp, but is sounded in the more rapid sequence of the *kee-kee* call. It is a rather frantic and pleading call that is made by young turkeys when they are separated from the flock and anxious to get together. This sound can be made on any type of turkey call.

Good turkey calling takes lots of work. Do your practicing during the off-season, and when that first turkey answers your calling and appears before you, you'll experience one of the greatest satisfactions that the outdoors has to offer.

The gunner for most upland species experiences a rather agonizing time of it when choosing a shotgun. Not so the turkey hunter. He has little concern for the niceties of stock fit, and the standard stock found on most over-the-counter guns works out just fine for him. Wing shooting is not the norm in turkey hunting. Anytime the hunter of turkeys is faced with a shot on the wing, it is an indication that something has gone wrong. Turkeys are essentially ground game, and their wings are used mainly in flying up to their roosts in the evening and flying down again in the morning. When danger threatens, they will most often trust to their legs and run off on the ground. When startled by the sudden appearance of a hunter in open woods with no cover nearby, they will sometimes fly up and away through the tall timber, and believe me, the sight of this great game bird becoming airborne is awesome. Unless the hunter's gun is loaded with large shot—not advisable for a reason I'll mention later—such rare wing shots should not be attempted. Unless multiple hits with small shot should strike the bird's head and neck, the heavy body feathers will impede the penetration of this smaller shot, and the bird will fly off with crippling wounds in the legs and wings.

The shotgun in turkey hunting is used in the manner of a rifle, in that it is aimed rather than being pointed and swung as in the wing shooting of other upland birds. The turkey hunter is essentially a big-game hunter, and his skills and methods of hunting are more akin to the seeking of big-game animals than to upland gunning. The gun is aimed so as to place a dense-centered pattern of small shot into the bird's head and neck. The shotgun is a deadly and most efficient instrument when used in this way, and very few turkeys will move more than a few yards after delivery of the shot.

All types of shotguns can be used in hunting the wild turkey, but the low-priced single-shots and bolt-actions will rarely be seen in the hands of an experienced hunter. The side-by-side double is the traditional turkey gun in some areas, but over/unders, pump-actions and both recoil- and gas-operated autoloaders are the choice of a great many hunters. Personally, I've used them all with the exception of the over/under, and have found all of them to be satisfactory.

More pump guns will be seen in the turkey woods than any of the other action types—probably because the pump gun is still the most popular shotgun in America. The autoloader is fast catching up with the pump in popularity, and it is probably the American gun of the future, but the pump gun is as trouble-free and reliable as any of the others and will be around for a long time. Which type do I prefer for my own use? Purely for the sake of tradition, I would rather carry a good side-by-side.

The different degrees of choke found in the two barrels of a double are of no practical value for turkey hunting, because what is required for this game is the tightest patterns obtainable. An ideal double gun for turkeys would deliver full-choke patterns from both barrels. The over/unders do not carry too comfortably in the hands because of the deep actions found on most of them. The side-by-sides, on the other hand, are comfortable to carry, but lack the single sighting alignment desired by some hunters on a gun that is to be aimed like a rifle.

A fault that shows up rather frequently in double guns is poor barrel regulation. A well-regulated double gun is supposed to place the pattern thrown by one barrel right on the other at 40 yards. It is surprising how often this is not the case in both expensive and low-priced guns of this type. One or both barrels may place their patterns high, low, right or left in relation to the point of aim. Because of the necessity of aiming the turkey gun, this fault should rule out such a gun for use on turkeys. As for myself, I wouldn't use such a gun for any purpose.

The 12-gauge shotgun is the main battery of the majority of turkey hunters and has probably brought more turkeys to earth than all the other gauges combined. The smaller gauges are seen more frequently as time passes, thanks to advances in ammunition which have allowed them to edge up to the 12 in the weight of the shot charges they will handle. The 16-gauge is used by many turkey hunters, especially in the South, and guns chambering the 3-inch 20-gauge magnum shells are being used more frequently in the turkey woods. The 28 and .410, because of their scanty shot charges, should not be used, and in fact their use should be barred by law. The 2¾-inch 20-gauge magnum shell with 1⅛ ounces of shot is a marginal load for turkeys, but can be used if the load, containing No. 7½ shot, shoots a dense pattern.

The killing loads for turkeys are those which can deliver a dense-centered pattern with an adequate weight of shot into the comparatively small area of the turkey's head and neck. If weight of shot charge were the only consideration of importance in the choice of a gun for turkeys, the 3-inch 12-gauge magnum would get the nod without question. However, guns chambering the 3-inch 12 are heavy and cumbersome pieces best suited to pass shooting on waterfowl from a fixed position. Turkey guns will be carried for many miles over sometimes very rough country, and the turkey hunter should choose a shotgun weighing not much more than 7 pounds, and throwing a minimum of 1¼ ounces of shot.

This 1¼-ounce shot load can be obtained in the 2¾-inch 12-gauge high-velocity load, the 12-gauge pigeon load, the 16-gauge magnum load and the 3-inch 20-gauge magnum load. Guns chambering any of these 1¼-ounce loads are eminently suited for the hunting of turkeys if their barrels deliver the required tight patterns. If the hunter of turkeys feels that he must have a heavier load, he can go to the 2¾-inch 12-gauge magnum load with 1½ ounces of shot, but for many years the 1¼-ounce load was the *heavy* 12-gauge duck and goose load. It was the favorite load of the old-time market gunners.

Current literature put out by most gun and ammunition manufacturers persists in recommending No. 2 shot and even BBs for use in turkey hunting. This information was evidently first put forth by people who had never hunted this game, but reasoned that because of the large size and great weight of this bird, large shot was required. Even for body shots at turkeys—not recommended if they can be at all avoided—No. 4 shot has enough remaining velocity and penetration to get through the turkey's heavy body feathers, provided the range is not over 30 yards. The larger No. 2s and BBs, of course, have this velocity and ability to penetrate in greater measure, but their patterns are not dense enough for sure killing.

Since most knowledgeable turkey hunters prefer the head-and-neck shot, the vast majority use heavy loads of No. 6 or 7½ shot. My own preference is a stiff load of 7½s for the first shot, followed by No. 4s in the magazine or second barrel of a double gun for follow-up shots if the first load is not effective.

The hunter who wishes to use a rifle for turkey hunting because of certain conditions of terrain or turkey behavior can use just about any centerfire cartridge of .22 or .24 caliber. However, most cartridges will require loading down to less than factory velocities to avoid spoiling a good deal of meat. The .22 Hornet cartridge is the exception to this rule, and if there is a perfect rifle cartridge for turkeys, the Hornet bears this title. None of the .22 rimfires should be used on turkeys, as they lack sufficient power to anchor these big birds. The 5mm Remington Rimfire Magnum might do a creditable job, but I have no personal experience to draw on in assessing its suitability. The .222 Remington cartridge in its factory loadings is a bit too powerful, but when loaded down to give approximately the performance of the .22 Hornet, it is a fine turkey cartridge. Considering the scarcity of good rifles chambering the Hornet, the .222 is probably the best choice.

Since most shots at turkeys in the spring will be taken in the early morning, and in the fall seasons in late afternoon or early evening, the turkey rifle should be fitted with a scope sight. A good-quality four-power scope is just about ideal for the purpose. The ranges at which turkeys are taken with the rifle rarely exceed 100 yards, and the good light-gathering power of a quality four-power glass will be appreciated. Plain cross-hair reticles of fine to medium thickness sometimes fail to show up under dim light conditions or become confused with branches or brush. The reticle in the scope mounted on a turkey rifle should be heavy cross hairs, a post or those which combine a thick cross hair at the edges of the scope's field with a medium cross hair at its center.

The return of the wild turkey to much of its former domain, and the imminent prospect of its further spread into as yet unoccupied territory, are reasons for great expectations among the sportsmen of America. If what I have set down here helps in some small measure to bring these expectations to full realization, my efforts will have been well repaid indeed.

UPLAND GUNS

BY JIM CARMICHEL

SOMEONE once said that appreciating a fine upland gun requires a "certain state of mind."

"Picture a gentleman of the old school," he went on, "properly attired in suitable tweeds, a soft felt hat, pipe in teeth, setter at heel and gun on arm with familiar ease. That gun, undoubtedly a fine double, will be an upland shotgun. . . ."

Try as I might, however, I've never been able to conjure up that image. Something always gets out of kilter in my mind's eye. My stepfather was one of the most avid upland gunners I've ever known, and if I substitute a cigar for the pipe the physical description fits perfectly—right down to the setter at his heel. But the upland-gun part always comes out wrong. Instead of a fine double, all I see is a Model 97 Winchester pump, worn to silver brightness on the outside and silky smoothness on the inside.

His Model 97 was what Winchester used to call the Brush Gun, with a 26-inch cylinder-bored barrel. I think Winchester stopped making this model about 1930 or so. The magazine capacity was five rounds plus the one in the chamber, and (before our state required a maximum capacity of three rounds) he could shuck those six rounds so fast his gun sounded like a chain saw. He hunted with three dogs then, and more than once, after a single rise of bobwhite, I saw all three dogs bring in dead birds and go back for more.

That old 97 pump was the antithesis of everything one might expect in a classic upland gun, yet when it came to actual application it was the most effective I've ever seen. Anyone attempting to match such a performance with a "proper" upland gun would have been pitifully outclassed.

The reason I mention all this is that we occasionally need an antidote for the spell—call it mystique—of the upland gun. However, I'm certainly not advocating that everyone rush out and start looking for old 97s. Rather, I'm only making the point that when we talk about upland guns we're talking about a lot of different kinds and types of shotguns. The same thing goes for "upland" hunting.

I've hunted grouse among the high ridges of Tennessee and North Carolina, chukar in the high passes of Idaho and Nevada and sage chickens and Hungarian partridge on the high plains of Montana. Each, without a doubt, is upland hunting. But I've also shot quail in the low deserts, snipe at absolute sea level and doves at points below sea level. Is this upland hunting? My working definition of "upland" game is "any game bird that ain't waterfowl." This can even include wild turkeys, depending on how you hunt them.

From so broad a description of upland game, one might deduce that an upland gun is "any shotgun that ain't a waterfowl gun." Actually, this isn't so far off the mark; at least this has been my experience. You see, I'm a pragmatist; I believe in using whatever gun works best for any particular job.

A few years back I carried what might be considered a "typical" upland gun on a chukar hunt in northern Idaho. The gun was light, had short barrels and was choked so as to throw a nice, wide pattern. As it turned out, however, the chukar were flushing wild, way ahead of me, and as a result too many birds were slipping through the pattern. On the second day of the hunt, I borrowed a full-choked trap gun. I wasn't looking for a trap gun in particular, just any sort of full-choke, but the trap model was all I could borrow.

That day, when those chukar came up way ahead of me, I just

leveled down on them with that trap gun and cut 'em a dusty, and by noon I had a full limit. On my way back to the car I happened across a game officer, who expressed amazement at my full bag. According to him, that was the first full bag limit to be taken in that area all season! Now, I'm not all that good a chukar hunter, and I'm not much of a trapshooter either. I was successful simply because I matched the gun to the situation.

This is the secret of a good upland gun: a gun that is matched to the situation. I'm certainly not advocating the use of trap guns for Idaho chukar, but I do advise liberal thinking. For example, when it comes to selecting shotguns, a dove shooter in Arizona shouldn't copy the habits of a Georgia quail hunter just because quail and doves are both "upland" game.

Assuming that you're totally confused by now, let's start putting some basics together. A common trait of nearly all types of upland shooting is that the bird will flush out of cover and try to get out of range as fast as possible. (The principal exceptions are doves, which Bob Brister discusses in his chapter.) The hunter has to get

Here, Jim Carmichel gets in a quick shot at a departing grouse. Guns for this sort of situation—quick flushes in heavy cover—must be fast-handling and open-choked.

the gun to his shoulder and fire at the fleeing target in one quick motion. If he hesitates in order to get his cheek in the right place on the stock, or tries to sight the target with the front bead, he will lose too much time and the bird will probably get away.

Thus, a prime requisite is fast handling. By this I mean a gun that easily snaps to the shoulder and fits the shooter well enough so that he is looking down the barrel without any conscious effort.

"Proper fit" is vitally important, but the term is so grossly misused that I hesitate to employ it. I've heard lots of supposedly knowledgeable shooters insist that the way to determine whether a shotgun stock fits is to place the butt in the crook of the arm, inside the elbow, grasp the stock at the grip and place the trigger finger on the trigger. If the trigger meets the finger at about the first joint, the "fit" is pronounced correct. If shotguns were fired from the crook of the elbow, this might be a pretty good way to determine correct fit. But as it is, we shoot them from the shoulder, and this complicates the hell out of things!

Frankly, I don't think stock length is all that important anyway. If we got down to the real nitty-gritty of stock fit, we'd find that about 90 percent of all hunters use a stock that's too short. But this really doesn't harm one's performance all that much. I've found that I can tolerate considerable variation in stock length with little or no harmful effect on my shooting, and I think most other shooters can too.

In my opinion, a far more important consideration is proper fit in regard to drop at heel and comb. When a shotgun is snapped to cheek and shoulder, the eye should be looking exactly where the barrel is pointing. A good test for this is to close both eyes, snap the gun into position, then open the eyes and see how they line up with the barrel. If the eye is looking at the rear of the receiver, there is too much drop and there will be a tendency to shoot under the target. If the eye sees all of the top of the barrel, there is not enough drop and there will be a tendency to overshoot.

If I had my druthers between these two evils, I would take a stock with not enough drop, because even if a shooter sees too much of the top of the barrel he still has a fair idea of where the shot will be headed. A stock with too much drop is really miserable, because you can't see where the barrel is pointed.

Unfortunately, most shooters who suffer from an ill-fitting stock are shooting stocks with too much drop. This is especially true of those using older shotguns. I'm not going to go into a long comparative listing of stock dimensions here, because cold measurements per se don't tell the whole story. Dimensionally, a stock may appear to have too much drop at the comb, but if the comb is rather thick the effect is much the same as if it had less drop. Conversely, a stock with a high but too-thin comb may shoot like one with a comb that's too low.

The best solution to this problem, short of having a custom stock made, is to try a lot of shotguns for fit and, using the old closed-eye trick, see how they measure up for you personally. I think that if a lot of shooters would keep an open mind about such things, and buy accordingly, they would get better results in the field. But who ever heard anyone say "I'm going to a gun store and buy the shotgun that fits me best"? Instead, everyone already has his mind made up, and almost always the decision is based on factors other than stock fit. The one saving grace, I suppose, is that we are pretty flexible and can learn to shoot almost anything fairly well.

Earlier, when I mentioned that a prime requisite of the upland gun is "fast handling," I was careful not to say "light weight and fast handling"—the reason being that light weight and fast handling do not necessarily go together. I've used ultralight guns that were also superclumsy.

The speediest shooting of all is International Skeet, in which the competitor is required to bring the gun up from below his belt after the target appears. Yet International Skeet shooters don't, as a rule, concern themselves with light guns. Instead they tend to use shotguns that range toward the heavier end of the scale. This is not to say that they always prefer heavier guns, but simply that the guns they prefer tend to heaviness.

Thus, as I see it, shotgun weight is to be considered only in terms of how much weight you want to carry around on your trips afield. Just don't make the mistake of equating light weight with fast performance—or vice versa.

By now you're no doubt getting the idea that there are a lot of variables affecting the so-called "upland gun." Good. Once you understand this, you're safe from the lout who takes you by the arm like a Dutch uncle and makes such pontifical statements as "Look son, if you're going to be a pheasant hunter you're going to have to use a super double-slip automatic . . ." Even if he has shot a dozen ringnecks a day since Moses was an altar boy he still hasn't the slightest idea what gun you're going to shoot best.

If someone were to take a survey on the numbers of upland game birds taken with each shotgun gauge, I expect we'd learn that at least three out of five are taken with the 12-gauge. Probably more. This doesn't mean that it takes a 12 to kill effectively, but only that most folks own 12s. Of late, the 20-gauge has gained a tremendous amount of ground, but it still has a long way to go before it seriously challenges the 12.

A lot of shooters are finding that the 20-bore is plenty for their upland shooting, but I don't think this is the main reason for the 20's rise in popularity. Instead, I think it is due to the increasing number of really attractive shotguns, especially the imports, available in the 20-gauge.

I've noticed lately a certain snobbishness among some souls who use the 20—especially those who have started using one only recently. Perhaps this is part and parcel of the upland-gun "mystique." Oh well, if it gives them any happiness to be holier than you (or me), I suppose it does no harm. However, when their

Probably the greatest controversy among connoisseurs of upland guns is which is superior, the repeater or the two-barrel? Advocates of the former say that pumps and autos (such as the 20-gauge custom-stocked Winchester Model 50 at left) offer a quick third shot, which is often a great advantage. Double and over/under fanciers, who would opt for the 12-gauge Ithaca SKB side-by-side at right, cite better handling qualities and an instant choice of two chokes. The birds in the center are grouse.

One of Carmichel's favorite guns is this Model 42 Winchester pump in .410. It must be pointed out, though, that if there is such a thing as an "experts-only" gauge, this is it. The .410's very thin pattern requires that the shooter be precisely on target in order to get enough shot into the bird for a clean kill. Those who are looking for a light, fast-handling gun would probably be better off with a 28-gauge.

company gets a trifle tedious I can't resist getting out one of my .410s and then doing my holier-than-thou act on *them.*

Frankly, I feel that virtually every modern bore size, except possibly the 10, has its place in the upland-game field. This notion is based not so much on opinion as it is on experience, and not so much on isolated experiences as it is on exposure to a wide variety of circumstances.

Some time back, I had very fine results on ringnecks with a nice little 28-gauge skeet gun. This was at a preserve—pretty easy shooting, but nonetheless every time I dumped a bird the guide and dog handlers would break into something sounding like epic poetry over my prowess with the little 28. By the end of the day they even had me believing that the 28-gauge was perfect medicine for ringnecks. And in fact, under those conditions it was. The birds were coming up almost underfoot and flying so slowly that I was on them before they'd gone 15 yards. If I hunted at that preserve for the rest of my life, I couldn't be persuaded to use anything other than that sweet little 28-gauge skeet gun. Likewise, if game-preserve shooting were the limit of my ringneck-hunting experience, I would be very much of the opinion that the 28-gauge was plenty adequate for all pheasant and would tell everyone who would listen.

About a month after that experience, I happened to be hunting "natural" pheasant in some corn strips in Iowa. The cornfields had been harvested except for strips about ten rows wide, running the length of the field. As we walked these strips, the pheasant would run ahead of us until they reached the end of the rows. Then they would take off like rockets. Usually we were quite a few yards from the birds when they flushed, and this, with the additional yardage they piled up in the first split second, made the shooting mighty tough. Fortunately, I was carrying a 12-gauge autoloader with an adjustable choke, so I screwed the choke down good and tight and had a pretty good day. Now, if I were an Iowa farm lad who had only hunted pheasant in those long corn strips, I would never be able to visualize using a 28-gauge for pheasant. Just the *opposite* of my earlier experience!

Thus, whenever I read, or hear, that such and such a gauge is too big, or too small, for a certain type of game, I instinctively become a bit suspicious.

If I could have only one shotgun, I think it would be a 20-gauge with 3-inch chambers; but if there were a 12-gauge gun available that I could shoot the least particle better, I'd get it instead.

Of course, gauge alone doesn't tell the whole story; a lot of one's success—or failure—depends on his choice of shot size and choke.

Doves, quail, snipe, woodcock and birds of that sort don't need a lot of killing. A few shot in the wings or torso and they fall. Pheasant, on the other hand, as well as various grouse, prairie chickens and to some extent chukar, seem to be able to take a pretty good dose of shot and still get away. I've seen a pillowcaseful of feathers knocked out of a pheasant and watched him fly away. This is why No. 7½ to 9 shot will do fine for the shore birds, doves, snipe, woodcock, quail, etc., but No. 6 is better for pheasant, grouse, etc. The heavier 6s penetrate deeper and disable better.

Of course, when we talk about getting a certain size shot into a game bird, we are also talking about getting a certain *amount* of shot into it. This is a matter of choke. With few exceptions, all

Unlike most upland birds, pheasants are heavily feathered, tough and tenacious of life, and the best shot size for them is No. 6. This brace of ringnecks was taken with a Winchester Model 101 over/under, choked skeet and skeet.

of the upland shooting I've done, and expect to do, called for a pretty much open choke.

I used to have the notion that pass shooting at doves required a fair degree of choke, but I've even gotten over that. Back during my school days, a pal of mine and I dove hunted nearly every day of the season. I even kept a record of the number of birds I bagged per day, how many shots I fired and the approximate range. I used a 12-gauge shotgun with a modified choke most days, but in areas where I expected the birds to be especially high I used a 12-gauge Merkel over/under with both barrels tightly choked.

My pal, however, who carried a 20-gauge autoloading skeet gun, seemed to get his share of the doves despite what I thought was a pretty serious handicap. To satisfy my curiosity on this point, I tried an open-choked gun for a couple of days and, except for a few really high shots, fared as well as I did with the tighter choke. Also, I picked off a few birds that seemed to be more or less "marginal" (that means that my swing was a bit awkward and/or I wasn't too sure of my lead). From that time on I've used an improved-cylinder barrel almost exclusively for doves, the exception being when the birds are flying high, fast and straight, or when I use a .410. In this latter case I use my Winchester Model 42 pump with a modified-choke barrel.

There seems to be a current swing toward buying shotguns with a more open choke. This is a good sign, in my opinion, because it shows that hunters are giving more serious consideration to their actual needs. Back when I lived in the hills of east Tennessee, we had two major game birds: ruffed grouse and bobwhite quail. Dove hunting wasn't big then, and waterfowl was almost unheard of. Yet nine out of ten new shotguns that were sold by the various hardware and sporting-goods shops had long, full-choke barrels. The reason for this, it was explained to me, was that a longer, more tightly choked barrel represented more gun for the money than did a shorter, open-choked one. But I don't think a lot of people believed this, because it was not at all uncommon for the pur-

This photo, taken many years ago, shows upland hunting as it used to be. The gun appears to be a Winchester Model 12 pump with the long barrel and full choke that were fashionable before shooters became more enlightened.

chaser to cut 2 or 3 inches off the barrel shortly after he bought it, opening up the choke to cylinder bore, the least possible constriction!

If there is such a thing as a classic American upland bird, the bobwhite quail must be it. For whatever it's worth, this is the bird most associated with visions of gentlemen bird shooters, beautiful dogs and fine guns. Since I was a southern boy, born and bred, Br'er Bobwhite was as much a part of my early hunting adventures as squirrels and rabbits. Everyone in our neighborhood kept two or three bird dogs, and quail hunting was, during the fall and winter months, an almost-daily affair. Yet of all the hunters I knew, and all the guns I saw in the field, I can recall very few hunters who used a double.

This is not to say that doubles were uncommon in my corner of the world; they were, in fact, quite common. It seemed that there was a Parker, L. C. Smith, Ithaca, Lefever or Baker in every household. In fact, we had a nice old Fulton ourselves. It's just

Resting in the seat of a plantation carriage is a high-grade Italian side-by-side. Among those who ride to the quail coveys in such conveyances, a side-by-side or over/under that is worth the price of a good car is the only fitting gun to take along.

that pumps and autoloaders were vastly more popular.

It's interesting to consider the fact that only recently have doubles, either side-by-side or over/under, come to be considered a prestige item. Back in the 1940s, when I was first starting to notice such things, it was the autoloader that was the real prestige gun. How many Parkers were traded in on autoloaders is hard to guess, but the number is considerable. Not only were autoloaders, and to a lesser extent pumps, impressive items to have standing in the gun cabinet, but they also netted more birds per covey rise than did doubles. When one was faced with the support of two or three bird dogs plus a family of devoted quail eaters, the numbers of birds that went into the pot was a factor to be seriously considered.

Today the situation has changed from what it was during my youth, not only in the South but all over. There aren't as many bird dogs, there aren't as many birds, there aren't as many places to hunt and the bag limits aren't nearly as generous as they once were. But by the same token, the average fellow who goes afield for quail doesn't plan on feeding his family on the results of his marksmanship. Thus he can carry the shotgun that gives him the most pleasure to shoot, carry and own.

I once lived in a little town that was near one of the country's best ruffed-grouse-hunting areas. The nearby mountain slopes were thickly covered with laurel, evergreen and hardwood, a perfect haven for grouse. Needless to say, grouse hunting was virtually a way of life. With almost every man and boy in the community hunting the same general area, encountering the same terrain and facing nearly identical shooting situations, one might think that a more or less universal opinion on the "ideal" grouse gun would have evolved. Such, however, was not the case. The hunters displayed a remarkable degree of disunity as to what constituted a good grouse gun. In fact, it seemed to me that the more they discussed their basic shotgun philosophies, the wider became the chasm between their individual opinions.

The only time I can recall their being of more or less one mind was when Winchester introduced its superlight, fiber-glass-barreled Winlite autoloader. This became a great favorite among the grouse hunters—but only after the barrel had been cut to about 20 inches!

Be that as it may, I expect I will use a side-by-side double for upland game for the rest of my life. This is mainly because I have some nice side-bys that I enjoy carrying and shooting. I like to thumb the release levers, drop the barrels and watch the empties kick out. And I'm especially fond of shooting a side-by-side in the presence of shooters who claim that they "simply can't hit anything with a side-by-side." Actually, if a person is already a good shot I can teach him to shoot the side-by-side in about twenty minutes. But usually I don't mention this, preferring to keep him in the dark so he'll continue to think I'm some sort of shooting wizard. Perhaps this also is part of the "mystique" of the double.

At the same time, however, I don't harbor any illusions about the double. It shoots only twice, and there have been plenty of

This is Carroll Dale, former pass receiver in the National Football League. Carroll is an avid grouse hunter in the avid grouse hunter in the mountains surrounding his home in east Tennessee. The shotgun is a Winchester Model 59 with a fiberglass barrel.

occasions when I sure would have appreciated a third shot. Some guy all hung up on doubles once wrote that two shots were plenty adequate for all situations. This, of course, is silly. Anyone who has done enough hunting for it to be worth mentioning has experienced plenty of instances in which a third shot was, or would have been, mighty handy.

A lot of this "two-shot" balderdash has come from our British cousins. They are great for writing articles and books about a "proper" shooting attitude, and scream to the high heavens about vulgar pumps and autoloaders. But at the same time, they advocate the use of matched guns and a loader. The idea of this, obviously, is to keep up a continuous stream of fire. One of these tweedy types once had the gall to tell me that a "true sportsman" never fired twice at the same bird. If the first barrel missed, he insisted, the only polite thing to do was wish the missed bird good health and go on to another bird for the second shot.

I hold the opposite view. Even if the bird does not fall, it is not unreasonable to assume that it may have caught a few stray shot—enough, possibly, to cause its death later on. Thus, when I start shooting at a bird I feel that I have an obligation to stay with it until it falls or my gun is empty.

But then, it wasn't written that man must hit with every shot—especially when he's upland-gunning.

PUDDLE-DUCK HUNTING

BY NORMAN STRUNG

I'VE BEEN known to be prejudiced on occasion, and I'm afraid that's the case when it comes to puddle-duck hunting. But my prejudice isn't without reason.

Duck hunting has a substance to it that's unique—a rich history that has its roots in Colonial times, in Currier & Ives prints and in the misty tales of old market gunners. From those earliest times up to the present, decoys, duckboats and a hunter's dogged dedication to deceiving a bird have been a valuable source of folk art. A more-than-considerable body of knowledge is required of the sport, too—an eclectic education in diverse subjects such as weather patterns, migration routes, mixing colors, habits of individual species, camouflage, ballistics. You never learn it all. Every time you go afield new knowledge is gained, new theories formulated.

Duck hunting is also therapy; the moment I consider designing a new decoy, or step into a marsh, my mind has room for no other thoughts. I become a duck hunter, to the exclusion of taxpaying, television watching, love affairs and other mundane pursuits of everyday life. A pitifully rare but extremely healthy state of grace in these troubled times. But to our subject:

The term "puddle duck" includes the following species: baldpate, black duck, Florida duck, gadwall, mallard, mottled duck, New Mexican duck, pintail, shoveler, teal (blue-winged, green-winged, cinnamon and European), widgeon and wood duck. Some of these are far more common than others (just which ones we'll discuss later), but this is the complete roster of the puddlers.

A puddle duck's habits center around the evolution of the creature. I think the most important item on the list that's headed "Things every duck hunter should know" is the location of a puddle duck's legs. They're close to the center of the body, suggesting a creature well adapted to walking on land.

This affinity for terra firma as well as water has a direct influence on its behavior; for one thing, a puddle duck is a creature that likes to be close to land whenever possible. It favors swamps, potholes, ponds and watery marshes rather than big, open water, like the diving ducks.

Puddlers are also called dabblers, a name derived from their feeding habits on water. Rather than totally submerging themselves, these ducks bottom-up, their tails poking skyward while their underwater head scavenges the bottom for food. Again, leg placement has a lot to do with this; a puddle duck's legs act as a point of balance, a fulcrum for the tipping body. This habit, in turn, has a direct bearing on where you hunt puddlers. They'd not normally feed in deep water; they simply can't reach the bottom.

Their takeoff too is influenced by those feet. Located so close to the weight center of the duck's body, they make for a combination launching pad and springboard when the bird takes flight. A puddler always leaps into the air, rather than running across the water like a diver. When he comes to stool, he flutters straight down—or very close to it—much like a helicopter landing.

Perhaps the most important aspect to the hunter of this land/water affinity is the puddler's damnable desire (in almost every case) to swing around the entire prospective landing area before he'll sit down. When you're hunting from shore, this is bound to bring him overhead, a vista from which hunters are most commonly revealed. It's this trick (or the lack of it) that makes me feel that divers are a lot easier to hunt than puddlers. It takes an Act of Congress to get a diver to swing over land, so hunter concealment is a much easier proposition.

Puddlers commonly feed both around water and in dry fields, usually on grain, and when it's available, they'll always rest on water. This makes for still another interesting aspect of their behavior: they usually have two distinctly different stops for feeding and resting, and they can be counted on to fly to and from these spots regularly under normal weather conditions, twice daily—once in the morning, once in the evening.

These ducks aren't especially gregarious, either; while they'll migrate in huge flocks, stopovers usually find them breaking up and moving around in small groups—rarely more than a dozen birds, and more likely two to six. This in turn has a direct influence on the number of decoys you have to set out to be attractive and effective to them.

There are three ways of getting puddle ducks onto your evening's menu: jump shooting, pass shooting and luring them into a spread of decoys (which is actually a form of pass shooting). My heart lies with the decoying tactic, but the other methods have their points, so let's start out with jump shooting.

As you may have guessed, jump shooting means "jumping" a flock of ducks by sneaking up on them. You can crawl on your hands and knees, Indian-fashion, to the edge of a farm pond, or drift a canoe down a meandering stretch of water where a flock is resting . . . the ways are many.

Jump shooting's major asset lies in the fact that its quality is likely to hold up throughout the season. Both decoy and pass shooting slump between the first week of shooting and the time when major migrations get under way, as native birds learn quickly where hunters will be and avoid those places. But by virtue of the fact that the mobile waterfowler goes to his quarry, not the other way around, any resident birds are susceptible to "jumping" tactics.

Successful jump shooting requires that you concentrate on feeding areas and feeding periods. Generally speaking, resting areas will be in places where the birds are unapproachable. The feeding areas must have good cover, too; a small, slow, meandering stream near the edge of a grainfield and a pond or marsh surrounded by cattails are two examples of top spots in which to ply this aspect of a duck shooter's trade.

Camouflage clothing is as important to the jump shooter as it is

Camouflage hats and coats, such as these hunters are wearing, are a must for duck hunting. Some gunners cover their hands and faces as well. When using camouflage, be sure that it matches the surrounding scenery.

to any other waterfowler. It will mask his approach to likely-looking spots, and when he gets a shot, chances are good he'll put other birds into the air. When he can slip into some brush and blend into the background, there's always the possibility that the birds might swing near, offering a pass shot.

Another valuable tool to the jump shooter is a duck call. Quite often, a few soft quacks will elicit a response from the real thing, revealing a duck's position and eliminating at least some element of surprise as a wild ball of feathers bursts into the air at your approach.

Pass shooting involves nothing more than concealing yourself somewhere along the route ducks use when flying to and from their feeding areas, then picking them off as they fly overhead. But as in many things, the doing is a bit more difficult than the telling.

First, ducks don't always use the same route day after day. When native birds are shot at frequently from one spot, they'll avoid it. Newly arrived migrants establish their own routes, and weather and changes in feeding areas cause these patterns to vary too.

So the successful pass shooter spends as much time glassing as gunning. A whole morning identifying the routes he'll intercept in the evening would be both typical and wise. Pay special attention to places that cause birds to either flare or gain altitude: a line of trees, a windmill, a water tower or whatever.

One of the best-laid plans of this particular mouse went awry under just that circumstance. There's a federal preserve near my house in Montana that's thick with mallards about midseason. Each morning and evening clouds of the birds lift off the ponds and marshes to feed in the nearby grainfields, and there's some great gunning to be had if you post yourself along the preserve's borders.

Bob Norton and I spent a whole morning plotting the path the majority of the mallards were using. It took them across a grain-field and a small marsh and over the border of the preserve along a break of trees next to which flowed a small, brushy stream. We knew the lay of the land well enough to realize it was an ideal setup. There was plenty of good cover near the stream, so we wouldn't have to build a blind, and the birds were crossing the border at treetop height.

We arrived at the carefully determined spot at around 3 o'clock —the time the birds began to move out for their evening feed.

I can't remember a time so frustrating. Flocks of mallard lifted off the precise spot we'd predicted and beelined for our location, and then as they approached to within 400 yards, they flared—and I do mean flared. They gained altitude; they split left and right; they pirouetted, danced and whirled like a shower of sparks.

Bob and I heard no shots, so we theorized that someone must be walking across the grainfield. But a half-hour later, the birds were still doing the same thing. We finally decided to look, and after bucking brush, fording the stream and slogging through the marsh, we discovered that the farmer who owned the grainfield had put up his straw in a stack that day, right on a line between us and the ducks. The mallard's distrustful unfamiliarity with the big stack had done us in.

It's decoying that I feel represents the most productive form of puddle-duck hunting, but much of its technique is applicable to tactics employed while you're pass or jump shooting, so if one of those be your interest, there's meat here for you too.

At the core of decoy hunting is, of course, the decoy. A trout you catch on a fly you tied and a rod you built is bound to be a notch above one caught on tackle you bought. The same thing holds true with a mallard that swings into a block you made yourself. To put it plainly, I highly recommend making your own stool (raft of decoys), but space doesn't permit a thorough discussion of the how-tos here. If you'd like to try your hand at it, I'd suggest reading *Duck Decoys* by Eugene V. Connett (Durrell Publishers, 1953).

In lieu of building your stool, you can buy one, and indeed, that's the route most gunners go. Dollar for dollar, I think the best buy in modern decoys is Styrofoam or molded plastic. In most cases, I prefer the Styrofoam; its pebbly surface resists glare even when iced up, it's light, it will absorb shot until it sinks from sheer weight of lead and it's cheap. The one exception I make to Styrofoam is when detail is important. The long, slender tail of a pintail can't be workably cast in this stuff, so when detail counts, consider molded plastic.

When buying decoys, make sure a self-righting feature is incorporated into the body. And removable heads are a good idea too; they can be replaced if they break, and usually can be set in any direction you wish. Herter's, Inc., Rural Route 1, Waseca, Minnesota 56093, carries both these types of blocks, and at reasonable prices.

The old rule about ducks' coming to species other than their own, yet of their own type (puddlers or divers), is quite true. Mallard will come to black stool, shovelers to mallard blocks and so forth. But I think that in the field that rule of thumb deserves more expansion and artistic concern than it is commonly given.

Each section of the country has a different majority species: the coastal marshes of the upper Atlantic Seaboard have the black duck; the Deep South, the wood duck; the Midwest and Southern Perimeter States, mallard and pintails and the Far West, the mallard. When building or buying your stool, you should do so with the primary local species in mind, but don't forget minority species.

For example, my basic rig for shooting puddlers on Long Island contains fourteen black duck decoys. Although black ducks are definitely in the majority, there are quite a few mallard on Long Island too, so I also include a brace of mallard in my rig.

For all practical purposes, there are no black ducks west of the Mississippi, and around my home in Montana mallard predominate. But there's always a handful of pintails around. So there my decoy spread includes sixteen mallard and four pintails.

Carrying this rule a little further, the lake where I do most of my hunting in Montana is lousy with coot, or "scoter," which, being inedible, are not game birds. Seldom do you see a flock of feeding birds without a few of these comedians around, so I also rig out two coot. Salt marshes don't seem attractive to coot, so in New York I don't use them. In both places, however, I rig out two Canada geese.

These big birds frequent both areas, so there's always a chance the two decoys might lure the real thing close enough for a shot. But more important, geese are wise, wise birds, and their presence in a rig indicates to passing birds that all is well; they function as a confidence decoy. There's also the matter of size: they're plainly visible from far off—which brings us to another thing to consider when acquiring a rig.

Most manufacturers offer their decoys in "oversize" models— larger-than-life replicas. The thinking is that because they can be seen from far off, they'll prove more attractive to trading birds. While I find the theory generally accurate, it has some inherent drawbacks; the main one is that because they're so damned big, you can't lug as many of them around the marsh as you can normal-sized blocks, and I do think numbers are important—more so than size.

So my recommendation is, if transport of decoys isn't a problem, go oversize. But if you've got to do a lot of carrying and walking with your decoys, stick to life-size, and bring along two geese to perform the function of long-distance attraction.

The number of decoys you should use at any given time is largely a matter of the number of birds you commonly see. I'd recommend tripling the number of the average flocks you see afield when the weather is pleasant, and quadrupling or quintupling that number during nasty weather. Speaking for myself, I've used as few blocks as nine and as many as forty-eight, depending on conditions. I'd say the elusive "average" number of blocks I rig out is around seventeen.

When you're hunting a lot, decoys will have to be painted yearly. But most waterfowlers make a big mistake when it comes to sprucing up their stool. They do it just before the season starts.

At this time, birds are just coming out of eclipse plumage; they're dull and mottled, not bright and gaudy—so it pays to do your painting around midseason, when the birds are approaching mating plumage. The use your decoys will get during the rest of the season should dull them up just enough to match the condition of the real ducks at the beginning of the next season.

Something else to consider when painting is done is sex (of the ducks, that is). The temptation is to go heavy on the drakes; they're the more eye-catching, and there's something in their colors that brings out the repressed artist in us. In fact, you're better off to paint the great majority of your stool as hens. That eclipse-plumage stage is part of the reason, but more important, the hens of most species are rather look-alikes. A hen mallard is practically a dead ringer for a black duck and comes reasonably close to a hen teal, gadwall, pintail—even females of the diving-duck species. I firmly believe the predominance of hens in a decoy spread makes for wider potential appeal, and more shooting.

The type of paint you use on decoys is, of course, important. It's got to be of the exterior type, and dead flat, with no glare whatsoever. I like to mix my own colors, so my trick is to buy a top-quality exterior acrylic, two quarts, one black and one white. You can then buy individual tints in small tubes that will produce any color you want. Mixing of colors does require some savvy, though, and if you've got neither the time nor the talent, Herter's sells complete paint kits for each species and includes diagrams of what color goes where.

Rigging of decoys deserves some discussion too. It's wise to make all your anchor lines the same length. That way you have an accurate notion of how far apart to set the stool to avoid their bumping into each other—a real giveaway to any passing duck. While short anchor lines will afford more accurate decoy placement, I'd recommend making the lines at least three times as long as the depth of the water you commonly hunt in. You're sure to be doing some gunning in heavy weather, and this ratio of line to

These commercial decoys are, clockwise from lower left: broadbill and black duck by Herter's, mallard by Victor and goose by Tren-D-Coy. Of the anchors shown, the ringed mushroom (center) is the best.

water depth will give your anchor a purchase that will hold tight in a strong wind.

The material of anchor lines is important too. The stuff you get when you walk into a store and ask for heavy string just won't do. First, the color, usually white, stands out like skywriting when viewed from the air. Second, most "string" rots quickly when exposed to water. Third, it's seldom strong enough to withstand the wear of windblown decoys working the line against keel and anchor. Opt for olive-drab nylon lines or the old commercial fisherman's "tarred" line. Both types are dull in color and will last through many seasons. I prefer at least 80-pound-test for a long life, and I lean heavily toward the nylon rather than tarred line because nylon will never rot.

Anchors are most efficient when they're of the mushroom type, and they're most convenient when they ring the decoy's head. This discourages lines from unraveling when in transport and working into a tangle impossible to undo in the blackness of 4 A.M. Unfortunately, I know of no such anchor available commercially. I cast my own—the base in muffin tins, and before the lead hardens I insert a fist-size ring of heavy copper wire.

Although we all have fond dreams of shooting out of a walled and heated grass blind, most of the time duck hunters have to be satisfied with more makeshift accommodations—something thrown together, or carried into a likely-looking marsh for a one-day stand. So let's examine what can be done in a real-life situation.

First, I've learned the hard way that it's foolish to assume there will be any blind at the spot you're going to—or even that there will be sufficient natural materials to make one. So I always carry a basic blind with me. If I luck out and there's a blind there, or good cover to make something sophisticated, so be it. But if there isn't, I've still got my minnow seine.

That's exactly what my blind is: a 25-foot-long, 4-foot-high fine-mesh seine net. Its color is marsh brown, and with the addition of four 5-foot-long 1x2s for corner supports, I can quickly construct a 9x4-foot enclosed blind—plenty of room for two gunners and my big black Lab.

This basic blind can, of course, be further elaborated upon. Cat-tails can be piled against it, marsh grass intertwined with the mesh; or better yet, when there's some sort of natural cover or a blind already there, the net can be suspended above your head to provide additional camouflage.

This overhead protection is extremely important in the hunting of puddle ducks. These birds invariably make several passes at a spread of decoys before settling in, and those passes almost always carry them over land. If you have no overhead cover, they're likely to spot the glint of your gun, shells or thermos, the bright color of a shell box or some other giveaway.

So when it's possible and practical, consider bringing with you still another part of a "blind"—an aluminum johnboat.

This square-bowed boat is as light as a feather: a 10-footer weighs about 50 pounds. Sears, Roebuck sells such a model for under $100. Paint it a dull dead-grass color and support it upside down over your head on your flimsy posts driven into the sand or marsh. Throw a few sprigs of native vegetation on top of it, and combined with the seine, you've got a top-notch blind that will keep the weather off you too.

Realize that the boat is more than just a blind. Assuming you can get to the water's edge with your car, truck or camper, there's no easier way to carry guns, decoys and assorted gear to the place you pick to hunt. And the boat means you'll be able to retrieve every cripple.

A permanent blind, if you've got the location, legal status and time to build one, is infinitely better. It can and should be constructed so that it provides maximum comfort for the shooters: all-weather protection, comfortable seats and a means of heat; usually a catalytic heater is sufficient.

A permanent blind is easiest to build if you design it around standard exterior-plywood dimensions—4x8 feet. A blind with this floor will comfortably house three gunners—four in a pinch.

Easily the best way to put one together is at home. Precut and brace the floors, walls and roof and paint them. Hinge the door, lay out the seat and so forth. When you transport the blind, do it with the structure knocked down. Once you reach the water, you can then float the components into position, or carry them across the gunwales of a boat. Setting it up should then be no more work than erecting walls and nailing everything in place. If you'll do the actual erecting with double-headed nails, you'll be able to take your blind down as efficiently and quickly as you put it up.

Another possibility is a floating blind. This amounts to an enclosed structure built on a barge or platform with oil-drum or pontoon flotation underneath. Floating blinds offer even more of an edge than a permanent blind, since they can be towed and anchored anywhere. As a season progresses, ducks often change their flight patterns—leaving, coming to feed and resting in very different places from those they favored early in the season. With a floating blind, you're in a position to change with their whims—even to the point of anchoring out from shore and gunning them over their resting areas.

Understandably, a floating blind is a lot of work—both to build and to maintain. Ideally, it should be located someplace where you keep an eye on it to protect it from heavy weather and vandals. In these days of short seasons and low limits, it's doubtful if it's worth the effort unless you'll be gunning every day. So you might also try what I consider to be the epitome of the modern blind: the grass boat.

I use "modern" advisedly, for grass boats are nothing new; antiques dating back to the mid-1800s are still in use on the eastern marshes of Great South, Barnegat and Chesapeake bays. But they are exquisitely suited to the situation that confronts the contemporary waterfowler.

Here is a walled and roofed floating blind, high and dry at low tide. Blinds like this offer flexibility in that the gunner can go where the birds are, but they're work both to build and to maintain.

The most sensible arrangement for the serious waterfowler is a grass boat. It affords both a portable blind and easy transportation for all your gear.

Grass boats are small and light—seldom more than 10 feet long and, ideally, less than 100 pounds. Their shapes run the gamut from pumpkinseed to a square, boxy barge. What they boast in common is a low profile, a lot of decking and room for the gunner to lie down.

Their gunwales are even with or close to the water, and contoured decking gently slopes upward to a keel-to-deck depth of 12 to 14 inches. Thus constructed, the boat can be slipped in next to a low, marshy bank or literally dug into sand or a marsh. The shooter slides his legs and torso under the decking and lies down in the cockpit. In this position, he's totally invisible from any angle but directly above, and even then, only his head and upper body are exposed. To put it plainly, these boats are deadly.

There are a few other advantages to a grass boat. They'll hold more than enough decoys for a good puddle-duck spread and all the gear you'll need during a day in the marshes. They can be set up anywhere, so you don't have to worry about someone's setting up next to your permanent blind before you get there. Their only drawback is that they're essentially a one-man proposition. Because they're light, however, two or even three of the boats can be trailered or tucked into the back of a pickup.

Surely the neatest way to use these boats is typified by the arrangement employed by "Frosty" Dick Freidah, a veteran of the salt marshes of Long Island and an old friend. One of Dick's boats has an outboard bracket, to which, when we go gunning, he clamps a small 3½-horsepower, pivotal-reverse outboard. Towing his two other boats, train-style, makes access to any part of Moriches Marsh fast and no work at all.

Tied inextricably to blinds and the necessity for concealment is a thorough knowledge of camouflage and how to achieve it. I don't know exactly what place ducks hold on the evolutionary scale of intelligence—probably not too high—but I do know that either instinct or experience has taught them to be very wary of places where a hunter can be easily concealed. For example, I occasionally hunt a small pond located several hundred yards from a big grainfield in Montana. The pond is rimmed with thick willows and greasewood—so thick that unless you knew it was there, you'd never suspect the thatch of brush to hold water.

The place is highly favored by mallard. They can get a full

meal of plump wheat, then fly to a drink without any effort whatsoever. But because danger is so concealable around that pond's
perimeter, they swing around and around, low and high, sometimes for five minutes, before dropping in.

Conversely, when I hunt the eastern salt marshes with a grass
boat, the birds often come to stool without so much as one swing
over land, just like divers. The reason why is plain: the salt hay
is no higher than a few inches. The birds assume that nothing
could be hiding there.

Remember this point when choosing a site to pass shoot or set
out stool. Admittedly, if you don't have a grass boat, you're not
going to be able to set up shop in a crew-cut meadow, but pick a
spot with low cattails or rushes, rather than thick, tall mushroom-
ing brush. Choose rivers or lakeshores with flat banks rather than
towering cuts and water-deposited mounds.

Next, when building your permanent or temporary blind, be
very careful about choosing material native to the area. Often,
grass or reeds gathered just a few hundred feet from your blind
site will have a very different color, consistency and appearance
from the truly native cover. Although cut brush makes for an easy
blind in a hurry, if it's not naturally growing along the water's
edge, don't use it.

Strive for natural appearance in terms of vegetative stratifica-
tion too. The place where water joins land could be sandy yellow
or muddy brown. Early in the season, the stems of grasses and
rushes might be green, the blades golden brown. The effect is one
of rough horizontal lines of color and texture. Try to imitate it as
closely as possible.

The cardinal rule of camouflage is to break up outlines, so pay
careful attention to straight, obvious lines: the roof line of a covered blind for instance, or the top line of a stretched seine net.
These can be effectively broken up with just a few well-placed
sprigs of grass—not much work at all, but it must be done if you're
going to have the kind of concealment that finds ducks dropping
into your lap.

Grassing is something of an art unto itself. Most permanent
solid-walled blinds are covered completely with native grasses
for camouflage, and of course, the decking on grass boats is too.

There are many ways to do this, but I think the fastest and eas-

Random patterns of stapled-on marsh grass make this shooting box blend in with its surroundings.

iest is with a staple gun. Just take a thumb-thick hank of grass you've cut and twist it two or three times. Stamp a staple through the clump into the wall or decking below the twist and another above the twist. Keep doing this until no piece of wood is exposed. Strive to keep from establishing a pattern; staple the twists running this way, then that, and try to get at least a few strands extending beyond straight edges—the corner of a blind, or the edge of a cockpit. Correctly done, grassing makes a blind or boat virtually invisible. More than once I've climbed out of a grass boat, walked around to warm my feet, then done a double take when the boat didn't seem to be where I had left it. With camouflage that perfect, you're bound to fool even the most educated black or mallard.

It's something of a truism that puddle ducks don't like open water. Under certain conditions they might raft up way out in the middle of a lake or bay, but for the most part these birds prefer, and are most easily lured to, shoreline areas: coves, cuts, sloughs, ponds and marshes.

This rightly leads the wise gunner away from places like long points or a straight shoreline facing a large expanse of water. Even though you might observe birds trading around these areas, getting them to come to a rig is going to be tough work.

Another rule of thumb worth remembering is always to rig in a lee—a patch of calm water fully protected from wind and weather. Lees are natural resting spots for birds, and their relatively calm water means your decoys will stand out in plainer sight. Then too, gunning of a lee usually means the wind will be at your back and birds will land straight at you—easy shooting, and pretty to behold.

When setting out your stool, begin with the blocks that are not your majority species: geese, coots, widgeon or whatever. In nature, birds tend to segregate by species anyway, and by setting them apart from your main stool, you've got a handy yardstick to measure distances. Pace off yardages and set the decoys at a predetermined range. I usually set my widgeon or pintails at 45 yards straight out from the blind and my geese or coot at 60 yards to my right or left, depending on the wind conditions.

Always rig in a lee (shown by the shaded areas). The calm water will keep your decoys in plainer sight, and ducks will land straight in toward you. (All illustrations by Sil Strung)

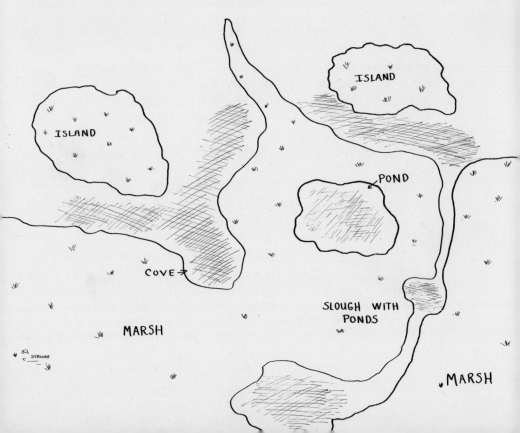

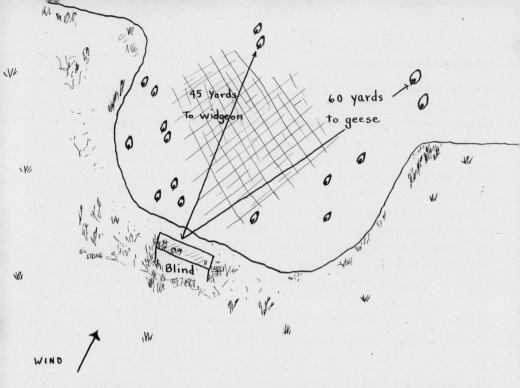

In this typical warm-weather "C" rig, the crosshatching indicates the probable landing area of the ducks.

The precise positioning of the rest of the decoys is largely a matter of the species you have and of weather. In the warm weather common to the beginning of the season, I prefer to rig out in a small cove or pond, patterning my stool in a "C" configuration with the open end of the letter pointing away from the blind. This closely approximates what ducks would do naturally: fan out along the curving shoreline to feed in the shallows. The "C" also affords incoming birds a ready place to land—inside the letter.

The area covered by the stool amounts to a half-circle, 35 to 45 yards in diameter. Decoys are not evenly distributed, but rather bunched in small groups of two to four birds, with a loner or two evident.

In stormy, windy or cold weather—the kind you can expect toward season's end—the pattern changes quite a bit. Real birds bunch up so that their mutual presence will break up wind and waves and provide some warmth, so at this time I rig in an "I" pattern.

In this situation, I prefer to rig off a small point—not a long lead of land stretching into big water, but the kind of point that would occur where the aforementioned small cove opens up into a modest-sized lake or river.

Rather than having the wind directly on my back, I like a wind quartering my back in this situation, so I try to set up my blind accordingly. I also think it's wise to use more decoys at this time than you did during warm weather. Thirty or forty isn't too many if it's practical to lug that many blocks to the blind sight.

Minority species are still set at predetermined ranges, away from the main body of decoys. When birds come in to this rig, they tend to land either in the middle of the "I" or between the shore and the upwind end of the configuration—so when setting stool, make sure your blind is in ideal gun range of these two

Heavy-weather rigs are best anchored off a point. The crosshatches show the birds' likely landing spots.

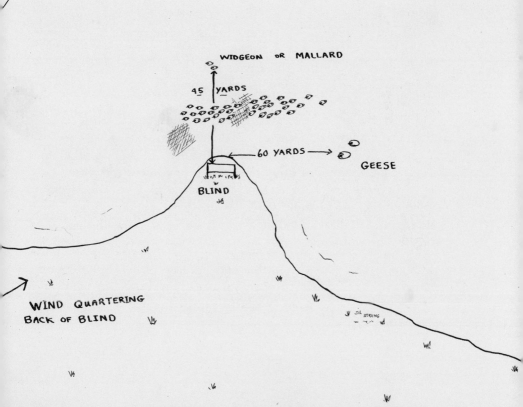

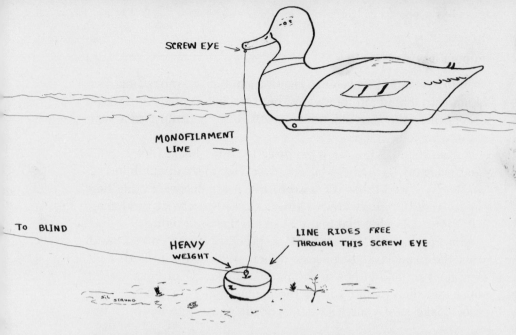

To make an effective "dabbler" decoy, fasten a screw eye to the bill and run the line to another screw eye on an anchor weight. The line then runs to the blind and is pulled from there.

places. It's also a good idea to leave a little space in the middle of that "I" so that birds have a place to land if that's their notion.

A carefully placed, well-manicured set of decoys will pull plenty of birds on its own, but there are some things you can do to enhance its effect. When the wind's flat, decoys don't move but remain immobile and lifeless. Anything you can do to add motion to that static rig is going to help bring birds near.

Easily the most effective trick is to make a dabbling decoy. Screw a small eye into the underside of a decoy bill, tie light monofilament fishing line to the eye and run it through another eye that's cast, screwed or otherwise affixed to a heavy weight on bottom. Run the line back to the blind and keep it reasonably taut. When ducks are in sight, yank the line hard, and the decoy noses under, exactly like a feeding duck. Realize, too, that the wavelets created by the dabbler also give some slight motion to other decoys—all in all, an attractive addition to your rig.

Using this same idea, you can also rig decoys to a trolley setup so that they swim back and forth. I've seen this done in the Midwest and along the Eastern Seaboard. But because of the rather sophisticated machinery required to achieve the effect, it's best suited to permanent blinds, leased lands and clubs or guides, rather than the average weekend gunner.

Flagging is an old market hunter's trick that's seldom employed anymore, and I really don't know why. The tactic is based on a natural activity of ducks—preening and rearing.

After ducks preen and oil their feathers, they stretch their wings and rear up off the water. They'll do this several times, until their feathers realign themselves. The visual effect is a sudden flash of activity; often, because of it, you'll be able to locate a distant raft that's otherwise invisible.

That some sign of activity is attractive to a duck is undeniable. Just think of how many times birds have come close when you're out in the decoys. And waving a 2x2-foot black flag roughly approximates a preening and rearing bird.

You don't wave the thing like a banner: just one or two fast up-downs. And you don't flag close birds—nothing within 300 yards. But try this trick on flyspecks drifting across the horizon or closer flocks that have obviously passed your rig by. You'll be surprised how many of them do an about-face and swing by your blind for a closer look.

Calling, like flagging, is an effective trick, but one that can be overdone. Probably the best instruction you can ever get in calling is to be around when a real duck starts to feel mouthy.

It's happened to me a lot, primarily because I often rig out in the spring to observe and photograph waterfowl. Because I'm not potting every bird that comes close to the rig, many of them sit in and stay for a while, giving me a good chance to chart their noises.

I've found that ducks call only their own kind. A mallard will call another mallard, a pintail a pintail and so forth. Because not all ducks quack (teal chirp and squeal; widgeon squeak and whistle, for example), it pays to be able to identify your birds in the air and "highball" only those types for which you have a call.

Understandably, you've got just so much room on your neck for calls. I pack just two—and one is a goose call. So my duck call, like my decoys, is attuned to the majority species. Since mallards and blacks call in almost identical fashion, their call is the one I use the most.

When you see a mallard or black in the air, the call to use is the highball. This involves five or six quacks, the first being loud and rather long—about three or four seconds' duration—and the others getting progressively shorter. Generally, you have to do this only once. If it seems attractive to a bird, it will be enough to produce the desired effect and he'll tip in toward your rig. If the bird ignores it, you might try one more highball—but chances are that all the calling in the world won't appreciably change his mind about your spread and just might help sour it.

When other species are near, I call too, but I don't sound the highball. Just an occasional, contented "quack," the kind you're bound to hear near the shore of any duck pond filled with civilized mallard. I don't think this literally "calls" other ducks in, but it does lend some realism to your layout and, I think, produces extra shots.

It would be misleading to get into brand names. I've found that all manufacturers produce both good calls and lemons. They just don't seem to be able to standardize the quality of the reed. What I do is blow the thing before I buy it, keeping the following in mind:

When blown hard, the call shouldn't fade into a squeak, but should maintain its throaty resonance.

The call should be capable of producing a "quack," low but audible, when blown very softly. The hard-blown call is the first note of the highball; the soft one, the contented lone "quack" of ducks peacefully feeding. You need both.

The tone shouldn't be too low, or the reed limp. If you're familiar with music, a note reasonably close to either side of middle C is ideal.

You can never divorce a gun from its user's personality, so when some grizzled old duck hunter tells you that his Model 12 Winchester was the best shotgun ever made for waterfowl, you've got to take the adventures he's enjoyed with that smoke pole as part of his recommendation.

And I'm the same way. I've got my favorite for ducks—a Browning Double Auto in 12 gauge—but it's my favorite partly because every time I look at it on the wall or feel its heft, some fond vision of a crumpled mallard or pintail leaps into memory.

With this in mind, I'll try to maintain some semblance of objectivity in my recommendations, which should be adapted to the type of hunting you expect to encounter.

For close-in shooting—birds that consistently decoy within 35 to 45 yards—nothing beats a 20-gauge chambered for 3-inch magnums. Their punch is equivalent to express 12s, and the light little 20s have snap and speed that make them a delight to feel on your shoulder.

They're the kind of gun that always feels "on," and whenever they make sense, I'd recommend them. But in the same breath, there just aren't that many Shangri-las where you can count on birds landing in your lap.

So I feel the all-around gun is the 12-gauge chambered for 3-inch magnums. It packs plenty of killing power at long, long ranges—40 to 50 yards—and it's distances like these that make up the bulk of a modern waterfowler's opportunities. It's also excellent for geese—work that the 20s, no matter how powerful their shells or large their shot, are not cut out for.

Whatever gauge you choose, I'd recommend 28-inch barrels with a modified choke. Full-choked 30-inch barrels are the old standard, and I've used them much, but I've come to the firm conclusion that they cost me more ducks than they get me. Their pattern is just too tight for moderate ranges, and you either miss completely or reduce the bird to a puff of feathers. Full chokes and long barrels are, however, wise choices if you're primarily a pass shooter rather than a decoy hunter. When they're covering distances, ducks commonly fly 40 to 50 yards up, and the extra reach will put more birds into your bag.

Although you may have some personal preference as to action, there's no debating that the automatic is the most efficient, no matter what gauge you choose.

Stock length is a far more variable matter for the waterfowler than for other aficionados of scattergunning. Most duck seasons get under way around midfall, a time when the weather's still warm across the nation. Understandably, you wear fewer and lighter clothes than later in the season when hard north winds sweep across your stool, and those clothes take up less room between your gun's butt and your shoulder than a heavy parka and insulated underwear. So unless you make some provision for the addition of heavy clothes, you'll end up with a too-long stock that doesn't shoulder properly toward the end of the season.

The best solution to this problem that I've found is to match your stock length to the heavy-clothes period. Generally this means a stock about two inches shorter than would be normal for you. Then, in warm weather, simply add a cushioned, pullover rubber butt boot to your stock. This not only gets it in the neighborhood of proper stock length; it also cushions the blows of heavy shells at a time when you don't wear enough clothes to soak up the shock.

At one time or another, duck hunting involves the use of all three shotshell categories: low-brass, high-brass and magnum loads.

Low-brass is ideal for cripples. Once a bird is out of the air but still alive, it must be dispatched. Although puddle ducks don't swim underwater with the fishlike ease of the divers, they are quite capable of submerged movement. And above water, they can make some pretty fast time. With a wind at their backs, a wading hunter can seldom catch them in waist-deep water.

There's no need for the power of a heavy load to stop them, and you should keep your shot for cripples small. I favor 7½s. The most vulnerable spot on a cripple is the head, a rather stingy target. The close pattern of small shot is sure to place a few pellets there. Then too, those small pellets won't penetrate the denser body feathers, so you don't end up with unnecessary lead picking at plucking time.

High-brass, or "express," loads are the ones to use on those days when birds are decoying close or when you're jump shooting. But I don't recommend using them exclusively. When you shoot at a bird that comes to stool or jumps up out of a marsh, if he has a few buddies with him you can count on another shot at a fast-retreating duck at a respectable range. So use high-brass for your first shot, and magnum loads for your second and third.

Straight magnum loads are the wisest choice when birds are decoying at a distance or when you're pass shooting. In standard 2¾-inch lengths they're capable of clean kills at 40 to 50 yards, and the 3-inch magnums add another 5 to 10 yards to that reach.

In terms of shot sizes, I flatly favor 4s for all situations but dispatching cripples. No. 2 or BB shot will kill at a longer range, but

In the space of a single season, a good retriever can recover his own weight in ducks that would otherwise have been lost.

at 50 to 60 yards, their patterns aren't dense enough to ensure the three- to four-pellet contact required to drop a bird cleanly.

Once you've got ducks on the water, you have to recover them, and this you can do by wading out yourself (if the water's shallow enough), rowing out in your boat (assuming you have one) or sending a retriever to do the job. Of these, the last is by far the most enjoyable.

Although other breeds (such as the Brittany spaniel) can be used for retrieving over water, only the "pure" retriever breeds have the size, strength and heavy coat to really handle the job. The three most popular retrievers are the Labrador, Chesapeake and golden, but of these three, the Lab is the overwhelming favorite.

In terms of sheer efficiency, the Chesapeake is tops. He can handle cold, rough water and heavy birds that would overwhelm either of the other two dogs. But the Chessy is hardheaded, surly and limited strictly to water retrieving; he's useless in the uplands. The golden has a wonderful disposition, but does not take as well to water as the Lab (who is equally sunny-tempered) and is not as strong a dog. All things considered, get a Lab. You just can't go wrong with one.

I see many waterfowlers who go to exquisite lengths to paint letter-perfect stool and build palatial, fully grassed blinds, yet forget the piece of equipment most important to camouflage—themselves.

The human body is unique and distinct to wildlife. No other form of mammalian life walks erect, or uses hands and arms for the same purposes humans do, or possesses such a light face with eyes set very near the middle of that flat plane. And all these attributes, singly or in concert, will quickly alert ducks that there stands their greatest natural enemy.

It follows that if you can successfully mask these signposts, you'll go a long way toward luring ducks within gun range, be you a pass, jump or decoy shooter.

One of my most persistent reminders concerning some semblance of personal camouflage comes when I'm caught flat-footed out of the blind, either emptying cold kidneys of a half-gallon of coffee, adjusting a few blocks or getting back onto numbed feet. As any duck hunter knows, undertaking any one of these operations is a guarantee that birds are going to come within range. "Freeze" is the command most often called out by your compadres, but freezing seldom works. If you're standing erect, no matter how stock-still you remain, birds will flare. They spot that erect form and the bright mirror of your face.

If, on the other hand, you slowly bend at the knees and the waist, hunch over and look at the ground, better than half the time the ducks will continue to approach. I've had them land right next to me while I was out in the rig—a rather uncomfortable feeling when there are two guys in the blind who haven't had a shot all day, I might add.

But the important thing is the effect. Birds don't seem to pick up slow movement—the aforementioned hunkering down should take five or six seconds. In that position, your outline is also rounded like a rock's, not straight like a man's. And your face is hidden from easy view. That's very important. Every bird who's sat next to me jumped into frantic flight when I turned my head to look at him.

This lesson can and should be carried over into your blind or duckboat. First, when there are birds in the air, don't make any fast movements. You might have to put down a cup of coffee or reach for a gun, but do it very slowly. And whatever you do, don't raise that gun to your shoulder until you're ready to shoot, or make any other motion that will plainly reveal your arms.

Never stand when you're hunting ducks. Sit down in a blind; lie down in a grass boat; make every effort to avoid presenting that sticklike profile.

Perhaps the toughest discipline involves your face. You shouldn't look at a duck directly. Old-timers have told me that birds can see the glint of your eyes. I don't know if I fully swallow that, but I do know that when you look directly at anything, you present the greatest surface area of face to that object—a face that reflects an awful lot of light and that plainly reveals the location of your eyes.

Wear some sort of peaked hat and keep your head down. Obviously, you've got to look at a bird sometime, but do it by peering up from under the brim or from the corner of your eyes. Follow a bird's path with your eyes alone, not with your entire head. You'll be flabbergasted at how many more birds will be willing to come in really close, and how few ducks will flare wild, yards beyond your gun range.

Along with this personal camouflage goes the clothing you wear. Always strive to match the color of the surrounding cover. Olive drab is a color long favored by duck hunters, either in a solid shade or in the army camouflage pattern—and in most cases it's about as concealing as a Santa Claus costume. Olive drab is a great color for camouflage in living woods—the dappled greens and browns of summer—but the color of a fall marsh is a rich brownish gold, and it's that color that will hide you best.

Hats are important too; the brim breaks up your face with shade and helps hide those giveaway eyes. You might also consider using burnt cork to darken your face. This is a trick I firmly believe in, especially when you're in a position from which you're doing a lot of looking up.

Your gun should use some camouflage too; an archer's bow cover twisted on and taped to your barrel is the easiest way to achieve this. Many times I've spotted concealed hunters by the glint from their gun barrels, and I know of one day when the reflection from mine, poking just beyond the front of my blind, was spooking birds. A buddy mentioned it, I then cradled the gun on my lap and birds decoyed freely thereafter.

To a very real extent, that incident illustrates both the secret of successful puddle-duck shooting and the essence of the sport. You've practically got to think birds into range.

The tidewater marshes of the East are the place where duck shooting was raised to the status of an art. And there, when you're a top duck shooter, you're called a gunner. I've had the pleasure of knowing a few gunners in my day: "Frosty" Dick Freidah, Joe Steigerwald, Joe Arata. They're men who constantly bring to bear all the knowledge of past experience and apply it to present—and future—problems. In and out of the blind, they're always dreaming up new twists, tricks and methods of placing a decoy that will, hopefully, fool ducks so completely that every bird in sight will be lured to cup his wings, drop his legs and come to stool scant feet from their blind. To me, it's the same kind of knowledge, involvement and creative energy that goes into the making of a painting or a sculpture.

Michelangelos of the mud, Leonardos of the cattails . . . duck hunting requires you to be these and more. But the rewards are great, and the effect addictive. You *become* the sport, fanatically committed to building better decoys and blinds, and are drawn to the marshes at every opportunity. It's a complex and immensely satisfying pastime that is the ultimate in outdoor recreation.

DIVER-DUCK HUNTING

BY GEORGE REIGER

WHY DO YOU DO IT? What compulsion drives you to get up when the rest of the world has just gone to bed?

Sometimes you're awake even before the alarm goes off. You lie a moment, relishing the early-morning quiet, but then quickly get up for fear of going back to sleep.

Your clothes are carefully laid out over a nearby chair—insulated underwear on top, shell vest sitting heavily beneath. Your waders and decoys are already packed in the car. Perhaps you didn't even take them out after the last trip. But your shotgun is waiting downstairs, along with an instant breakfast. Soon you're out the door, carrying a canvas bag full of lunch and spare shells in one hand and your gun in the other.

Maybe there's a retriever to take along. Happily, your partner will have one if you don't. There's little nuisance in having a handsome Lab or golden jump up on you, sharing your excitement for the day ahead. And later there will be pride when he comes ashore—pouring and shaking water, but with his mouth grinning-full of a fat broadbill drake.

When you reach the dock, there are already hints that it will be a good morning for shooting. (But then, doesn't every morning have hints like that?) Today waves slap up around the pilings, and a glaze of ice shows everywhere the spray flies, and the dock lights shine.

Out across the marsh, everything is darkness. The moon has long since set, and there's not yet even the first suggestion of dawn. There will be a wet, potentially dangerous run to the blind, and for a moment you and your companion plan the where and how of getting there. Planning is useful, for if nothing else, it relieves the anxiety of the trip ahead by first taking you there in your imagination.

You start out.

There's reassurance in the quick spark and steady roar of the outboard. Primed by the run the day before, she coughs to life at the first pull of the starter cord. At least this much you can control. Out there are tides and wind and bitter-cold water that draw at the edges of your life and warmth. But with your hand on the tiller, guiding the boat through a maze of shadows and dim reflections, those fears, for the moment, seem remote.

Now time begins to quicken. The first tentative light is seen in the east. You're almost at the blind, but the decoys must still be put out. Above the roar of the outboard you hear the *quack, quack* of a startled puddle duck. Then you see it. Sometimes more than one. Dark, blurry shapes whirling away across the low sod islands of marsh grass.

The blind looms suddenly near. You feel pride in having once again unraveled the maze of creeks and markers and found your way without delay. You idle the boat down against the wind and current and start putting out the decoys, one at a time. Perhaps you take off your woolen gloves and put on an insulated rubber pair—the kind trappers or divers wear. This is wet work, and you don't want to have stiff fingers when the shooting begins.

Despite your desire to set each decoy with care to keep its back and head dry (and therefore free of ice), there's impatience in the air. Your partner has seen a bird buzz by, and he takes time to unsheath his gun from its case and load up. Then the dog gets restless and unexpectedly plunges into the water and swims for shore. He'll be shivering with the cold soon enough, you think. But right then you don't care. The dog almost upset the boat and wet half the decoys when he left, and if he gets cold this time, perhaps next time he won't be so foolish.

The starlight is gone now, and every second brings the dawn nearer. But finally you're done. You run your companion in toward the blind and then take the boat to a creek mouth a little way along the shore. You leave your now-empty gun case in the boat, load up and start back across the flooded marsh. The dog meets you halfway, galloping out of the gloom and leaping about with enthusiasm. Already you've forgiven him for splashing overboard, and his excitement further charges your own.

A shot! You go down on one knee and try to see the bird without turning your head too much. The dog has stopped, and from a half-crouched position, he too scans the horizon. His ears are cocked slightly forward, and his expression is intent. He knows there's work ahead, and his pose is so striking that for a moment you watch him and not the water.

The birds suddenly whisk by and down the channel—a trio of mergansers. You get up and continue to the blind, where your companion makes a few apologetic remarks about firing before legal light, about shooting at sawbills, but mostly about having missed.

You say nothing, but with the dog on his own small platform at the edge of the blind, you squeeze in and take your seat. It's always at this moment that you know that whatever the cost in time, trouble and money, it has all been worthwhile.

Out ahead of you is a flotilla of decoys. Two Saturdays of other activities that-might-have-been were spent getting that peculiar mix of wooden and plastic birds ready for the season. At the time, opening day seemed far away. But when it was done, you were glad. At least now if you have poor shooting, it can't be blamed on the quality of your decoys.

Full light comes rapidly. The stiff breeze limits the number of shore birds you see this morning. A drake bufflehead suddenly appears around the point. Your dog sees him, but no one else moves. You don't shoot bufflehead anymore. But to put their presence to use, you've invented a little game of superstition: If the bird flies by the outside of the stool, so will the rest of the ducks that day; if it sits in or flies over the stool, you'll have good shooting.

The bufflehead decides to land. Pert, immediately suspicious, the colorful drake sits on the water and nervously looks about. For some reason you think of all the millions of people who are still asleep and will never see such a sight. No nonhunter has ever craved the perpetuation of wildfowl more than you, who suffer all the agonies of an arctic environment to pursue them. But this one species you don't kill anymore. And there's nothing to explain.

The bufflehead is suddenly up, pattering across the wave tops, and away. Then your companion grips your arm. Down the channel and coming fast is an airborne line that writhes and weaves like something serpentine. The line approaches and is quickly discernible as the first large flock of greater scaup moving from the inner bay to larger water and the clam beds beyond.

A final glance at the dog and decoys, and you crouch lower, just your eyes peering through the edge of broken reeds that rattle in the gusting wind. Most of the birds angle away to keep direction with the channel. But a contingent of sixty or so continues straight for the blind. On they come, wings beating a blur, and now you can begin to distinguish the drakes from the hens. As they close the last few yards, some cup their wings, sliding wildly like planes about to overshoot a runway; others come low, wings merely trembling to hold them above the wave tops. Then they're there, swirling over the decoys. Off goes your safety and up you go. A shot, two shots, and four birds fall! Two of those are your partner's. In the excitement, you didn't even hear him fire.

The rest of the ducks are already gone. "Vanished" is the word. Far up the channel, fragments of that once-connected serpentine line diminish rapidly from sight. It's over so fast.

While the dog does the work that your patience and centuries of selective breeding have trained him to do, you stand and stretch to draw the adrenaline from your arms. But the dog is not yet back with the last bird when your partner says, "Down!" And then up the channel once again comes a line of birds such as you hope to see in Paradise when you get there. There's simply no finer or faster gunning in all the world than the hunting of diver waterfowl.

Today, the scaup is king. Both the lesser, also known as bluebill, and the greater, or broadbill, have replaced the canvasback and redhead as our principal diving-duck quarry since the can and

The greater scaup has reigned as king of the divers ever since the canvasback and redhead were put on the protected list. Ever watchful over the water, scaup are even more so when they come ashore.

redhead were put on the protected list. Overshooting by men who took these birds for granted and, more important, the destruction of prime nesting grounds in the north-central United States and Canada, as well as enormous man-made changes in their coastal wintering grounds, are the causes most responsible for the decline of these former monarchs among waterfowl.

Most scaup nest farther north, where, hopefully, drainage projects and development will never come. And until that perfect day when canvasback and redhead populations are restored to pre-1900 levels, bluebills and broadbills will be relied on to keep alive the grand tradition of open-water, late-season hunting that is the most rugged and invigorating form of North American waterfowling.

While most diving ducks breed on fresh water, the majority move out to the coasts during the fall migration. In fact, divers seem to delight in confounding the neat little arrows on flyway maps issued by various governmental agencies. These ducks will sometimes spend as many days traveling east or west as south. An example is the greater scaup, which regularly breeds in the Northwest Territories and Alaska, but which divides its wintering populations between the Pacific Coast north of Mexico and the Atlantic Coast from the Carolinas to Cape Cod.

Those waterfowl that stick closest to the ocean are called sea ducks, or "coot," by most hunters. They are really scoters, and their family includes the American, white-winged and surf subspecies. We'll get back to these later on.

The redhead, canvasback, greater and lesser scaup and ringneck (which I insist on calling ringbill because the two bluish-white rings on the bird's bill are *always* present in *both* sexes, while it's sometimes difficult to distinguish the vague chestnut collar on the lower neck of even a mature drake) are all members of the genus *Nyroca*, which is a Latinized form of the Russian word *nyrok*, meaning a diving duck. The importance of this is to suggest the many similarities among these five birds. While lesser scaup and ringbills are often found wintering on large fresh water lakes, and redhead, canvasback and greater scaup appear to prefer the coastal bays, each species is likely to show up in the other birds' preferred habitat. In addition, they're all generally late migrants, staying just ahead of the worst winter storms. Many redheads, canvasbacks and broadbills don't even arrive at the extreme southern range of their wintering grounds until December or even January.

In recognition of this fact, many coastal states have extended their duck-hunting seasons by a week or two in order to provide the cold-weather gunner with a bonus period. As a result, some diving-duck specialists in the Mid-Atlantic States don't even bother to hunt in November anymore; they bring their boats and decoys to the coast only after the first freezing weather in December.

Other ducks of the open bays are the American and Barrow's goldeneyes (both commonly called whistler), the ruddy duck, the bufflehead and all three species of merganser: American, red-breasted and hooded. Except for the winter plumage of the ruddy, these are among our most beautiful waterfowl. With striking contrasts of white and dark iridescence, their color patterns mirror the contrasts of winter—dark skies and falling snow; black waves crested by white. Merely the sight of a drake bufflehead zigzagging over the decoys is enough to make the adrenaline flow.

One of the most intriguing aspects of most of this group—the goldeneyes, the bufflehead, and the American and hooded mergansers—is that they're all tree-cavity or stump nesters. They prefer to brood their eggs at some elevation from the ground or water and frequently use enlarged woodpecker and flicker holes to do so. However, any suitable height with a nesting platform might be adapted. As a result, some people with summer homes in Ontario and Quebec have arrived in late spring to find an American goldeneye family in residence on some portion of the roof, perhaps even attempting to occupy the chimney itself.

The average number of eggs in a tree nester's brood is ten. As soon as the young hatch, they are called to the ground by the hen. Using claws on the tips of their tiny webbed feet and beating their wings furiously to provide stability, the ducklings climb the inside of the nest cavity and, without pausing, tumble one by one to the ground. The hen then guides her brood to the nearest water, where they commence feeding on small water animals—snails, mosquito larvae and the like. On the wintering grounds, this diet is merely adapted to local conditions in which small crabs and mussels replace the summer's insects. And it's in intercepting these birds as they trade back and forth between their favorite coves and channels in search of shellfish that the duck hunter experiences some of his finest shooting.

Late last season, John Cadwallader and Mike Greata, two New Englanders, came down to hunt quail on my farm in Virginia. We found few birds, and rather than see the boys go home disappointed, I asked whether they'd like to try some pass shooting for ducks. I added by way of inducement that such shooting might be the severest test of their considerable shooting skills. My friends were interested but skeptical, mumbling something about ruffed grouse being the severest test of anyone's shooting skill. But a neighbor, Wes Corson, and I took them out and divided them between two points of marshland jutting into a channel through

Big bag limits on mergansers and sea ducks attract many gunners to this specialized form of diver-duck shooting. Here's a hunter with part of a two-man limit of red-breasted mergansers.

which good numbers of whistlers, bufflehead and red-breasted mergansers flew. We provided a dog for each man, so all they had to do was shoot and keep shooting until they had their limits. They thought this would be a snap—until the first bird came through on a tail wind.

I have no idea how fast that little bufflehead was moving, but my two friends undershot him by an embarrassing number of yards. The shooting continued like this until each gunner had gone through more than a box of shells. Then they called it quits. Grand total: three bufflehead. My friends conceded that diving ducks, along with ruffed grouse, were the severest test of any shooter's skill.

Neither one of these men is a bad shot. In the upland coverts, they more than hold their own. But being used to a generally slower target in wooded areas with ample range marks to aid instinctive lead, they found their introduction to waterfowl shooting a humbling affair. Pass shooting—particularly pass-shooting birds on a healthy tail wind over flat, indistinguishable marsh or water or up against a monochromatic sky—offers few clues as to range and lead. If, on top of that, the gunner is unfamiliar with the true size of his target, he may frequently misjudge distance and, therefore, the shot. The only way I know for any man to improve his lot as a pass shooter is to practice as often as he can. However, since this involves many pounds of wasted shot as well as a high proportion of unrecovered cripples, it's not a sport I participate in much anymore—except to host a pair of upland-gunning friends and to exercise a pair of eager dogs.

Though diver-duck hunting is done throughout the continent, it's primarily a coastal sport. In the days of the market gunner, mallard were the most popular waterfowl sold in Chicago; the canvasback always took the prize in New York and Baltimore. Most of the divers taken in the Midwest are merely bonus birds to a day of sport with puddlers or geese. One afternoon I had excellent bluebill shooting over a South Dakota stock pond—but only after we had spent the morning hunting honkers along the Missouri River.

When divers first cross the border from Canada, they come in readily to almost any sort of stool. A few diver decoys in the lot almost guarantee success. However, by the time the survivors reach the coasts, they're not quite so easy to fool. Therefore, the hunter who plans to do well on them learns to specialize, and he generally starts by making sure he has a large number (anywhere from two dozen to a hundred or more) of the sturdiest, finest replica diving-duck decoys he can afford. The only exception to this kind of investment is if you plan to do mostly pass shooting. There you can get by without any decoys or, perhaps, with just a few to bring the birds closer to where you're hidden. There's also the practical fact that lugging a load of decoys (plus gun, shells, etc.) across the marsh without a boat is no way to start a day of shooting requiring maximum concentration and coordination.

Since I usually set out decoys from a boat, where crowding, not weight, is the only limiting consideration, I prefer to use wooden blocks. There's an esthetic appeal to shooting over well-maintained wooden birds (perhaps even ones you've made your-

Putting out decoys can be a finger-numbing process, and collecting them when they're wet is even worse. Rubber gloves come highly recommended for this work.

self). But there's also the fact that cedar or white pine will hold up better than most synthetics in freezing salt-water use season after season. Equally important, pine and cedar blocks (and to a lesser extent, pressed cork) have ideal weight and riding characteristics for the choppy water conditions most often associated with diver-duck shooting. Properly balanced, a solid wooden decoy will bounce and bob far less than any synthetic yet devised. Further, it will be less inclined to turn over in a crosswind and carries a load of ice better than most plastic birds.

I stress solid wood over hollow wooden decoys because, while hollow decoys were popular on such grounds as Barnegat Bay for close to a century into the 1940s, they were developed primarily as a means of reducing the weight per decoy so that more blocks could be safely carried aboard a small punt or sneak boat. If weight is a factor today, a variety of plastic decoys can be found that weigh even less than a more costly hollow wooden bird—that is, if you can still find someone other than yourself who will carve one for you. Outboard motors in combination with large-capacity, lightweight boat hulls make it possible to carry far heavier average loads per gunner than were feasible even twenty-five years ago. Therefore, once again, solid wooden blocks—many in "oversize" designs—are returning to fashion.

When stooling out on a cold day, *never* throw your decoys helter-skelter, relying on the keels to right the birds. For starters, you should have a pretty clear pattern in mind as to how you want the birds set out—leaving ample space within and around the stool (and still within range) for birds to land. Divers normally land in the middle of or at the head of a stool, so you should arrange your decoys to have the birds within easy range as they set their wings for landing. There's been much mumbo jumbo about various patterns for a stool. But I find there's no way to make such recommendations other than underwriting such general designs as the fishhook, the open circle and the broken line.

Another reason not to throw the birds out indiscriminately is to prevent water from getting on their heads and backs on a freezing-cold day. No matter how many ducks are already on the move, take time to do the job right. On some cold, choppy days, ice will form so fast you'll have to make several trips out to the stool to knock the stuff off. (Be careful how you do so; you don't want to knock off the paint or part of the decoy.) If ice continues to accumulate on a decoy, it can actually cause the block to sink. While there may be some mornings when a little ice on a decoy doesn't seem to discourage birds, more often it does. Finally, if you can safely manage it, take your gun along when you wade out into the stool. I've shot many a diver while standing in the middle of my decoys.

Repair and paint your blocks soon after the season ends. This is merely a personal opinion, but I find doing work of that sort easier in the dead days of February and March than trying to catch up on the work in late summer or early fall, when there's so much else to distract an outdoorsman.

Burlap sacks are the time-honored tote bags of the duck hunter. Particularly when you shoot over a salt-water marsh, you don't want or need anything finer to bag your decoys. However, a can-

Most self-respecting ducks wouldn't come near this spread. The white, shining faces and the gleaming outboard motor are a dead giveaway that something is badly amiss.

Get your decoy-repair chores out of the way in February and March. Such work is doubly difficult to do in the distracting days prior to the opening of the season.

vas bag for shells is a good investment, especially if it's to be tucked inside a watertight plastic sack for storage under a boat seat where bilge water could slosh over it. Metal and wooden shell boxes are simply impractical. They'll rust or corrode in salt water (the metal hinges on the wooden boxes give way), and their extra weight makes them undesirable to carry any distance. (The weight of your shells will be enough.) Finally, such boxes tend to be noisier and more awkward to stash than fabric containers.

I recall when some years ago a manufacturer came out with a shell-box-and-swivel-shooting-seat combination that, in theory, seemed the perfect item for pass shooting. But the contraption weighed more than the shells it carried, sank immediately out of sight into any kind of soft ground—especially when I dropped my 200-pound bulk onto it—and sat so low in proportion to my height that my knees ended up under my armpits whenever I tried to swivel for a shot. A small wooden post with a foot to retard its sinking into mud, topped by a section of board large enough for my posterior layered over with insulated clothes and waders, would have been all I required in the way of a shooting stick— and a whole lot lighter to carry, and less expensive to boot.

Use monofilament for decoy lines. This is a trick my brothers and I learned some years ago while hunting over a sand bottom and crystal-clear water on a bright sunny day. Despite several flights of birds, we didn't get a shot. The incoming ducks all flared away well out of range. A few circled for another look, confirmed their suspicions and flew on. We were baffled. We're reasonably meticulous hunters, and despite a thorough inspection of ourselves, the blind and the immediate vicinity, we couldn't see what was wrong. The birds continued to flare out of range. My older brother, Tony, then sought out a vantage point where he could see the area of the stool from a bird's perspective. He walked up a hill behind and to one side of the blind, and there the bright sun and clear water gave him the clue: our tarred cotton decoy lines showed as harsh black marks against the white sand bottom of the cove.

Johnny and I still weren't convinced this was our problem. However, Tony went back to the car, got out his tackle box and returned with a spool of 20-pound-test monofilament fishing line. With nothing to lose but more potential shooting, we pulled in the decoys, replaced the tarred line with transparent nylon and reset the stool. By noon, we had our limits. More important, we had our evidence: not a single incoming flight thereafter had flared away.

Today we use 30- to 50-pound-test monofilament (anything heavier tends to get stiff and unwieldy on very cold days) with dull-finished swivels at both the decoy and the sinker ends to keep the line from twisting. If we plan to shoot over a rock or oyster-shell bottom, we'll tie in a short dark length of heavy braided line between the sinker and the monofilament to reduce decoy loss through line abrasion. If you frequently gun over mud bottoms, of course, you may employ brown or dark green lines. However, since I use decoys over a variety of bottoms, I'd just as soon be rigged for any contingency. Our days afield are all too few, and I'd rather have some other excuse for not getting shots than something as easily controlled as the color (or lack of it) of my decoy lines.

There are a number of commercially made weights on the market, or you can make your own with a simple mold. However, you must make sure the weights of your decoys, whether store-bought or homemade, are every bit as inconspicuous as their lines. Rather than use them for one or two trips until the brightness wears off, do your color softening before the season begins. If the brightness doesn't fade through ordinary exposure to the weather, then don't hesitate to paint your sinkers. A spray can of flat black or brown is a nominal investment for further confidence that you've done all you can to increase your odds for a successful outing.

Likewise, if you're putting your decoys out by wading (versus setting them out from a boat), step on each weight as it goes down. This will not only further disguise its presence by burying it in a soft bottom; it will help anchor the decoy more firmly so that it doesn't start drifting away just when the shooting gets good.

When retrieving your decoys at the end of the day, you can use either the figure-8 or simple wraparound method for storing line on the birds. Wood has an advantage over plastic for decoy bodies in this regard because the mildly abrasive texture of wood helps hold the line in place better than the smooth surfaces of many plastics. Then too, the lead keel on a wooden decoy helps brace and hold the line if the wraparound method is used.

Make at least two turns of line around the neck before slipping your decoy weight over the bird's head or bill. Whether or not you use the slip-over type of weight, a neat aid for the modern duck hunter is a neoprene-rubber band attached directly to the weight or to the swivel joining the line and weight. This elastic band should be stretched over the decoy's head to help hold your weight firmly in place. Before the advent of this trick, most decoys, plastic and fiber ones included, ended the season looking like refugees from mob violence. Their backs and breasts were scarred or dented where sliding, banging weights had done them in, and in extreme cases, broken necks and bills occurred. A loose 8-ounce mushroom sinker at the bottom of a decoy bag can do a lot of damage. If each weight is strapped to the bird it belongs to, not only will potential damage from tumbling weights be minimized, but you'll actually be able to figure out which weight goes with which decoy when you're setting them out in the predawn darkness.

Regarding clothes, there's no form of gunning in which you're more likely to get wet, and once wet, miserable, than diver-duck hunting. Though there'll be days when a pair of deerskin shooting gloves will do (or even better, your bare hands), the best sport usually comes when conditions (and your body) border on frost-bite. For starters, take two pairs of woolen gloves with you—one to wear and a spare. The gauntlet style that protects the wrists is pref-erable. Long ago I learned to shoot passably well with woolen gloves on, but if you feel you can't, you might do some home modification on a pair to enable you to get your trigger finger free when the time for action draws nigh. Regular shooting gloves with this feature already built in just don't make it. I've yet to find the pair that can take the cold and salt-water exposure. As an old-time gunner once put it: "Wool's a wonderful thing—even when it's cold and wet, it's somehow warm and dry."

As I mentioned earlier, you might try a pair of rubberized gloves, preferably with insulation, for handling wet decoys and anchor lines. They will also be useful for push poling, stalking game on your hands and knees or any of a dozen sometimes un-planned activities during the course of a day's outing. If you can find rubber gloves large enough to slip right over your woolen pair, so much the better.

Some gunners wear woolen face masks to keep their cheeks, necks and ears warm and to disguise their faces from incoming birds. If you can wear one of these without getting unduly warm and without obstructing your peripheral vision, that's fine. I opt for a scarf, camouflage face makeup and an insulated gunning cap with earflaps that can be tied up across the top or under the chin depending on the weather. I simply have never gotten used to itchy wool on an unshaven face! With burnt cork on your cheeks, you may look like a parody of Commando Kelly, and it may be a little difficult to explain your camouflaged face to the patrolman who catches you speeding home, but I still find that happiness for me lies with this combination.

The rest of your clothing is no different from any outfit you'd wear on a polar expedition. One of the benefits of the snowmobile craze has been the perfection and proliferation of those magnifi-cent one-piece insulated suits which keep you warm with less bulk than anything else I know. Of course, for moderately cold days, insulated underwear, a wool shirt and a camouflage or dark non-reflecting parka over your shell vest are also fine. And while I'm about it, let me make an appeal to all clothing manufacturers. In addition to the usual run of tan and green camouflage clothing for deer and turkey hunters, please consider your duck hunter. Green, and even many shades of brown, just don't make it on the winter marsh. These colors are almost as conspicuous as a white sheet (which would be okay if you were shooting on the ice). Please, dear Mr. Haberdasher, come up with a camouflage design with shades of black and dark olive. That's the color of a wet winter marsh. And you may then also sell a few parkas to deer and turkey shooters who do their hunting in rain-soaked woods. But emerald green—not on my winter marsh!

As has been observed before, the key to maintaining overall body warmth is the feet. Duck hunters particularly suffer from cold feet, because they slog about a lot before the day begins, working up a considerable sweat under their waders or hip boots (if the darn things don't leak besides). Then they lie down in a boat or sit quietly in a blind while all that moisture falls from 100 degrees to freezing. Almost every duck hunter has had the experience of watching ice particles form on his boots.

Here again wool comes to the rescue. I generally wear one lightweight pair of cotton socks under a heavy pair of woolen socks and then my insulated waders. Even one pair of heavy woolen socks is far better than trying to squeeze on a dozen different pairs of socks, calculated to cut off circulation at the ankle and complicate a cold foot with frostbite. I also prefer this arrangement to the increasingly popular insulated bootee. But here I acknowledge being old-fashioned. The bootees are good too.

My last thought on footwear comes from a British friend who does a lot of waterfowl stalking in Scotland. He laboriously cuts patterns of his foot out of newspapers for each trip and then throws the sodden mess away when he comes home. Sometimes it takes a few vigorous shakes of the boot to get the last of the paper clots out, but he insists that newspaper is even better than wool for retaining heat. Maybe when dry, but doubtful when wet.

Speaking of heat, if you plan to stay out all day, you'll want to pack a lunch that is loaded with calories. It doesn't have to be large, but it should contain energy boosters like chocolate or nuts. My personal favorite is a peanut butter-and-jelly sandwich. A hot thermos of something is also advisable, and odd to say, a thermos of cold water should be available, particularly if you exert your-

self in getting to where you're going as well as out of consideration for the dog who might otherwise have to tank up on salt
water. A thermos is advisable because ordinary glass or plastic
containers have a way of freezing solid in cold weather.

Finally, litter. All summer long, the boater and fisherman is lec-
tured not to throw away his candy and sandwich wrappers. DIS-
POSE OF PROPERLY say the nonreturnable bottles. Well, the same
propaganda needs to be aimed at the hunter, for increasingly I
find marshes where his presence is all too apparent. This is doubly
dumb when you consider that every foreign item in the marsh in-
creases the odds of turning wary birds away from that area. Be
sure to bring in your empty shell cases. If appealing to your finer
sensibilities doesn't do the trick, consider these advantages: You
won't give away any clues to other hunters about what kind of
luck you've been having. You'll be making some youngster or gunning club happy with a donation of empty shells—and maybe
they'll be so busy reloading, they won't have time to hunt on your
favorite duck marsh. You'll save yourself some money by learning
to reload your own shells. If nothing else, think of all that wasted
brass in an age of diminishing metal supplies.

There was a time in my youth when I thought killing waterfowl
with a 20-gauge shotgun made me a better sportsman. Looking
back, I shudder at such an assumption. I know how many birds I
killed with my Fulton double. And I know how many I only crippled and then had to chase down. Consequently, I have an awful
inkling of the even greater number I merely peppered that were
to fly on and die elsewhere. You *can* kill a deer with a .22-caliber
rifle. But it's cruelty to hunt deer with such a small gun. Likewise,
you can do in a broadbill with a .410. But at what cost to what
other birds hit and lost? I use a 12-gauge today, and though I believe the man who packs a 10-gauge for most diver-duck shooting
is going just a mite heavy, better that than the other extreme. And
when it comes to pass shooting or sea-duck hunting, a 10-gauge
or a 12-gauge shooting 3-inch shells is right at home. (Here one
recalls the old-timer's advice about a 3-inch shell's being the best
retriever.)

In the way of gun types, it's a toss-up between a double-barrel
and the three-shot models. The double is the classic waterfowling
piece, and it's certainly easier to keep clean and salt-free than the

pump or semiautomatic. Then too, there's the psychological factor of knowing you have only two shots; thus you're often more
careful with the first, since you have only one to go. But many a
time a third shell in the magazine has kept a cripple from escaping, and that alone makes the pump or autoloader a worthy
companion in the marsh.

Express No. 6s are good for all-around, over-decoy shooting.
Sometimes I use 7½s if I'm gunning for a specimen to mount.
Then, since 5s happen to pattern in a most magical way from my
favorite autoloader, I use that size whenever I can get it. (Fives
are one of those odd shot sizes few country stores handle anymore.) Fours are so often acclaimed as the shot size that makes
for the all-purpose duck load that I hesitate to say I use them only
for late-winter (hence full-plumage and full-fat) duck shooting
and for sea-duck and pass shooting. With sea ducks, 2¾-inch magnums, 3-inch shells or a 10-gauge gun are a must, and if 4s don't
work, don't be ashamed to go to 2s. Scoters seem to be even
tougher to kill than geese, and you can't throw too many high-
power, large-size pellets at them.

Shock—that is, high-density impact—kills the greatest number
of birds. That's why I'm keen on 6s for most of my waterfowling.
But scoters carry a special kind of armor in their winter plumage,
and you'll want larger shot with greater velocity to get the penetration needed to stop these birds. Fives and 6s cut well through
the interstices of a scaup's plumage, but with scoters—well, I've
actually shaken some of my "sea coots" and had shot fall out and
go rattling over the boat seats and gunwales. This was shot that
never even made it to the skin!

Finally, a word about chokes. The standard recommendation
for the double-barreled duck gun is modified and full or full and
full. For the single-barreled gun, full is the choke most often mentioned. A lot depends on shot and gauge size, of course, but I've
found most of my duck shooting over decoys very well handled
with a modified barrel alone. And on days when I was shooting
borrowed upland equipment, improved-cylinder and modified
double-barreled combinations served as well. I suspect many gunners place too much emphasis on the fine gradations of choke, perhaps as a means of explaining missed shots. But as with any
target, improved-cylinder does best for close-in work, full or extra-

full for the long-range shots; and modified represents the happy
medium.

I've also used several variable-choke devices with success. And
though there are many who pooh-pooh such aids, most of the popular brands do exactly what their advertising says they'll do:
namely, create a variety of choke options for a single-barreled gun.
Some hunters argue that you'll destroy your patterns with the
things or that a duck blind is no place to start playing with choke
adjustments. But I've seen cripples recovered when a variable
choke was screwed down from modified to extra-full to provide
the concentrated pattern necessary to kill a swimming target. And
I've seen decoy hunters make the same switch—and bring down
birds—when the ducks refused to stool and passed by at extreme
gunning range. Now, this is not an exhortation to have you send
your favorite pump immediately off to the gunsmith for installation of a variable choke. Rather, it's more in the way of moral support for you fellows who already have such a gadget on the end
of your barrel and take a lot of flak from purists who talk self-
righteously about traditional shotgun design.

In the old days, it wasn't just the canvasback's large size and
swift flight that made him the king of wildfowl. It was his exquisite table qualities as well. For this reason, and by comparison,
the greater and lesser scaup are often disparaged and even dis-
carded by ignorant hunters. The truth of the matter is that the
taste of any waterfowl lies largely in what it eats and how you
prepare it, not in romantic traditions of what it should taste like.
Back in the days when wild celery was the canvasback's mainstay
on his wintering grounds, this bird was considered the premier
table fowl of North America. But wild celery is losing the battle
to pollution in many areas, and the canvasback that resorts to just
any food—including rotting fish—is as rank to eat as an aging her-
ring gull. Likewise, while I once took a bite of a broadbill that
tasted as if it had just come from an oil spill (and in fact, may
have), most of the greater scaup I consume match in flavor the
coastal black ducks I also eat. And while it's true that lesser scaup,
ringbills and ruddy ducks are smaller than canvasbacks and redheads (which was doubtless the reason they had a lower rating
in the marketplace), I regularly rank any one of this smaller trio
above the larger divers, simply because the smaller ducks spend

more time on fresh water than salt, where there are more desirable plants to be found. Cans and redheads largely subsist on a variety of inferior grasses, algae and shellfish wherever coastal development has destroyed the wild-celery beds.

My point is this: There's no reason to belittle "blackhead" divers as poor substitutes for the redheads and canvasbacks you may once have known. Scaup, ringbills, whistlers and others in the diver clan are outstanding game birds in their own right, and this judgment extends from the sight of them flaring over the decoys to those few you bring to the table garnished with wild rice and watercress.

I skin the diver ducks I bring home, because it's easier than plucking them and because, by doing so, I eliminate a possible source of rank flavor. If you worry about scorching the breasts of birds treated this way, I suggest you try laying bacon strips across them. This protects the birds from drying out and imparts a distinct and pleasant flavor of its own. Better yet, don't cook your birds so long. Wildfowl should still bleed when cut into with a carving knife. Otherwise, you've done your taste buds and the bird's ghost a great disservice.

Save the giblets for stuffing. Incredibly, I sometimes find I have to explain what giblets are to a generation of souls who know only about packaged chicken parts from the supermarket. Giblets are a bird's heart, gizzard and liver—which are not only edible and, therefore, foolish to waste, but downright delicious when chopped up with onions, celery, apples and bread and then basted with hot butter. However, some gunners I know are justifiably concerned about peculiar chemical concentrations in the livers of birds shot over such choice waters as the lower Hudson and Newark Bay. In these cases it might be wise to discard the livers. Also discard the giblets when they show discoloration or decay (probably because you were lazy and didn't clean the duck the same evening you got home from the hunt). No matter how tired you are, get this chore out of the way *at once*. It's harder to do after you've had a shower and a drink. And it's doubly difficult to do the next morning.

With some birds, I simply cut out the breasts. I'll occasionally treat a whistler this way, and always do the few red-breasted mergansers I kill. Ironically, the hooded merganser—despite its being a member of the subfamily *Meriginae*, the sawbills or fish ducks—can be one of the tastiest fowl flying. I've served them with black ducks at dinner parties and my guests were unable to distinguish them except by size. However, I don't eat more hairyheads (as they're irreverently called in the Mid-Atlantic States) because I regard the species as too unusual to kill. Except for a fine drake I had mounted a while back, I let the rare hooded merganser that visits my stool fly on. My pleasure is in knowing there are still some around.

The "must manual" for all waterfowlers is F. H. Kortright's *The Ducks, Geese and Swans of North America*. Someday (I hope) all hunter-safety courses will include a requirement that you be able to identify the game you plan to hunt and know something of its natural history. When that day comes, Kortright will be the assigned text for all waterfowlers. First published in 1942 by the American Wildlife Institute, it's now in its umpteenth printing. An outstanding book.

But since waterfowlers are traditionalists and romantics as well, we like a little literature with our nuts-'n'-bolts reading. Hence, make a trip to your local library or secondhand bookstore and get yourself copies of Dr. William Bruette's *American Duck, Goose,*

The year is 1915 and the place is Barnegat Bay, New Jersey. The hunter is standing in a typical Barnegat sneak box covered with dead eelgrass. In addition to their low profile and good stability, gunning boats like this one, when properly camouflaged, were nearly invisible.

and Brant Shooting (G. H. Watt, 1942) Eugene Connett's *Duck Shooting Along the Atlantic Tidewater* (William Morrow & Company, 1947), George Bird Grinnell's *American Duck Shooting* (Forest & Stream, 1901) and Van Campen Heilner's *A Book on Duck Shooting* (Penn Publishing House, 1939). All these books will provide much entertaining reading and give you some idea of what it was really like in the fabled days of yore. In addition, I've found some useful tips to apply in my own gunning today.

Finally, a word on bands. If you should be so fortunate as to kill a duck carrying a metallic leg band, report the number and complete circumstances of the kill (weather, hour, place, condition of the bird, etc.) to:

Bird Banding Laboratory
Fish and Wildlife Service
U.S. Department of the Interior
Laurel, Maryland   20810

Not all the information you send may seem meaningful at the time, but since I once had a researcher write me years after I reported a band to ask the precise shade of the bird's bill, it's best to put it all down at the time. Memory blurs an awful lot.

The folks at Laurel are busy and backlogged, so it may be a few weeks, even months, before they acknowledge, but the information is critical to our understanding and management of waterfowl. And you have to be something of a lout not to be curious or excited about a bird you've shot who was traveling with his life history strapped to one leg.

Hunters call the most popular of the sea ducks "coot." Not the true coot of fresh water (alias mud hen, blue peter, etc.), but the "sea coot," better known to ornithologists as the scoter. There are three species—American, white-winged and surf (commonly called skunkhead in New England)—that share the same wintering grounds and, hence, the same hunter's bag.

Also shot in offshore waters are the old squaw, the harlequin and the eiders—most frequently the American and king. Actually, of this group, only the old squaw shows up commonly in a sea-duck gunner's bag, with the exception of coastal Maine for the American and king eiders. This is not because the other species are so extremely rare. It's rather that a cold, cold winter is required before they'll come within popular gunning range along our more densely settled coasts.

Though old squaws nest farther north than the harlequin and many eiders, they winter as far south as the Carolinas on the Atlantic Coast and Puget Sound on the Pacific. Each winter on Chesapeake Bay this species seems to be more numerous, with one recent Bay survey showing old squaws numbering into the tens of thousands. Yet despite a generous season that begins in September and runs through January, few Marylanders or Virginians hunt sea ducks. Most know, September openings aside, that few old squaws show up in the Mid-Atlantic States until about the time the regular duck season begins. By that date, there are so many other, more familiar, targets available that most waterfowlers never get around to sea-duck shooting. This is a pity, for it's fast and unusual sport, and there's nothing quite like it in the entire realm of shotgunning.

New England hosts the greatest concentrations of sea ducks in America, and this is where the sport is practiced in all its variations. The hunter finds a local flyway and then contrives to intercept the birds—mostly scoters—as they move to and from their feeding grounds. Sometimes the shooting can be done from a sandbar or low neck of land. Most often it involves getting out in a dory with a string of nondescript decoys ranging from legitimate attempts at scoter facsimiles to bleach bottles painted flat black. Frequently the ducks will try to land among these dark bobbing shapes; more often, the stool acts as a magnet to the birds' curiosity, merely bringing them a little closer for the shot.

Sea-duck shooting has to be one of the toughest forms of gunning going. In addition to weather best suited to test the stamina of a polar bear, there are the birds themselves. I sometimes think scoters were evolved by ammunition manufacturers to provide them with a steady income. The amount of lead these birds can carry is truly astonishing. Doubtless much of the shot is absorbed by these birds' especially heavy dressing of feathers and fat. But sometimes their ability to endure is downright supernatural.

One afternoon three of us were shooting from a flooding sandbar in Long Island Sound. Scoters were flying low over the sandspit, and we thought it would be no time at all before each of us

had his seven-bird limit. Other than the fact that we had to retreat from the tide every fifteen minutes or so, we had almost continuous shooting. Yet only one of us got his limit. Our problem
wasn't in hitting the birds; it was in killing them.

Some of those big scoters reacted to the lead we fired as though
it were only rice. One of my companions swears a white-winged
scoter circled and came back to take a charge of ballast under his
right wing to balance the load he'd already taken under his left!
The range averaged between 20 and 40 yards, so our failure to
stop more birds didn't result from trying to sky-bust them. One
of my skunkheads was most memorable: I hit him about 30 yards
out. He shuddered with the impact, but kept coming. I hit him
again about 10 yards away and completely bowled him over, so
that he tumbled with a mighty splash into the shallows at the
edge of the bar. He came up swimming. My final shot patterned
a perfect 30-inch circle around the bird. He didn't even bother to
dive—merely shook himself and kept swimming! Finally I had to
chase him around the shallows and fire three more shots to finish
him.

To top off the day, on our run back to the dock, one of the birds
with a broken neck somehow contrived to get out of a burlap sack
and make it to the gunwales before one of us saw and stopped this
ghastly creature. Believe me, experiences like that give you
strange dreams.

Nearly as eerie is a curious and successful escape ploy often
used by old squaws. When fired at, they'll dive into the water as
though hit, immediately disappear and then come out *flying* some
yards away exactly as though they had been launched from beneath the surface. The first time this happened to me, I shot at
one bird in a flock of twenty or more. The entire formation fell to
the water and disappeared. Stunned, I stared at the spot where
they'd gone in. I imagined my old squaw "kill" was some kind of
world record for an ounce and a quarter of No. 4 shot. Then all the
birds suddenly popped from the surface about 70 yards from the
boat and sped away. It was more than a letdown; those birds had
contrived the perfect wildfowler's putdown.

Sea-duck shooting seems to represent a growing area of special
interest in the broad range of activity that is waterfowling. Limits
are still generous (in most states it's seven sea ducks a day, four-

teen in possession; in Alaska it's fifteen and thirty). And the birds generally nest far enough north so that it will be many years before the drainers, channelizers and other reclamation types reach the spring latitudes of these oceanic divers. Hopefully, by that time most North Americans will have developed a conscience about what we're doing to wildlife—and ourselves—and the whole process will have been slowed or stopped.

Other persistent threats facing diving ducks are the thoughtless high-seas skipper who flushes his oily bilge offshore and the tanker skipper who seeks to shave a half-hour off his Red Sea–to–St. Lawrence River run and ends up on the rocks. These men are villains in the traditional sense of the word, and it's often only the hunter, caring enough to holler about the outrage, who plays the part of conscience for an otherwise preoccupied populace.

The skies may never again be darkened by the spring flights of waterfowl. But if they are to be there at all, it is the hunter who will keep them flying. Close to a century ago, men like John A. Lacey and George Bird Grinnell decided to save waterfowling for future generations—and to save waterfowl in the process. We owe it to their efforts to maintain and enlarge our own levels of interest so that future generations may think as kindly of us as we think of these conservation pioneers.

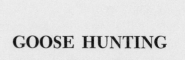

GOOSE HUNTING

BY ZACK TAYLOR

HIGH IN THE sky they make their decision. Wings cup into a parachute shape; calling slows, then stops. Steadily, majestically, thrillingly, the flock falls out of the sky, each bird maneuvering expertly in the air currents.

In the blind you hunker down, moving not a muscle. These are geese, and part of the reason for that long, slow guide into your decoys is so that every eye in the flock can scrutinize the area for possible danger. Suddenly they are in range, and you leap to your feet, pick a bird and down him. Perhaps you get another.

This act—drawing a flock of geese to a set of decoys—is unquestionably waterfowling's finest moment. Nothing compares with the excitement of it. Ducks are graceful creatures. But the goose is lord of them all, in giant sizes as big as swans (20 pounds for Canadas) and with a reputation for wariness and sagacity that is, under most conditions, unmatched. Challenge a goose flock and you take on the masters. Little wonder the sense of hunting accomplishment is so great when you trick one.

Yet in some ways I think the goose's vaunted reputation scares hunters off. Tales of the needs for hundreds of decoys, of superblinds and the high cost of leasing good goose-shooting fields turn

226

The Canada goose is the emperor of waterfowl. Despite his great size, he can fly for hours at speeds of 40 miles per hour. Holding one at arm's length requires a strong man: a big Canada will weigh as much as 20 pounds.

hunters away. On the old "They said it was impossible, so I didn't even try" principle, too many hunters content themselves with other waterfowl that come easier to bag. It shouldn't be. Populations of the popular blue and snow geese are stable at high levels. White-fronted geese also remain at satisfactory numbers. All are handling hunting pressure well, and unlike the situation with many popular duck species, their nesting grounds in the subarctic are not threatened by the urbanization of the Canadian Prairie Provinces. In fact, the only dark picture concerns Atlantic Coast brant; a two-year nesting failure caused by freak snow conditions has populations drastically down and seasons closed tight.

With Canada geese it is another story. Populations aren't stable. They are exploding! There are more Canada geese than ever before. In a game-management triumph that can compare only with the comeback of the antelope and the wild turkey, waterfowl biologists have introduced "homegrown" Canada flocks in almost all of the Lower Forty-Eight States. Chances are you have flocks

Blue and snow geese, as well as Canadas, are thriving. This photo was made at James Bay, Canada, near the birds' subarctic breeding ground.

near you. These are Canadas, born and raised in local areas, that may or may not migrate. Population expansions are everywhere putting geese into locales where they were never seen before. Add to this bright picture another population buildup in the regular Canada flocks that nest each summer in a subarctic band across Canada roughly below the Hudson Bay line. Each fall these birds, migrating south, fill farmers' fields and city parks and, in Westchester County, New York, give game wardens problems because they are taking up residence in—would you believe—swimming pools.

To convince a man with a swimming pool full of honkers that they are too smart for him to harvest would be difficult. Anyone can hunt Canadas with a reasonable chance for success. Like any game animals, they have periods of great vulnerability. Hungry or fatigued geese will decoy readily. Electronic "feed" calls so unerringly lure them to their doom that such devices have been banned. You can't do quite as well with a legal mouth call, but with practice you can come close. Any pass shooter knows that under certain conditions geese will throw their famed wariness to the winds and all but ignore danger.

What applies to Canadas goes for other geese to a greatly lessened degree. The Canadas lead in wisdom; all the rest rank down the line. Blues and snows are no smarter than mallard or pintails, and many would rate the ducks as more difficult to fool. The brant of both coasts are downright easy to hunt, at times almost too easy to decoy and kill.

The first, the easiest and somewhat the sneakiest way to kill a Canada goose starts before the season opens. While blues and snows tend to migrate in a series of long, purposeful flights, Canadas trickle down the flyways. They take their time and seem to thoroughly enjoy the golden days of fall. And if an area holds food they will hang around for days on end, usually using a body of water as their resting area and feeding in fields around it.

Scouting these flocks before the season will teach you their habits. If you find the flock is using a certain field, set up there in the predawn darkness with a few decoys and you'll stand an excellent chance of getting a crack at these birds.

The first few days of the season, even the smart old honkers are extremely vulnerable. Not only do they forget, but a typical Canada flock is Mama and Papa and five youngsters that have never heard a call or a gun. These young birds are so easy to fool that almost every survey of Canada goose kills indicates that year- or two-year-old birds outnumber older birds (they mate the third year) by four or five to one. In the old days of "tollers," when tame live geese called to incoming birds, it was common to have the juveniles break out of the flocks, like any unruly youngsters, paying no attention to their parents' shrieks of warning.

When the season is new, these young birds get separated, lost and confused and often put their searching mom and pop into situations and places they'd rather not be in. A few decoys and a good call are all you need to put a few Canadas into your freezer.

This shooting won't last long—a few days at most. The reason is that when the guns start popping, wise old flock leaders pour on the coal to get all hands to the sanctuary of one of the state, private or federal refuges found the length of every flyway. Here they will stay until spring. It's safe to say that today shooting Canada geese and, to a lesser extent, other goose species means shooting on or near a refuge. A federal study of band returns showed that almost 85 percent of geese killed were shot within several miles of a large federal refuge. Since smaller state or private refuges weren't always known to the biologists, they felt the actual percentage was probably higher.

No one will argue that refuges, mostly large federal refuges bought with your duck-stamp money, are concentrating geese. In the eyes of some southern hunters they are "short-stopping" the birds. The geese do not extend their southern range but stay in northern areas, thanks to the comfort and availability of the refuges. Mattamuskeet, in North Carolina, is a good example. It used to be an East Coast goose Valhalla. No more. Even though goose concentrations in the Chesapeake now reach the hundreds of thousands, only a tiny number of the birds—a few thousand or so—trouble themselves to journey the couple of hundred miles south to the huge, now-empty North Carolina refuge.

Game managers have tried just about everything to move Canadas south: harassing them with airplanes, providing less feed, increasing gunning pressure. Nothing seems to work. A refuge manager's job has some built-in problems besides this one. If he doesn't plant refuge crops, the geese descend on the fields of surrounding farmers, who howl about crop depredation. Too much food on the refuge and the geese won't leave, and hunters start objecting. Too little and the geese are forced out more, bird harvests soar, game managers get alarmed and the season slams shut. Balancing the various factors is tricky, and things don't always come out neatly.

The general pattern you can expect in any given refuge area is that the geese will very quickly exhaust the food available on the refuge. After that they follow the routine of many other birds and feed in the morning and afternoon, returning to the refuge to rest during midday and, of course, at night. There are generally two ways to hunt them: pass shooting as they fly into and out of protected areas and decoying them into blinds in fields surrounding the refuge.

The beginning goose shooter quickly learns the second hard fact of honker hunting. (The first is that they are usually too confounded smart.) There is no available free land around any major refuge in the country. You can ask farmers' permission to hunt for lesser species such as rabbits, quail and pheasant and probably get an okay. Not so with geese. Any farmer lucky enough to have fields that geese feed in will be solicited so often that he will consider gunning rights as another cash crop. If geese would fly far and spread the wealth around some, it wouldn't be so bad. But they feed first in fields near the refuge, gradually extending their range as forage is exhausted; generally 20 miles is the maximum distance they fly. Naturally, the fields nearer the refuge are more desirable, and the price of gunning rights is high. How high is hard to say, but you probably wouldn't be far off if you anticipated $1,000 per season.

This thins goose-shooter ranks quickly, to be sure. But you aren't out of business if you lack the scratch. By law every refuge must provide gunning areas. These either are free or require a small fee, a couple of dollars tops. Since there is usually more demand than supply, positions are generally chosen by some form of lottery. Usually you get an assigned station with perhaps a crude blind, most likely for pass shooting only. In some areas you can utilize a blind and set out decoys.

Pass shooting is mostly luck—luck in what spot you draw (some will be favored; others will not fare so well); luck in where the

geese fly (do they go over you or the next guy?); and to some extent it is luck in the most important elements—when they fly
(even *if* they fly) and how high.

My friend Dave Harbour made a 46-day study of the movements of geese on a Colorado refuge that confirmed what it takes
years of goose shooting to learn.

The first point concerns moonlit nights. To a certain extent all
waterfowl feed on nights of bright moonlight. The canny Canadas
take full advantage of them. If they can see well enough to fly
comfortably, they will feed all night and spend the entire day on
the refuge, resting, preening, socializing and jeering at frustrated
hunters waiting for them to come out.

There are some exceptions. Heavy cloud cover, for example, despite a full moon's presence above the clouds, might make it too
dark for the birds to fly. But usually you want to confine your
hunting to the days during the dark phases of the moon—the last

*For pass shooting, where the birds are numerous, a makeshift blind or
even a clump of bushes will suffice. This is the author, Zack Taylor,
waiting for a combined flight of blues and snow geese.*

quarter of the old moon to the first quarter of the new—so that you can be fairly certain that the geese spent the previous night in bed and will be flying when you're in position in the adjacent fields.

Geese are gentlemanly fellows and like their comfort. They don't normally follow the dawn and dusk trading times as closely as ducks seem to. Harbour found that they started out of the refuges around 8 to 9 A.M. and by 11 A.M. flocks were headed back in. The afternoon flight started somewhere after 2:30, and by 3:30 or 4 o'clock birds were on their way home.

On sunny fall or early-winter days, you can set up decoys and have a chance that the geese will be fooled by them and descend to you. On such days, however, your pass-shooting chances are greatly reduced. The reason is that the geese will lift off water areas and climb. By the time they get overhead, they will probably be at 100 yards and higher. Guns blast when this happens, but no one profits but the shell manufacturers. Up on James Bay I once saw a flock of Canadas fly over a waterfowl "expert." They were at least 125 yards up. He threw his automatic to his shoulder and emptied it at the geese, who took no notice whatsoever. Feeling somewhat foolish, he turned to me and smiled. "This is a nice gun," he said, "but it lacks killing power."

Later, we'll discuss how to put some killing power on your side, but what is needed to bring geese down to acceptable shooting range can be summed up in one word: weather—any kind, and the more of it the better. The more unusual and severe, even better yet. Winds, drizzle, overcast, foggy rain, fog, snow, snow squalls, frontal weather, winter thunderstorms, hail, ice, severe freezing cold—all are the waterfowler's friends, for all to a greater or lesser degree rob the geese of their caution. Since weather is so important, let's examine what it can mean to the hunter.

Ducks and geese don't like dense fog. They can't see far enough ahead to avoid danger. They can and do fly into things and kill themselves. However, patchy or light fogs offer favorable gunning conditions. For one thing, it's the only time your eyesight is on a par with the birds'. The fog robs them of the ability to subject your rig to their usual withering scrutiny—until it's too late. For another thing, they won't fly as high. Geese have built-in compasses, to be sure, but do much of their navigation by familiarizing themselves with landmarks. Fog keeps them low enough to see the ground. The silent, windless conditions associated with fog also make your call sound especially enticing.

Food locked out of reach under ice makes all waterfowl uneasy. Even the threat of this stirs the birds. For geese, feeding in the fields becomes harder when temperatures drop and the ground is frozen. Another reason why cold is good for hunters is that the birds' food requirements go up as temperatures plummet. More food is needed than the normal half-pound-of-grain-a-day requirement. The colder it is, the better for hunters.

A severe rainstorm is the only thing that puts you out of business. Ducks and geese sit tight if possible, probably because their visibility is so drastically reduced. Light rain, however, is good. Like fog, it hampers their seven-power eyesight and creates good calling conditions.

Storms of any kind put waterfowl on the prowl. The birds don't like them, become edgy and tend to trade around seeking shelter. In severe storms they may hole up while the storm is going on, having attempted to feed before the blow. Snowstorms frighten geese. They get more and more panicked the longer the snow covers the ground and will search long distances to seek out fields where drifting allows them to forage. Dave Harbour's study proved this conclusively. On days when it was snowing, the geese left the refuge early and stayed in the fields all day. They wanted as much food in them as they could get. Geese, incidentally, seldom starve in severe and prolonged snow conditions, as ducks sometimes do. They merely put that forty-miles-per-hour all-day cruising range to work and head south until bare fields appear.

The high winds that ruin other forms of hunting and knock fishing dead are made to order for the wildfowler. Ducks and geese don't enjoy being buffeted, and they'll seek shelter. Also, they have less control in the air in high winds and have to work harder to get where they want to go. All this takes their minds off you. The Harbour study found that geese fly into and out of refuges at much lower altitudes during high-wind days. Those days when a high-pressure ridge is moving through your area and winds shift to the north or northwest and blow like crazy are second only to snowstorms as the best days of all on which to hunt.

When conditions favor the hunter, the geese apparently feel

Geese generally like to settle in areas that are open all around. For terrain like this, stalking is one tactic that works—but only once for each flock. These blue and snow geese did not fly quite fast enough to get away.

the weather is the greater threat. At times they virtually forget that danger lies below. Whereas on normal days they will leave the refuge at 150-yard elevations, during inclement weather they'll sail right over the blinds at 20 to 40 yards, and if they see you, instead of flaring, they will only fly faster.

While pass shooting is the commonest form of goose hunting, every farm boy knows the most direct approach. You locate a flock, slither to within shooting range and bushwhack them. This isn't all that easy to do. Goose flocks maintain sentinels. At all times one bird or more has its neck extended, alert for possible danger.

You'll have to keep out of sight at all times on your stalk. Geese generally like to settle in land areas that are open all around, but at times there will be a fence or a rise you can utilize in your stalk. If possible, plan your approach upwind. The wind will muffle any sounds, and it is quite possible that otherwise the geese can smell you coming. Since it takes the big birds a few seconds to get into full flight, accepted bushwhack procedure is to leap to your feet and run the last few yards toward the flock. Obviously, bushwhacking works only one time per group of birds. The flock won't be back after suffering such an indignity.

Drawing geese within range by decoying them is the supreme art. The first requirement, of course, is a suitable spot in which to build your blind and set out the decoys. Geese used to be water-oriented birds and, of course, still utilize water areas as resting places. But the advent of mechanical crop-picking machines in the 1950s changed the whole character of where most geese are shot. The machines are not nearly as efficient as humans and leave a small residue of grain behind. Geese everywhere began taking advantage of this. Whereas goose shooting used to be a watery affair like duck shooting, the vast majority of hunting is now done on land.

This isn't true of brant, which are strictly water-oriented birds, disliking even to fly over land. But blues, snows and speckled geese also share the Canadas' love for stalking grainfields.

The amount of grain left on the ground skirts a fine line between legality and baiting. Around goose-shooting areas you tend

At one time, geese were invariably shot over or near water. But the advent of mechanical harvesting machines, which leave a residue of grain, have changed the birds to land dwellers for a good part of their time.

to find the most inefficient harvesting machines ever invented. But federal and state wardens will sooner or later arrive and note the excess and you get tagged. This, incidentally, leads to a pithy situation. Around any refuge will be found blinds that are rented on a daily basis—so much per man per day. The urge to bait is almost irresistible to the commercial guides who own these blinds. Baiting is, in fact, the only certain way they can draw the birds to their rigs again and again, day after day. The problem comes when a guide "sweetens" the mechanical pickers the night before. You go into the blind before dawn and, of course, can see nothing. Suddenly there is the law, arresting you along with the guide even though you had no knowledge that the field you were shooting was baited (or had been assured by the guide that it was not). You are as guilty as if you had performed the act yourself. You pay, and often painfully. Fines of several hundred dollars are not unknown, and you are branded in the newspapers as an outlaw hunter. About the only way you can protect yourself—aside from finding an honest commercial guide—is to take an inspection stroll around the field as the first light breaks.

All the aforementioned details about weather apply even more specifically to decoy shooting than to pass shooting. Those snowy days when the geese feed all day, trading from field to field, are perfect for decoying. Foggy weather too holds out great promise.

The first fact about decoying geese is that you need plenty of decoys. Commercial men sometimes set out hundreds of decoys, and seven hundred is not an unknown number. A great way to build decoys is to cut auto tires into thirds, roughly in the shape of a goose's back. Then screw on a neck and head cut out with a band saw. Paint the decoy gray and white to match the goose's body. Another common goose imitation is the silhouette. You face silhouettes to all points of the compass, so that some of the decoys are visible from any angle. The latest trend in Canada goose decoys is oversize silhouettes. These may be as much as 6 feet tall. Two decoys are cut from a single sheet of ⅜- or ½-inch plywood and each is bolted to an iron rod (fence or road-sign standards are best), which is driven into the earth with a sledgehammer.

There are numbers of variations on the goose-silhouette theme. Some hunters tack wings of killed geese to them for a natural look. The problem with full-bodied decoys is that they take up so

much room. You darn near need a pickup truck to transport fifty or sixty of them. Hollow-bodied decoys solve this problem some-what, as the bodies nest together. They take time to assemble, however, require maintenance and are a pain to set and pick up.

Probably of secondary importance is the decoy paint job. You want the white stern for its high visibility, the black neck with white neck patch and a flat gray-brown back. (The color scheme would have to vary for the different species.) But generally you are better off making new decoys than restoring the elaborate, every-feather paint job on older ones. The late Glenn Martin set out a spread of Canadas that were taxidermy mounts, no less. His guides told me he did no better than they did with silhouettes or neck-and-tire-body decoys.

How many blocks is enough is a subject of endless debate. My home-port Canada goose shooting takes place during a six-day pre-duck-season special season. If I'm lucky, the days coincide with the main goose migrations down the Atlantic. I've gotten reasonable shooting, and on a few occasions when I lucked out on major flights, I could have killed geese all day long. My total spread is eleven shell decoys—three full-bodied, two oversize and six regular-size water decoys. I arrange them so that it appears the flock has landed in the water (as it would do on a coastal marsh) and is marching up the bank to feed.

Those few decoys pull, and for several rather basic reasons. First, my geese haven't been shot at very much. The season is rela-

tively young when and where I hunt. Second, and more important,
I get a passing crack at thousands of geese. Flock after flock
sweeps over me (if I luck out and the birds don't fly south earlier
or later). I have a one-in-a-thousand chance that a particular
flock will be tired enough or hungry enough or just feel like settling down on me. The decoys and my call merely give them an
excuse. With all of this, the geese more often than not see to it that
I don't get an exaggerated sense of my own ability. I feel pretty
good if I can kill geese on two out of the six days of the season.
The other days I have a fine time watching them.

Other goose species are much easier to decoy, given equal conditions. All waterfowl get spookier and spookier as they are ham-
mered and the foolish and bold birds are combed out. But snow
and whitefront decoys work very well because of their high visibility. Pieces of newspaper, bed sheets, clods of earth covered with
paper and heads made of paper cups—all of these do duty as
decoys and work well.

Everything that applies to blinds for duck shooting applies
even more for geese. Keeping still is the all-important thing. I remember one time years ago I was out of the blind, asleep with my
head on the softest pillow of dried eelgrass you could imagine. I

*The decoys in the background are silhouettes, and they fooled the two
real geese in the boat.*

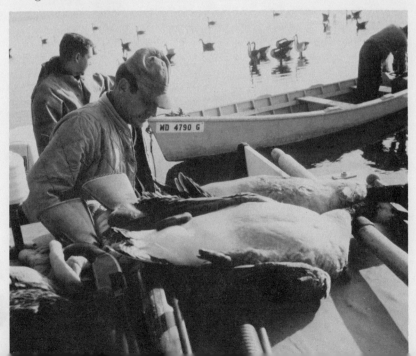

heard a whistle from my partner and went instantly into action the way any member of the Old Duck Hunters' Society would: I only opened my eyes and gripped my gun a little tighter. (You didn't think I'd disarm myself on a duck marsh, did you?) A flock of about five Canadas was decoying perfectly to our setup. They came in, decided they wouldn't sit down after all and started over our heads. By then it was too late. Partner and I knocked down two. The point is that I was in all kinds of plain sight and the geese didn't mind at all because I didn't move.

A pit blind is the traditional field blind for geese. It is warm and conceals the hunter extremely well when cornstalks are rigged to cover the top. Pit blinds are pains, though. They fill with water, cave in or both. You darn near require a pickup truck when you're building one to cart away the dirt. Scatter the dirt around too much and the raw look will be hard to conceal. And at the end of the season, usually when the ground is frozen rock-hard, you have to fill in the pit or the farmer will spill his tractor into it.

A foot pit makes a good compromise. You sit on a plank at ground level with a small blind built around you. This can be ply-

A pit blind works best when it's surrounded with brush or cornstalks— enough to cover the top loosely.

Geese are extremely vocal animals and are highly susceptible to good calling.

wood covered with cornstalks and/or evergreen boughs. (Don't ask me what the geese think about pine trees in a corn or soybean field, but they don't seem to spook from them.) Your feet go into a small trench that reduces digging and filling to a minimum.

Ability with a call is much more important for geese than for other waterfowl. Only Midwest forest shooting for mallard compares. Geese are tremendously vocal animals. Scientists have identified ten different calls that Canadas use, and the familiar honk has at least four variations. This advanced system of communication plus a gregarious nature makes them extremely susceptible to calling.

We were once on the marsh early, putting in a sinkbox. A great mass of Canadas was passing high overhead, maybe 1,000 feet. One of my partners had, only days before, come back from hunting James Bay. "You've heard those Indians call geese," I said. "Let's see you bring those birds in." This when we were standing out in full view on the marsh. "Okay," he said. We lay down and he started yelping like mad, face down into the marsh. I couldn't believe my eyes when the back of the flock of some fifteen hundred to thirty-five hundred birds broke off and came sailing toward us. There must have been a hundred and fifty birds swinging down. They didn't come all the way to us but sat down in open water, perhaps 200 yards away. The point is that even a very inexpert voice call pulled them.

I call as loudly as I can to every passing flock that I think can hear. If I'm gunning with a reliable partner, we both call. As birds get closer or start to decoy I soften the sound, call into the bottom of the blind to disperse it and slow down the rate of calling as they keep coming.

What applies to Canadas applies even more to the less-wary species. The James Bay Cree Indians do so well with their calls for several reasons: They have the first crack at the birds—the first guns these geese hear all season. Blues and snows aren't so smart; the Indians almost never call in Canadas. The Indians are superb mimics of game. You should hear them talk to a hiding cripple; they make little shushing, comforting noises until the bird reveals its position by responding. I brag that I can stop brant dead in the sky with a call. I can't quite—but they too, typical of all geese, love to be talked to.

Guns for geese should be appropriate to their size. Brant fall easily out of the sky, but the other geese come down hard. Cana-

The most effective goose gun is the one that holds three shots instead of two and fires the biggest shell possible. This means a pump or auto chambered for the 12-gauge 3-inch magnum, or the Ithaca Mag-10 auto.

das, blues and specklebellies are big birds and heavily feathered. The toughest of all are the Canadas, as tenacious of life as black ducks. So hard are they to kill that I've devised a special shooting technique. I call it the "hang in there" method of scientific shooting. When you get a Canada in your sights, you hang in there, shooting him until he drops. Sometimes over decoys you have the luck, a la duck shooting, to fold one bird and swing on another. But more often, the birds will shy away at the last minute and you'll fire at extreme ranges. As with the man who hit the mule with the sledgehammer to get its attention, your first shot often merely implants the idea in the goose that he has gotten himself into an extremely unpleasant predicament. The next shot you belt out may hurt him. Maybe with the last shot the danged fool has enough sense to realize he's done for.

I vary the preceding masterful style with the famed Taylor "get the lead out" technique. (Both methods, as you can easily tell, are born of extreme desperation.) Using this latter approach, I pick out a goose and empty my gun at him. The idea is to surround the critter with as much lead as possible in the hope he will fly into some and damage himself.

The trouble with killing geese, aside from the fact that they are so rugged, is that you are almost always shooting them at the end of your shotgun range. Anyone who has ever watched the average goose shooter in action realizes that said average fellow cruelly inflates the idea of what maximum range really is. I daresay if a Canada flock 125 yards in the air flew over a hundred gunners, between forty and sixty of them would blast full-tilt at the geese even though they could go on shooting indefinitely at this range with no chance of killing them.

A friend of mine did some experiments at Remington Farms, where some twenty-five hundred well-tended birds provide consistent and spectacular pass shooting. Over the years he'd worked out three general range categories. One was for those birds he felt comfortable taking. The next was for geese he would shoot at, but somewhat reluctantly. And the last, which he had learned from experience, was the very outer limit of his ability to kill the birds. One day Remington technicians broke out some fancy range-finding gear and accurately measured these distances. The "comfortable" birds were 50 yards away. At 55 yards, the shooter began to feel uneasy. Beyond 60 yards, he knew he could kill a Canada only with a lucky head shot. The gun he was shooting was the goose gun—a standard 12-gauge loaded with 2¾-inch magnum loads. My own goose gun is a standard gas-operated 12-gauge, and I shoot the biggest loads I can find, but I won't attempt a shot longer than 60 yards.

The long-standing rule that you can use to tell when a goose is within range is that you can pull the trigger at the moment you can distinguish his eye—actually make out the bird's eye.

If you increase the size of your armament you start inching out your range. But only by inches.

Because round shot lose their velocity so quickly, there is little difference in pellet speeds at hunting ranges, no matter how much powder you put behind them. What the big magnums do, therefore, is put *more* shot into a pattern than can a standard shell, while maintaining only a slightly higher velocity. In the hands of a very skillful hunter, a 12-gauge shotgun with 3-inch magnum shells can drop geese reliably at 50 yards. And, tall tales aside, the shoulder-cracking 10-gauge loaded with 3½-inch shells will extend that range only 10 yards more. Look at these gauges and loads:

This gunner is hunting the Susquehanna Flats and is watching his pals work among the decoys 150 yards away. The effective goose-getting range of the two (unloaded) guns in front of him is about one-third that distance.

Shell and Gauge	Shot (ounces)	Powder (dram equivalent)	Muzzle Velocity
3½-inch 10-gauge	2	5	1,335
2⅞-inch 10-gauge	1⅝	4¾	1,330
3-inch 12-gauge	1⅞	4½	1,315
2¾-inch 12-gauge magnum	1¼	3¾	1,315

The obvious goose gun, then, is a 10-gauge shooting 3½-inch shells. But before you race out and buy one of these cannon, I urge you to shoot one several times. The amount of recoil that one person can stand will knock another silly.

To give you an idea of comparative recoil, Remington Arms worked out this table:

Gun Weight (pounds)	Gauge/ Shell (inches)	Powder (dram equivalent)	Shot (ounces)	Free Recoil Energy (foot-pounds)
10	10/3½	5	2	51.3
10	10/2⅞	4¾	1⅝	38.7
8	12/3	4½	1⅞	47.9
8	12/3	4	1⅝	45.0
7½	12/2¾	3¾	1¼	28.6

I have a gunning buddy who uses the 3½-inch 10-gauge, handloading to the maximum of 2¼ ounces of shot and 5-dram-equivalent charge of powder. He is an extremely powerful man who holds down a physical job, but he can shoot his gun no more than six or seven times without getting a splitting headache. The 10-gauge cannons are mostly doubles that lack any recoil-dissipation devices, and they dish out significant punishment. Strong men are knocked dizzy by them. At the least your ears ring and you see stars. It is one thing to use them in deer hunting, in which you may have a single shot a season, but who wants to be slammed time after time? Sooner or later you start gritting your teeth and shutting your eyes as you pull the lanyard.

An excellent compromise is the 3-inch 12-gauge. Guns like this are made in gas or mechanical auto actions that soak up some of the kick. Recoil is not actually reduced, but is delivered over a longer period and thus seems much less. Another favorable factor is that they will take standard trap and skeet loads (though you may have to operate some of these shotguns manually when using light loads). So without its costing you an arm and a leg, you can remain friends with the brute between seasons, and there's no doubt that the added familiarity you gain from using the shotgun between hunting trips will pay off when the season opens.

Beyond some thought given to your gun, little extra gear is required for the budding goose shooter. You'll probably be in fields, so hip boots or waders aren't necessary. Field boots or snowmobile boots can be worn. The inevitable long underwear and down jacket keep the fires burning between flights, and hand warmer, thermos and earmuff hat are all part of the game.

Finally, the goose's unswerving diet of grain makes it one of the finest of all waterfowl on the dinner table. Even Atlantic brant, before they get on the sea cabbage, have an almost matchless flavor. You seldom get even a strong-flavored goose. The Canada is the mildest of all *if* you get a young bird. You'll have to be a lot cooler than I am to look for a young bird in a flock when you are shooting, but if you do have a choice out of the day's bag, pick the birds with the sharpest nails and smallest wing knobs. The nails are worn and the knobs exaggerated in tough old birds. Generally, the younger geese have some "blue" (actually brown or gray) in their white markings as well.

We were sitting around a clubhouse one night talking about the haunting quality that the Canada's call has. Especially if you hear it in the night, it echoes of the far places and a wild and free existence. Another fellow spoke up. He was a crass Georgia boy lacking couth. "The sound of a Canada goose I like best," he drawled, "is that *thump* when he hits the ground."

The gentleman may be woefully lacking in poetic appreciation, but I do admit he has a point.

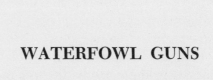

WATERFOWL GUNS

BY NORM NELSON

LET'S DESIGN a duck gun.

But what? A classic side-by-side double? A nicely balanced over/under? A racy-looking autoloader, or perhaps a homely but functional pump gun?

The best approach is to decide what we expect of a gun for duck hunting—in which, for convenience of definition, we can lump goose hunting too. If we decide what the gun is expected to do under what conditions, the gun should design itself.

Note that I specified a gun for duck hunting, not duck shooting. There is a difference. You can go to well-operated commercial game preserves and shoot flighted ducks while you're wearing evening dress, if you wish. But that's not duck *hunting*.

The *hunting* of waterfowl is something else. Duck and goose hunters merit the shotgunning equivalent of the Combat Infantryman's Badge. They go out in foul, wet, freezing weather, and even prefer it. They shoot from squall-tossed sneak boats on stormy salt-water bays. They stumble in the dark through water and mud in flooded pin oak flats down South or in cattail marshes up North. They crawl through wet gumbo cornfields or down muddy ditches.

247

Duck hunting is sometimes done in weather cold enough to cause instant icing of any stray spray that hits gun metal. In some regions, duck hunting is hot, dry and dusty. I've shot desert ducks from the foot of a blowing sand dune where eyelids and gun actions alike got gritty in five minutes.

And in all these places, the guns go along—to be dropped in water and mud; banged around boats under heavy, knobby decoys; drenched in salt spray or blast-frozen in the season's final hunt, when the northern flight is racing down ahead of a Canadian blizzard and the mercury is headed for the storm cellar.

All these harsh realities in that masochistic sport called wildfowling are known painfully well by the sons of men who voluntarily endure such madness, yea, even unto the second and third generations of muddy feet and runny noses. Obviously, our ideal wildfowling smoothbore had better be rugged, mechanically reliable and not finicky about digesting shotshells that may be wet or somewhat dirty or both. Common sense says this is not the place for fancily ornamented guns—all the more because elaborate engraving and metal inlays are moisture and rust traps.

General Sheridan wrote of frontier Texas that it was heaven for men and dogs but hell for horses and women. Wildfowling, it can be paraphrased, is great for hunters and retrievers but tough on boats and guns.

Now that we've established what a duck gun must put up with —lots of physical abuse and tough field conditions—let's take a

A waterfowl gun must be able to withstand exposure to rain, snow, ice, sand and mud without jamming. The one seen here is guaranteed to get splashed before the hunter comes ashore.

look at what we expect this gun to accomplish.

It's to be used for taking surprisingly tough, proverbially wary, winged targets, usually at longer ranges than upland gunning requires. A long shot for a ruffed grouse or quail hunter is almost point-blank range for a duck gunner. With the exception of the midget wildfowl, teal and bufflehead, ducks and geese are much harder to kill outright than thin-skinned, soft-feathered upland birds. When wounded, most ducks are great escape artists if the environment offers them half a chance. A goldeneye can dive and swim 100 yards underwater. In cattails flooded too deep to permit him to wade and standing too thick for him to swim through, a wing-tipped mallard can evade an AKC field-champion retriever all day long.

Therefore, the ideal duck gun should hit hard. Four decades of duck hunting have convinced me that for the average hunter in modern waterfowling conditions, this means a gun firing a minimum of 1¼ ounces of shot. Fortunately, today's wide range of shotshell loads makes eligible everything from the 20-gauge 3-inch magnum on up. But the 12-gauge offers the greatest choice of models, the most versatility in loads and the best resale or trade-in value—and makes the most sense.

Loads of less than 1¼ ounces are less than ideal for most waterfowl gunning, except perhaps on fragile species like teal or when used by the kind of expert who breaks 100 straight on the trap or skeet range and has a fine eye for range estimation over the water and decoys.

Anyone who simpers that lighter loads are more sporting for general wildfowling use (barring the exceptions cited above) is apparently too dull to realize that the name of the game is not to cripple the birds and allow them to escape as tormented pieces of live mink bait back in the marsh.

Crippling loss is a severe constraint in modern wildfowling. The ratio of wounded, lost birds to those making up the hunter's legal bag is far too high and should be reduced.

Minnesota game managers ran two extensive studies of crippled-duck losses. One was at a public hunting area close to the Twin Cities, thus likely to be frequented by many casual, less-than-expert hunters. The other study was at a far-northern hunting locale, several hours' drive from metropolitan areas, hunted by more serious and (hopefully) more determined and expert hunters.

Crippled-duck losses at the site close to the Twin Cities, used by the more callow nimrods, were highest—a shocking 50 percent. For each bird in the bag, another was hit and lost. Theoretically, to take a four-bird bag limit, a hunter on the average shot, and subtracted from the waterfowl resource, a total of eight ducks.

What about our expert hunters in the far-off-hunting-area survey? As expected, they did somewhat better. Even so, their crippling ratio was still a painfully high 30 percent—about one duck lost for every two in the bag.

Since waterfowl populations are uniquely affected by gunning pressure (unlike most other game, which tends to be regulated by natural food/cover factors), this kind of wastage is obviously a severe problem in management of the waterfowl resource.

Every duck hunter has a personal obligation to reduce that kind of avoidable drain on the "capital" that keeps him in business as a duck hunter. We simply cannot afford to waste ducks in that fashion.

There lies the argument for a three-shot repeater in duck hunting. The quick third shot is extremely useful for nailing cripples.

While the two-barreled gun offers the fastest second shot of any, its lack of a third is a distinct handicap.

Together with a good retriever, it keeps my personal crippled-duck loss, year in, year out, at less than 10 percent, even though I hunt mainly in thick-cover areas with naturally high potential for cripple losses.

One of the most durable canards in sporting lore is the ancient fiction that double guns (of either type) are "more sporting" than the plebeian repeaters. This, one strongly suspects, started as a class slur by the Establishment when low-priced, mass-produced repeaters began putting more low-income canaille into the shooting field to compete with the Old Guard.

Really, the double-gun user is not chivalrously handicapping himself. He has in hand the best-pointing, deadliest-shooting, quickest-repeating (for two shots) gun ever designed. The butt-light mounting characteristics of a good double and the muzzle-heavy pointing stability of that twin-tube weight out front make it a better game-killing piece, by and large, than most repeaters. Although high speed of fire is of dubious value, the double gun (at least in single-trigger models) is a faster "repeater" than either a pump gun or an autoloader.

However, the problem of the double gun, as we have seen, is lack of a quick third shot to smack a stricken bird in the air or on the water to save a cripple from escaping.

Admittedly, the third shot of a repeater is practically useless in many upland situations. Nor is the third shot all that useful in bringing down a third bird out of a flock of waterfowl, thanks to both the greater range of typical wildfowl gunning and the speed with which both ducks and geese can open up that range. A wise waterfowler instead learns to save that third shot to deliver the permanent coup (if necessary) on one of the birds he knocked down with the first two shots. Often, that cripple-stopper shot is needed. And anything that helps reduce the sizable percentage of the waterfowl resource written off as crippling loss is good conservation and hence good sportsmanship.

This is not to bum-rap the already-cited virtues of the double as a generally superior bird-hitting arm. Nor does lack of a ready third shot detract from the double gun in the upland field. Here, a live cripple on the ground rarely offers a third, polishing-off shot, thanks to ground cover. But years of using both repeaters and double guns have convinced me that the latter, although better-pointing (thus, better-hitting), create crippled ducks that dive or escape into thick marsh cover where at times even a good retriever can't get them.

That narrows the "ideal duck gun" field down to repeaters—either pump models or autoloaders. Low-priced bolt-action shotguns are far too slow in repeat fire and usually too poorly stocked to even qualify in the competition here. Cheap single-shots are usually a beginner's gun.

Similar in configuration, pumps and autoloaders vary from one model to another in handling and pointing. Autoloaders have a softer recoil. Their "power loss" diverted to operate the gun mechanism is insignificant. Don't think of them as faster-firing, because some pumps can be repeat-fired more rapidly than some autoloaders, and extremely fast shooting at waterfowl is both unnecessary and usually ruinous to scoring of hits.

Autoloaders generally are heavier than pumps and carry a bit more weight forward. This, in most cases, improves the balance and pointing characteristics for wildfowl shooting. The archetype here, a great gun, is John Browning's famous long-recoil autoloader, still produced under the original aegis of Browning Arms and made for many years in slightly modified form as the old Remington Model 11—both fine guns. The first thing you notice on picking up an autoloader of the old Browning long-recoil pattern is that it feels muzzle-heavy. Compared with many repeating shotguns, it is. That's just fine for wildfowling's pointing and smooth-swing needs.

World War II proved the feasibility of gas-operated weapons. This system quickly became the wave of the future in autoloading shotguns, but was not necessarily a step forward. First, typical gas-operated designs (including the "floating chamber" type) don't have as much recoil-motivated machinery out in front as John Browning's masterpiece did. Hence, they lose some of the lock-on-target handling that pleased just about any shooter who ever seriously used a Browning/Model 11 in the hunting field.

The worst of these was the post–World War II Winchester Model 50 gas-operated autoloader. The design used a compensating weight mechanism well back in the gun's buttstock. This was a pure disaster. The gun was unwieldly to mount, and the balance point, being too far aft, made it muzzle-light, whippy and miser-

The old "humpbacked" recoil-operated autoloaders, based on John Browning's original design and made by Browning, Remington and Herter's, among other manufacturers, has fine weight-forward balance and good reliability, but kicks like a mule.

able to point accurately. Guns of this model can often be found at surprisingly low prices on the secondhand market—guess why.

Second, no one to date seems to have come up with a gas-operated shotgun quite as reliable and stoppageproof as the original Browning long-recoil pattern. The model coming closest to this ideal is the excellent Remington 1100, perhaps partly thanks to the drastic improvements in shotshells brought about by plastic hulls. Older Browning and Model 11 autoloaders made their reputation for reliability back in the days of comparatively inferior paper shells, which, as you may recall, were great for getting damp and swollen in a wet jacket pocket (for duck hunters, is there any other kind?).

Another factor in considering autoloader performance is handloading, which in shotshells began a massive revival in the mid-1950s. Granted, plastic reloads in today's excellent reloading machines are far superior to the weak-mouthed, paper-hull reloads produced with the truly primitive reloading systems a few of us struggled with in the early '50s. Even so, good handloads are not quite as good as the equivalent factory shotshell. This can cause problems in a system as sensitive to ammunition variations as the autoloader.

A duck hunter wants fairly powerful loads. These require slow-burning shotshell powders. Such powders don't burn as cleanly as faster powders. In some gas-operated autoloaders, the buildup of burned-powder residue from such loads can cause problems. The gun functions by tapping off a small amount of powder to drive an operating piston, thus introducing burned-powder residue into the piston assembly. Over the years, I owned three different versions of the same basic gas-operated autoloader made by High Standard. With an excellent stock design and enough weight forward for stable pointing, these were fine game getters—when they worked. Unfortunately, stoppages from firing residue were all too common, with both factory ammo and handloads, although stripping and thoroughly cleaning the gun after every shooting session helped somewhat.

To sum up, most autoloaders are good-shooting pieces, thanks to their weight distribution. What weakens them as wildfowling guns is the painful reality that any autoloader needs consistently high-quality ammunition in order to work properly. A handloader who shoots an autoloader had best resign himself to occasional gun jamming.

Even if a hunter sticks to factory shotshells, the normal conditions of wildfowling still tend to conspire against the autoloading principle. Cold weather can cause an autoloader to malfunction, particularly when overlubricated. Mud and moisture can cause jams. Dirty ammunition, no rarity in muddy blinds or field pits, can stop the most reliable of autoloaders.

To guard against these problems, the user of an autoloader must discipline himself to ensure strict quality control of his handloads, using the best of reloading equipment; carry out careful, regular gun cleaning and maintenance; and take pains to keep his shells clean afield.

Finally, we have pump-action repeaters as an option for the generally ideal wildfowling gun. In my four decades of wildfowling I've used fifteen different shotguns, including doubles, autos and pumps, while hunting with many fine waterfowl experts and noting their choices of guns. Today, I'm more convinced than ever from these experiences that the pump gun is the best compromise for duck and goose hunting.

The pump gun is far less vulnerable to jams than any autoloader. A good pump is the best dollar buy, since pumps are lower in price than autoloaders of comparable grade and much cheaper than a medium-quality double gun today. The better pump designs have enough weight forward for good pointing characteristics.

At best, the pump gun is an ugly piece of ordnance, looking vaguely as if it belonged in the water tank of a toilet. A pump totally lacks the classic sleekness of a side-by-side double or the appeal of an over/under. With the underslung magazine tube looking like an afterthought, the pump doesn't even match the unglamorous autoloader for looks.

But the pump is a classic of operating reliability. Most specimens will keep working under the worst of conditions at least as long as the hunter himself can function. The only thing that will stop a good pump in the field (outside of rare breakage of a part) is ice forming on the exposed operating rod or ammunition in really bad physical shape.

The American pump-action shotgun is very old, going back to the late nineteenth century. Since then, literally dozens of models have been made by practically every American manufacturer of long arms, not to mention foreign pump models. Inevitably, some of these designs have been dogs; some have been angels.

The best-known is the Winchester Model 12. If there's a classic pump gun, the Model 12 certainly is it. Its action is of an archaic, somewhat complex design, although highly reliable in functioning. This meant relatively steep manufacturing costs which eventually killed off production of the lower-grade Model 12s in 1963.

What made the 12 an American classic over the years was both its reliability and its fine handling qualities. A standard Model 12 seems to fit most shotgunners naturally. With the exception of a lightweight version, the conventional Model 12 is a fairly heavy gun for a pump. As in the case of the autoloaders, much of this weight is properly forward. This makes the gun point with stability for consistent hits.

Basically, that's why the Model 12 outlasted many would-be competitors, outsold those competitors that did survive, became the commonest gun in clay-bird competition and is still a sought-after model on the secondhand market. Its Winchester successor, the Model 1200, unfortunately does not have the Model 12's reputation for reliability.

Perhaps the single greatest testimony to the excellence of the Model 12 is the fact that popular demand "brought it back from the dead" just ten years after its manufacturing demise. Through the use of the investment-casting process, Winchester was able to drastically cut down on the amount of machining required to produce the 12, and hence could reintroduce the gun at a competitive price. Although nearly a year has elapsed, at the time of this writing, since the Model 12's resurrection, the factory is still tens of thousands of guns behind in filling its orders. And despite the idiot claims by some people that investment castings are inferior to machined forgings, the new Model 12s are every bit as good as the older ones.

Of the homely pumps, the best-looking is the Ithaca 37, thanks to the sleek, unbroken receiver wall made possible by lack of a side ejection port. The last of the prewar generation of milled-parts pump guns, the Model 37 has a simple action, much easier to strip for cleaning than the complicated Model 12. One of the 37's faults, common to three guns of this model I've owned, is a relatively weak extractor that sometimes fails to withdraw a problem shell.

Another drawback in field use is the ease with which a Model 37 can be fired accidentally when the hunter is closing the action. The 37 has a too-small trigger guard, and a gloved forefinger is almost certain to rest against the trigger. In the heat of action, the trigger can be unintentionally held back, with the result that the gun will fire as soon as the action chambers a live round. Some

The huntress in this photo is holding an Ithaca Model 37, an extremely popular pump gun with a simple action that's protected from the weather. The 37 is handicapped for waterfowl shooting by a stock with excessive drop and light weight.

One of the very best pump guns for waterfowling is the High Standard Flite-King, which was initially sold under the Sears label as a J. C. Higgins.

other guns can do this, but none seem to do it as readily as the 37.

But the main objection to the 37 for a waterfowl hunter is the gun's lightness—which is one of its selling points. A light gun is not advantageous in most waterfowling situations. With heavier shot loads in 12-gauge, the Ithaca's recoil is severe. The gun is too light up front for accurate pointing and tends to wave around when the shooter throws down on a fast-moving bird. The lightness of the 37 also makes it more possible for the shooter to unconsciously indulge in the mortal sin of stopping his swing on a fast, crossing shot. Finally, the Ithaca's buttstock in most models has too much drop at the comb for most shooters, causing a tendency to shoot low on rising targets.

The two best pump guns for the money on the market today are the Remington 870 Wingmaster and the High Standard Flite-King, both medium-priced, reliable, sweet-shooting guns with no bad habits. The Remington is a postwar design with stamped parts. But unlike the Winchester 1200, it has a reliable, trouble-free action and over the years has become a popular shotgun.

The High Standard is a real "sleeper" that made its postwar debut under a Sears, Roebuck proprietary label of "J. C. Higgins," aimed at the low-priced market. The gun quickly became successful in spite of its mail-order aura, something that can make the more snobbish gun enthusiasts snort, rear and roll their eyes like a quarter horse colt seeing his first rattlesnake. When Sears discontinued the gun, High Standard continued marketing it under its own name as the Flite-King.

The action is one of the smoothest ever developed for a shotgun. When you hold a High Standard pump vertically and push the action-release button, the action falls completely open from its weight alone. It's also an easy action to strip down for cleaning or parts replacement. The gun is very well stocked for most shooters and has the proper balance. Trigger pull, important for wing shooting and often overlooked by hunters, is excellent.

If High Standard succeeded in producing one of the worst of the gas-operated autoloaders, it more than blotted out the sin by producing one of the very best pump shotguns in history. Lacking the historic appeal of a name like Remington or Winchester, the High Standard has never been a widely popular gun. Even in these inflationary times, good High Standards under the "J. C. Higgins" label have been selling secondhand for as little as $40 to $50, a fantastic bargain considering the inherent virtue of the piece— for the shooter, not the status seeker.

In summary, the superior pointing qualities of doubles aren't enough to undo the serious handicap of their lack of a third shot to reduce crippled-waterfowl losses. Autoloaders handle well and provide the third shot, but they pose some problems of reliability and demand extra maintenance. This leaves the pump gun as the best for most waterfowling situations—but only if it's not a poor-pointing, hard-kicking lightweight, and only if it's mechanically reliable.

In any event, pick a duck gun that is of medium weight or a hair more and that has a slightly muzzle-heavy balance. Avoid a light, whippy gun. Okay for fast snap shooting at close upland birds, arms like this are not ideal for the more deliberate, semi-aimed shooting typical of waterfowl gunning.

Breathes there the duck hunter, with soul so dead, who never to himself hath said, "That bird I just missed would be in the bag if (pick one alibi): A. I had a tighter-choked gun; B. I had a more open-choked gun; C. I shot fours instead of sixes; D. I shot sixes instead of fours; E. I had a ten-gauge magnum instead of this lousy twelve-gauge"?

The fault, dear Brutus, lies not so much in loads and chokes as in ourselves.

Duck and goose hunters spend far too much time worrying about chokes and shot sizes but not enough time practice-shooting on the trap range or at good varmint targets like crows or rural blue rock pigeons.

The typical American solution to any problem is twofold: First, if some is good, more must be better. Second, when in doubt, spend more money. An American sportsman buying himself a duck gun is likely to know that there are three basic shotgun chokes, of which the tightest and longest-ranging is full choke. With visions of ventilated ducks falling at 60 yards, he's powerfully tempted to buy a full-choke gun.

Then he reads somewhere that 3-inch 12-gauge magnum shells have 1⅞ ounces of shot; and the mental scenario becomes mortally smitten mallard at 70 yards. After all, nearly 2 ounces of shot makes the conventional 2¾-inch 12-gauge magnum load of 1½ ounces appear anemic, while the 1¼-ounce looks ridiculous. And think what those Roman-candle magnum loads would do to geese!

But the tiresome realities are:

1. Only a minority of duck hunters today know how to lead a duck at 40 yards or more.
2. Tighter choke, heavier shot and more shot will not make up for clean misses due to poor shooting.
3. Even very big Canada geese can be killed with surprising consistency with normal waterfowl loads and medium-size shot like No. 5. The range of heavy No. 2 is limited by thin patterns.

Most of us tend to overestimate the range at which we're actually killing wildfowl. A beneficent Deity has kindly arranged that all my life has been spent in good duck country. When I pass on, my wife plans to have me laid out in the casket in duck-hunting togs and waders, to ensure that natural look considered desirable in the funerary visitation period. Despite these many seasons joyously misspent in the pursuit of both waterfowl and lobar pneumonia, I still find myself overestimating the actual range of duck shots.

As an example, last fall found me slipping down a winding

stream, jump shooting from a canoe. As I veered around a fallen snag at a bend, a mallard flushed from a shoreline willow patch. He went straight up, an easy shot, and fell straight down. I smugly congratulated myself on my wisdom in using a tight-shooting (75 percent) gun and No. 4s in order to pull off sure kills at 45 yards like this. Forty-five? Heck, he must have been closer to 50 yards!

When I landed to pick him up by the willow patch, the angel of truth nagged me to leg it back to the shoreline snag whence I had fired the shot: 34 paces. That translates to about 31 yards. Add some charity because of the slant-range hypotenuse and I probably nailed the bird at 36 honest yards. Sky-silhouetted, he looked farther.

I've done all my decoy hunting on public waters used by other hunters. Watching hundreds of other gunners shooting, I've been convinced over the years that most waterfowlers get 90 percent of their ducks *inside 35 yards*. They shoot much farther than that, including sky-busting attempts at 100 yards or more, but rarely do any except close birds fall. For this kind of hunting, nothing tighter than modified choke, rated roughly as putting 45 to 55 percent of the total shot into a 30-inch circle at 40 yards, is needed. A good modified pattern is also surprisingly useful for many jump-shooting or pass-shooting situations up to 45 yards. In short, it's the best compromise pattern for wildfowling when a reasonable amount of shot is used.

For decoy gunning, a normal improved-cylinder choke that patterns from 35 to 45 percent of the shot under test conditions is adequate, *if* enough shot is used to ensure pattern density complete enough to hit even small waterfowl. However, a modern American shotgun with improved-cylinder boring in anything other than short, 26-inch barrel length is very rare. Barrels this short usually have the muzzle-light pointing characteristics already described as less than ideal for duck gunning.

Older guns tend to be choked more tightly, since they were made for the loosey-goosey shot-pattern performance in the days of less effective gas-wad sealing and long before the modern plastic shot-protecting cup wad. With modern shotshells, these older guns may shoot tighter patterns than what the legend stamped on the barrel indicates.

An ancient Winchester Model 97 owned by my father shoots astonishing 80-percent patterns despite a heavily pitted bore dating
from the corrosive-primer era. He's a fine enough shot to capitalize
on this gun's tight patterns and ranging qualities. But he's also a
hunter with sixty-plus seasons behind him, harking back to the
predrainage days when a wildfowler easily and legally could
shoot a skiffload of birds. Today, no one has a chance to develop
that kind of shooting experience on wild ducks.

If life isn't complicated enough, some guns, when shooting the
larger shot sizes, have an overchoke problem that results in
spewed-out, irregular patterns. I once got rid of a stout duck gun
that shot fine patterns with everything but what I wanted to use
in it—No. 4 shot. Barrel lapping and/or choke reaming often cures
this problem, paradoxically tightening up patterns with the larger
shot.

These are reasons why a shotgunner who doesn't pattern his
gun is as blind as a deer hunter who doesn't sight in his rifle. Only
through pattern testing can you find out what patterns your shotgun is really shooting and what sizes of shot and ammo brands
work best.

Patterning may also reveal that your shot charge is not centering where the gun seems to be pointing; the gun may be shooting
high or low because of a poor stock fit, a bent barrel that you
didn't know about or a badly installed variable-choke device. Patterning is a time-consuming chore, but can be important to your
shooting success.

If you're a handloader, an easy way to achieve more waterfowl
hits through looser patterns is simply to develop loads without
shot cups. Use separate plastic overpowder wads, since these
largely prevent the occasional blooper misfires that, believe me,
were the curse of pioneer handloaders back in the early 1950s. In
my experience, handloads without shot protectors are good for
about five fewer percentage points of pattern performance. Example: One of my repeaters, marked modified, actually produces 60-
percent "improved-modified" patterns with good handloads using
shot cups. Without shot cups and with the same size shot it shoots
uniform 53-percent patterns.

This gives me a variable-choke system without any devices on
the muzzle. I use the looser-patterning loads over decoys when

the birds are cooperating nicely, as in the predawn legal shooting period when well-called mallard will come almost into your lap. When shots tend to be longer, I switch to the other loads (color-coded for identification) shooting a noticeably tighter pattern.

Variable-choke devices are available either as factory options or custom-installed. Such hardware has a long history, dating back to the 1930s.

They won't cure bad shooting habits. If you're a swing stopper, shooting behind birds, or an unconscious flincher, some hardware added to the end of your gun is not going to solve the problem. It's interesting to note in gun stores that a surprising number of the secondhand shotguns for sale have variable chokes on them. In each case, the owner presumably had a choke installed to correct some problem. The fact that the gun ended up for sale may indicate that the choke didn't cure the problem, whatever it was, or didn't meet his expectations of magical performance.

With a new variable choke installed, the shooter spends too much time changing settings in the field. It finally dawns on him that the sky doesn't rain dead ducks simply because he now has Nine Full Degrees of Choke at His Fingertips. Soon, he finds himself leaving the choke at one setting or using one tube only; and most of the time for a duck hunter, that probably will be modified choke.

All too often, our hero's shotgunning problems will have been worsened. Most variable chokes raise the front sighting line of the gun (which most wing shooters use, knowingly or not). This, if not compensated for in some fashion, will make the gun shoot lower. That's exactly what you *don't* want a shotgun to do on typical, rising targets. On a low-stocked gun like the Ithaca Model 37, a fat choke device up front can destroy your shooting results.

The best solution is to restock the gun with a higher comb. In effect, this raises the "rear sight" (i.e., the comb of the stock) to compensate for the jacked-up frontal sighting point. Still another solution is to have a careful and knowledgeable gunsmith bend the barrel gently to put the shot-charge placement higher. Bending the stock tang of a pump or autoloader and refitting the stock is also practical.

Another common problem with interchangeable choke devices is a bad installation job that causes the shot charge to shoot off to one side or the other. Actual remounting of the choke may be the best remedy.

Choke devices with built-in recoil reducers actually do reduce recoil. Muzzle blast is sharply increased, however, making you unpopular with other gunners in the same blind. If recoil is a problem, the gunner should drop down to less powerful loads, get a heavier gun or have a recoil-reducing weight installed in the stock.

Among wing shooters, waterfowl hunters are unique in having long-standing, utterly sincere clashes over appropriate shot sizes for the sport. This rarely occurs among upland hunters. Ruffed-grouse gunners tend to stick with 7½ or 8 shot; the majority of pheasant hunters would be happy if no shot size other than No. 6 could be bought, and so on.

But get three waterfowlers together to talk shot sizes, and chances are there'll be three table-pounding arguments going.

"For decoy gunning, number six shot is best," says one wildfowler.

"Oh, yeah?" says another. "All you really need is seven and a half."

This hunter has wisely equipped the stock of his Ithaca Model 37 with a rubber cheekpiece to compensate for the higher line of sight created by the addition of a Cutts Compensator.

Young birds and/or early-season birds, such as these mallard, can be taken with relatively small shot sizes.

"You're both crazy not to use number fours," says the third shooter.

All three hunters can be right.

The No. 6 man may be talking about general gunning for medium-size ducks, like widgeon or lesser scaup. The 7½-shot enthusiast may be hunting teal or little divers like ring-necked ducks or bufflehead. The third hunter may be a jump shooter taking rear-end shots at big, tough mallard that he must drill deep to drop cold.

Not only the type of hunting and quarry, but the gun's choke should influence the choice of shot. A man hunting with a fairly open-choked gun will miss some small ducks with No. 4s simply because of lack of pattern density. He'd probably better stick to 5s and 6s or, if small waterfowl are his typical game, 7½ shot.

Even the time of the year influences shot-size logic. Early-season ducks tend to be less wary, are typically taken at closer range and include many juvenile birds with minimal feathering and no fat. Late season finds ducks fully feathered out with the heavy garb they'll wear until next summer's eclipse molt. Underneath, they may have a quarter-inch of very solid fat to soak up shot energy in a nonlethal fashion. The smaller shot sizes that creamed early-season mallard won't be as effective on big, northern flight ducks armored with added feathers and fat—unless the hunter's individual shooting style causes a high percentage of head-and-neck hits from almost overleading the target. The latter gunners are the kind who swear in all truth that heavy shot is not needed on big, hardy waterfowl—and they're right, for *their* style of shooting. Less skillful shots like me tend to make body hits when we hit at all, and here, heavier shot is definitely in order for deep, lethal penetration on big ducks and geese.

One oft-used argument is that smaller shot penetrates better than bigger shot because of the lessened cross-sectional resistance that feathers, fat or flesh offer to the small pellet. In practice, that's not realistic. Out where the target is, the heavier shot pellet will arrive with more hitting energy and greater penetration than the ballistically inferior smaller pellet, even though they both leave the muzzle at approximately the same speed.

I tend to be a large-shot user. My favorite mallard shot, even over decoys, is No. 4. With big shot, there's less carcass mutilation (not more, as fable hath it), because there's normally less of it to smack into the target. Also, more of the big pellets will pass completely through the bird, a fact that both I and my dental fillings appreciate at the dinner table.

In addition, larger shot sizes are blown less off aim in high-wind situations, which is when some of the best waterfowl shooting often occurs. Finally, larger shot is the better breaker of wing bones. This is important on strong-flying ducks like mallard, widgeon and pintails. The puddler species in general have what an aero engineer calls low wing loading. These birds have lots of wing area available to carry their body weight, compared with stubby-winged diving ducks like scaup. All too often, a strong-flying puddler takes mortal hits, sets its undamaged wings and glides beyond practical retrieval. Years ago when I switched to heavier shot, there was an immediate reduction in that kind of cripple loss as more birds instantly fell with completely deactivated wings. It meant (at least for me and my style of shooting) quicker, more humane harvest of the quarry and fewer lost cripples.

Highly useful for the open-water gunner is to have some small shot loads at hand for polishing off swimming cripples. The greater pattern density of No. 7½ shot will do a better job of cleanly kil - ing a low-swimming cripple at longer range than the harder-hitting No. 4s, for example.

It's a question of simply scoring hits, not how hard the pellet strikes. A semisubmerged cripple at 40 yards is a very tiny target to hit at a flattened angle with the coarse pattern of heavy shot. You can churn up the water around a hunkered-down, swimming cripple with a full salvo of 4s, and through no fault of your own still not score a hit. But with 7½s, the chances are greatly increased that some pellets will hit the head and neck.

Geese make up the waterfowl category wherein the ultramagnum enthusiasts run amok. The size and desirability of this peerage of the wildfowl kingdom simply addle the wits of normally rational hunters, not only in the field but even when it comes to abstract thought on the subject.

The goose resource has been the one bright spot in American waterfowl management in the last three decades. Duck populations have been clobbered by overhunting due to state and flyway rivalries, plus drainage and occasional drought. But careful management, development of captive "seed" flocks and the natural ability of geese to take good care of their hides have built up fine goose-shooting opportunities in every major flyway.

Along with this has developed a goose-gunning mystique, to the pleasure of some of the more incurable shotgun nuts and certainly to the profit of arms and ammo manufacturers. The extreme position among the former is that no rational man will attempt taking medium or big geese without, at minimum, a 12-gauge 3-inch magnum firing 1⅞ ounces of shot. Further, he'd be much better off with a 10-gauge magnum firing 2 ounces of shot, since the use of a 20mm Oerlikon antiaircraft cannon isn't quite practical for the average hunter.

Just thinking about this kind of ballistical pornography leaves many hunters panting and clammy-palmed. But the dull and dowdy fact is that all goose species can be taken very adequately

Because of their great size, Canada geese appear to fly more slowly than they actually do, and most misses end up far behind them.

with conventional duck guns, down to and including the 20-gauge magnum or any other 1¼-ounce load.

The average hunter needs a 10-gauge magnum for geese (or long-range ducks) about the way he needs a 250-horsepower V-12 Jaguar to commute through city traffic. The King Kong magnums have a recoil factor that will progressively pile-drive a hapless wildfowler up to his knees in marshy loon litter, unless the gun he's using weighs 10 pounds or more.

That weight is too much for reasonable shotgun handling. A more modest magnum like a Winchester Model 12 in 12 gauge with 3-inch chambering weighs in at 8½ to 9 pounds, depending upon the wood density of the stock and how many shells are in it. Although I'm a fairly husky 6-footer with long arms for good leverage, I find that my Model 12 magnum as described here is just about all the gun I can handle with reasonable dexterity.

Furthermore, the longest shots I've made on geese were 50-plus measured yards, where nothing more apocalyptic than 1½-ounce short magnum loads of No. 4s—shootable in any modern 12-gauge of normal gun weight—scragged the targets very cleanly, including producing completely shattered wing butts on big western Canadas up to 10 pounds. Meanwhile, many serious shooters like Oregon gun writer Francis Sell find 1¼-ounce loads of 5s to be excellent roast-goose converters. Although I part company with Brother Sell on the virtues of 20-gauge double guns for wildfowling, I agree that his load choices consistently kill geese well into the 40-yard bracket, which is as far as the average gunner could hit them with anything. While it's true that a 10-gauge magnum load of 2s can take geese at 70 yards, most of us would be incapable of doping the fantastic lead angle required at that range.

Many hunters honestly feel they need more gun for geese because of past failures to knock down honkers at apparently easy range. Their problem is that what appeared to be a big Canada at 40 yards was actually at 80 yards. An 8-pound goose is not the biggest of the species by far. Yet it looms huge compared with a 3-pound mallard and gigantic alongside a 2-pound scaup or widgeon.

The real secret in nailing geese is the patience to let them come within decent range. When a honker looks as if he may be close

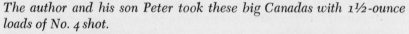

The author and his son Peter took these big Canadas with 1½-ounce loads of No. 4 shot.

enough, he's not. When he looks quite close, he's probably within possible, but not certain, range. Only when he is as huge as a Goodyear blimp coming in to moor do you have him within dead-sure range of 40 yards or less.

Admittedly, letting him approach this close is hard on the nerves and fire discipline of the hunter. The thrilling yelp of in-coming geese and their seemingly slow-motion approach give the crouching hunter severe shakes, heart fibrillation and a spastic bladder. But the agony of suspense is justified when you rise up to take a startled, flaring honker, sure that he's yours before the gun butt hits your shoulder. (Incidentally, scared geese are very fast on the getaway, despite their stalling approach, and thus it is easy to shoot behind them.)

Therefore, good choices of duck guns for the average hunter will make useful goose guns for most situations. If there are any special guidelines, they'd be basically to use No. 4 shot for big Canadas in lieu of smaller shot and to use full-choke pattern density for better killing power on big geese. Smaller geese like whitefronts, lesser Canadas, snows and blues can be taken with any gun/load combination that can be counted on to take mallard. The smaller goose species are no harder to kill than mallard, less likely to escape when crippled and actually easier to hit because of slightly greater target area.

Despite their strong opinions on shot sizes, waterfowl shooters rarely discuss, let alone argue about, powder charges of various factory loads.

Probably it's because many of them are confused by this aspect of the subject. My favorite uncle, a veteran duck hunter, once cut apart a factory shotshell, weighed the smokeless-powder charge and discovered it was far less than the "3¾-dram equivalent" the box said. I pointed out that a much smaller charge of smokeless did approximately the energy work of 3¾ drams of black powder of the old days and that 3¾ drams of smokeless powder would be over 100 grains avoirdupois weight and would constitute a triple charge that would blow to flinders the best shotgun made.

I never did convince him that it wasn't all an anticonsumer rip-off by the arms companies. He said that at best, it amounted to misleading labeling. In a sense, he was right. The powder charges labeled on factory shotshells are a holdover from the black-powder era. Unfortunately, no one has come up with a better nomenclature system. Actual powder content would be a meaningless guide, since this can vary with the kind of powder and a particular production batch of that powder used by the ammo manufacturers to achieve X amount of velocity within Y range of pressure limits.

Don't worry about it. The slight velocity difference between "maximum" or "magnum" loads and "field" or "target" loads is not a significant factor either in the lead you allow on flying game or in the striking energy out where the game is. The amount of shot and the size of that shot are reasonably important and the more meaningful guides when you're selecting factory ammunition. The savviest handloaders I know cut their powder charges a bit, kill game just as dead and just as far anyway and reduce both their powder costs and their guns' recoil by a modest but welcome amount.

The information in this chapter is all based on the use of lead shot pellets, which, as this is written, are legal for waterfowl. However, it is pretty certain that during the 1975–76 waterfowl season lead shot will be illegal along the Atlantic Flyway, and that by the following year it will be forbidden altogether.

The reason is this: Each season, an estimated 600 tons of spent lead pellets are deposited on our marshes and wetlands. Waterfowl, in their search for food, ingest these pellets and ultimately die of lead poisoning. The number of ducks that actually die from this cause is open to dispute, but the most reliable studies to date indicate that they run well into the millions every year. And this loss is utterly unacceptable.

With the advent of nontoxic steel shot, waterfowlers will have to adjust to a new set of rules. First, it will be necessary to use larger shot, since steel has a far lower sectional density than lead. For example, No. 2 steel shot is about the ballistic equivalent of No. 4 lead. Second, it is quite probable that the 3-inch 12-gauge magnum may become the standard wildfowl load, as only this long shell can hold enough of the bigger shot to give sufficiently dense patterns. Third, we may well see the popularization of 10-gauge guns, and there are rumors that one company has developed an 11-gauge especially for steel shot. Finally, steel shot (because of its hardness) can bulge the tubes of old double-barrels—

it will not harm modern single-barrel repeaters—so you'll have to retire any elderly side-by-side or over/under from waterfowling.

There has been a violent objection to steel shot from some quarters on the ground that it is a crippler of birds. Although they lack the weight of lead shot, steel pellets produce better patterns (because they deform less in the barrel), and they can be propelled at higher velocities without additional recoil. It is true that beyond 40 yards steel pellets are ineffective, but then, for all but a very few expert shots, so is lead.

Waterfowlers are simply going to have to part forever with the dream of busting ducks at the length of a football field and take that 35-to-40-yard limit as the gospel.

Rarely do the tens of thousands of words written annually on shotgun wing shooting get into the subject of shotgun sights.

The actual sighting mechanics by which a shotgunner points his gun is terra incognita. Usually the subject is dismissed with the trite chaff that "Shotgunners don't aim; they point."

Not true. Most shotgunners, I believe, aim. That is, they use physical reference points on their guns in order to shoot ahead, above, straight at or (in the case of descending wildfowl or plunging doves) below the target.

The best duck shot I know is a Minnesota game-warden pilot with the fine Swedish name of Patrick Emmett McFall. Pat and I shared a North Woods backcountry boyhood that offered some pretty fair duck hunting. No clay-bird man, Pat learned to shoot on live targets: assorted birds with a 12-gauge Remington 11 and later, Wehrmacht *Herrenvolk* with an air-cooled Browning .30, circa 1944–45.

Pat could always wipe my eye in bird shooting, and I tried to learn his system. Like almost all good wing shooters, he could not tell me how he was pointing and leading, because it's largely an instinctive reflex. But he did declare that he was not aiming. "I just point out there," Pat said. "I don't know why they bother putting front beads on shotguns."

Came the day when we got into great bluebill and redhead shooting after Pat had broken the front bead off his shotgun on a canoe gunwale. Out of the first flock of white-bellied scaup that whistled in over the decoys, I knocked down two while Pat scratch-hit one. I was astonished. He was frantic.

"Can't hit a damned thing without that bead," he swore. "Got any gum?"

I pulled out a stick and tore it in two. We both chewed furiously to get the gum wet and sticky, because more ducks were coming down the lake. Pat bit off a small chunk of gum, rolled it into a ball and plastered it on the Model 11's rather tall front-sight ramp. He smacked two out of the next flock, lost his gum off the muzzle and missed the third shot. We had a couple of lively cripples swimming fast out of range. Reloading, Pat fired, sans front sight, and missed his crippled duck by yards, shooting way high.

In other words, this very deadly wing shot was utterly dependent on a frontal reference point in aiming his gun, even though he didn't know it all those years. (Unabashed, Pat said only that he'd have shot better with Juicy Fruit.)

Perhaps a quail or ruffed-grouse gunner could get along without a front bead on his shotgun, but ducks are usually shot at farther ranges than close upland birds like quail, woodcock and grouse. The clay-bird game that most closely simulates duck gunning is trapshooting, and veteran trapshooters are extremely sensitive to their sighting systems. Many of them are heavily dependent on a ribbed gun barrel. Why? Because they're using it as a sight. If they were relying purely on proper cheeking of the gun and clear vision alone, a rib and a front bead would be superfluous. A skeet gunner, by contrast, may tend to be more of an instinctive shooter, blasting at closer, acutely angled targets with, as a rule, a much more open pattern and finer shot. But that's not a simulation of *typical* duck hunting.

A front sight such as a shotgun bead is not a reliable reference point by itself. Euclidean geometry makes it obvious that the front sight is reliable only when its relationship to the shooter's eye is constant. Getting the shooter's eye to the same place each time is partly a function of the shotgun stock's comb.

This is a crude rear-sight system. Many misses are due to variations in how the shooter shouldered and cheeked his smoothbore. The commonest error is to cheek the gun sloppily, hold the head too high (thus in effect drastically raising the "rear sight") and shoot well over the target.

The safeguard or control point here is how much barrel ap-

pears in the shooter's visual picture. If he's seeing a lot of it, his
eye is high, and the shot charge will shoot high, just as a rifle with
iron sights shoots high when the rear sight is raised.

The rib serves the same purpose as the barrel, only it's more
clearly defined to the shooter's eye, thanks to its flat surface and
square edges. I suspect that I use a rib much as other shotgunners
do, whether they are aware of it or not. When I want to shoot
high at a steep-rising mallard, I stretch my neck up a fraction, see
more rib under the front bead and cut loose. All this is done by
learned reflex action, since there's little time to consciously think
about it.

All this contributes, I suspect, to why so many shooters naturally do well with side-by-side doubles. Most doubles have a rib
of sorts. In addition, the twin-barrel structure is a pretty obvious
reference point to indicate to you how you're cheeking the gun.
If your head is high, that double path of steel tube and rib out in
front is instantly very prominent and should tell you something.
With a little experience, the message is almost instantaneously re-

*Both the pump gun at left
and the over/under at right
are equipped with sighting
ribs. Standard equipment
for competitive target
shooters, they are invaluable for the hunter as well.*

ceived and acted upon without conscious decision making by the gunner.

This is important to the wildfowler, because much of the time he doesn't want to shoot very high. Divers shot at over decoy situations are often flying very low and level, easily missed with too high a shot-charge placement. Mallard are often shot while going straight up. But they're also shot coming down over decoys at steep, full-flap descent angles, so that you must actually shoot well below the bird. Another common shot in wildfowling is a duck high overhead who is going away from you. Just the reverse of the oncoming high bird, the outgoing high bird is best taken with a gun that doesn't throw its charge high. In effect, you must shoot well under him.

An upland gunner is usually blasting at a fast-rising bird. In duck and goose hunting, there are *some* fast-rising targets, plus birds coming head-on at a high, overhead angle, and in these instances a naturally high-shooting gun (e.g., such as a straight-stocked trap gun) will give you a nice, convenient, automatic lead factor.

The guns that serve me best on waterfowl are those which center the shot pattern just a few inches high at 40 yards. Although this would not be so hot for steep-climbing pheasant, it is the best compromise for many waterfowl shots in decoy and fly-by pass-shooting situations. But when I go out to jump shoot fast-climbing puddle ducks, my choice is a smoothbore that shoots a good foot

Jump shooting means taking on targets that are flying straight up, and a shotgun that places its pattern high is more effective than one that hits dead-on. These mallard have gotten up at 40 yards.

or more high at the arbitrary 40-yard mark, rather than one of my somewhat "level-shooting" duck guns.

If all this strikes you as complicated, you're so right! Of all shotgunning, wildfowling is the most complex in terms of varying situations, radical differences in the behavior of (and tactical approach to) different kinds of birds and so on. That's what makes wildfowling an incurably fascinating sport for those who get seriously hooked—yea, surpassing the love of women and the pursuit of wealth and even inducing them to forgo other pleasurable forms of hunting to acquire a case of catarrh in a half-frozen marsh.

We have seen two basic ingredients in the thorny problem of hitting wildfowl with a shotgun. One, most of these targets are relatively small because of greater range—a mallard at 40 yards is a more difficult mark than a pheasant at 20, obviously. Two, the classic sighting system of cheek/eye relationship to the front end of the gun is not too reliable. An excited gunner shooting too fast with his head up or with an ill-fitting stock will miss too many birds. Such devices as ribs, sometimes with auxiliary midlength beads in addition to the front bead, can help prevent overshooting or undershooting, but are still somewhat primitive sighting systems.

Therefore, it's odd that duck hunters, above all other shotgunners, haven't stampeded in the direction of optical sighting systems. If any game-bird shotgunner can best use an optical sight on his smoothbore, it's the wildfowler.

Lack of equipment offered has not been the problem. Bill Weaver, the scope maker who really introduced American riflemen to glassware on guns, had a good shotgun scope on the market not long after World War II. He used it for all kinds of tough, quickie targets, including quail, and preached the virtues of a shotgun scope to any who had an ear. Not many did; and the Weaver Company eventually dropped its one-power shotgun scope from its product line.

In its place, the Weaver people came out with a gadget called the Qwik-Point. It's a well-thought-out variation on the basic idea of a reflector sight. The idea is to give the user two things: a good, unimpeded view of his target and an optically projected aiming point that is a fixed constant in terms of where the gun barrel points. Even if the shooter moves his head a smidgen, which can ruin him in conventional shotgun sighting, he will still hit if he properly relates that optical aiming point to the target.

In other words, the optical sight is a great truth teller. If it shows that you are on a straightaway bird, by golly, you *are* on him, whether your head is a quarter-inch high or not.

The effectiveness of this system was proved decades ago in wartime use. Aviation-gunnery experts wanted something better than the crude steel-ring-and-front-post sight. A scope sight offered improved aiming, but a fighter pilot scrunched up against a scope sight atop his instrument panel wasn't likely to see much else, which could be disastrous.

Then someone doodled up a little glass window that could be looked through easily while still permitting normal perspective all around it. A small mirror with an image etched on it was set at a slight angle below and in front of the little glass window. It projected the image onto the glass mirror as a bright ring. In the device's advanced form, of course, the projection was done with a small lamp so that no skylight illumination was needed.

The system was a great improvement over ring-and-post arrangements. The first Flying Fortress models that had a tail gunner used the old ring-and-bead. Although this gunner was usually firing at straight-on, no-deflection targets astern, it wasn't too effective. When those "stinger" twin .50s in the tail position were given the reflector sight, more enemy fighters developed Browning bellyaches.

To train aerial gunners, the Air Force mounted similar sights on shotguns and took the boys out to clay-bird ranges. A friend of mine was assigned as cadre at one such base, where he had a chance to do a lot of free trapshooting with these reflector-sight shotguns.

Fairly experienced with a conventional bead-sighted shotgun, at first he could not hit his hindquarters with both hands using a reflector sight on an Air Force Model 11 Remington autoloader. Suddenly he made a breakthrough and annihilated clays better than ever before.

Basically, this GI-model reflector sight was the forerunner of the interesting but short-lived Nydar shotgun sight that was briefly on the market in the late 1940s.

The Nydar failed to catch on with shotgunners. A big reason was that wildfowlers, the most logical users, found it too vulnerable. A piece of mounted glass sitting up at a right angle atop the receiver of a hard-used duck gun is subject to all kinds of accidental demolition. Second, the glass was too much exposed to getting spattered with rain and snow. Third, it wouldn't fit into a conventional gun case. Fourth, shotgunners are traditionalists. To them, an optical sight on a shotgun looks too kooky to put up with.

The last reason is probably why the good Weaver K-1 shotgun scope never really got off the ground in terms of sales. A conventional scope is fairly rugged, and you can get a gun case that will fit a scoped shotgun. Also, hinged lens caps keep a scope usable in rain and snow. But show a shotgunner a scope-mounted wing-shooting smoothbore and nine times out of ten he shudders involuntarily and turns a delicate green around the gills. Serious rifle nuts are gadgeteers and don't worry much about their guns' looks—the esthetic monstrosities that populate the ranks of the highly functional free-rifle class are a perfect example. Shotgunners, however, have some definite ideas about proper appearance, and scopes on shotguns are outside the pale, in the view of most.

They are missing the biggest bet of their wing-shooting lives. An optical sight on a shotgun is highly effective on waterfowl. It's

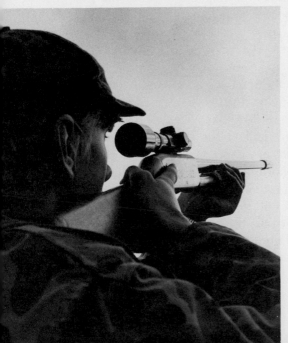

The sadly ignored optical shotgun sight (this one is a one-power scope from Herter's) is invaluable, as it eliminates the sighting errors caused by improper head position on the stock.

far superior to conventional shotgun point sighting in the weird half-light of dawn or in a stormy, premature dusk, when some of the best wildfowl gunning offers itself.

Best of all, the optical sight frees the shotgunner from his vulnerability to hasty, improper cheeking. Within reasonable limits, he can have his head and eye high, low or off to one side. As long as he steers the optically projected image of something like the Weaver Qwik-Point or the reticle of a one-power shotgun scope into the right relationship with the target, he will hit. With an optical sight, the previously all-important shotgun stock now becomes just a handle and a way to steady the gun.

There are problems to overcome. First, an experienced gunner, like my buddy using the old Nydar at the Air Force shotgun range, must unlearn his old shooting habits. After years, it's hard to break yourself of using the shotgun muzzle's bead (which can be seen easily in the wide field of an optical shotgun sight). The best way to kick that habit is to get out onto a clay-bird range with the new shotgun scope or Qwik-Point. It's not too difficult, and probably only a couple of rounds of trap will get the shotgunner grooving on his new optical-sight picture.

At this writing, the Qwik-Point is somewhat superior to the other shotgun scopes on the market. The Qwik-Point projects a luminous, large dot which makes a beautiful aiming point. Get that onto or properly ahead of a bird and there's no way you can miss. Solving vertical or horizontal lead-angle problems is still a reflex action—a problem for that minicomputer called your brain. But the Qwik-Point reveals exactly where you're aiming your gun —something that can be very deceptive in conventional shotgun pointing.

By contrast, the other shotgun scopes on the market today don't have that good an aiming point. Just as the first automobile makers designed vehicles that looked like horse carriages, shotgun-scope makers so far haven't kicked the habit of designing rifle-style reticles. Of the shotgun scopes currently on the market (Herter's and Bushnell), not one has a reticle ideally suited for wing shooting. Needed is a reticle that's simply a big hollow circle subtending maybe 30 inches at 40 yards. Cross hairs are useless as an anticanting control, because the game gunner is going to be concentrating on that ring aiming point. If his eye starts wandering around the field of the scope to align cross hairs with the horizon, etc., the distraction will be fatal to concentration on his sight picture and lead.

And for heaven's sake, forgo all temptation to have any "lead calculating system" in the form of dots or bars, water-witching forks or signs of the zodiac cluttering up the magic-circle reticle. Any scope designer suffering preliminary hallucinations along those lines should purge himself with a strong laxative, take a cold shower and then just pick up a drafting compass to draw that thick-walled circle that a good wing-shooting scope cries out for.

My testimony on the deadliness of the shotgun scope is valid, because I've used one for the past couple of seasons. Mine is the Herter's, but all three makes currently on the market are similar— 1-inch tubes, zero magnification and enormously wide, bright fields. Oddly enough, I have found myself hitting satisfactorily while ignoring the inadequate reticle of the Herter's shotgun scope. The eye seems to home in automatically on the center of even that huge a field. But a large, circular reticle would be better.

A shotgun scope, of course, must be sighted in. Adjust it to look right dab in the center of where your scattergun puts its pattern. That seems to work better than sighting in the gun to print the pattern a bit higher than the scope or Qwik-Point's point of aim. But to each his own—you might want to experiment for best results.

One problem with optical sights on shotguns is weak mounting. A scope tube is best anchored with a side mount to snug it down as low as possible for comfortable cheeking. The higher the mount, the more the comb of the stock is going to be down along your jawbone, a poor place to absorb any untoward recoil. Receivers of some repeaters may be too thin in the sidewall to take enough screw threads to anchor the mount against the hefty recoil of a normal shotgun. There's usually thicker metal in the top of the receiver, and your gunsmith may advise a top mount for that reason, particularly on aluminum receivers.

To sum up, optical sighting systems are highly effective. Because there's no geometrically dictated alignment problem in aiming such a gadget, *they're faster than conventional aim pointing.* Because they overcome the common sins of improper shotgun mounting and cheeking, they lead to some very deadly shooting once the gunner gets used to the different and radically better sight picture.

No treatise on wildfowling gunnery is complete without mention of a few side items. Foremost is the need for a good gun case to help protect the duck gun when it's being transported in a boat full of gear or in a car trunk. Pick a tan or dead-grass-colored canvas model—not plastic. It will wear better and is less slippery to handle when cold or wet. Second, pick one that has a full-length zipper, so that the case can be opened up to dry when wet. Nothing rusts a gun faster than a wet gun case.

Fancy guns take a beating in normal wildfowling. Their usual high sheen is a tactical error, to boot. Ducks and geese have too-sharp eyesight without your flashing any heliograph warnings to them from a glittering gun barrel.

At archery shops, camouflage tape can be bought to put on the gun barrel of a musket used for serious wildfowling. It also helps protect the barrel from nicks and dings. I went to this system after experimentally painting a perfectly good Remington autoloader with duckboat paint. A gunning friend who stopped by took a horrified look at the atrocity of paint's being applied to a gun, muttered something about a day that would live in infamy and stalked off into the night. Later he made me an offer for the gun that I could not refuse, just so that he could get out the rags and paint remover to redeem the arm, as he put it, from unspeakably vile servitude. Actually, the dead-grass paint served the purpose of camouflage very well. But camouflaged bow tape is even better and can be removed without any ill effects on the bluing, stock finish or resale value.

The mechanisms of duck guns should be cleaned fairly regularly. Exposed frequently to moisture, they're likelier to get rust inside than a more pampered upland smoothbore. Don't ignore the trigger assembly. I once mournfully sat out an hour-long fly-by of thousands of Mississippi Flyway redheads with a gun whose hammer-sear mechanism was too badly rusted to function, thanks to a previous hunt's rain.

Bore leading isn't much of a problem today, because of harder lead shot plus plastic protector sleeves. When leading occurs, it can be scrubbed out, after a fashion, with a brass brush. What works better is to run through the bore a patch smeared with pharmaceutical blue ointment, a mercury-based salve. Leaving it in the barrel overnight lets the mercury amalgamate with the lead fouling, which then comes out cleanly with a couple of fresh patches next day.

Overoiling leads to dirt collection and jamming. Use oil sparingly. If you hunt in cold climates, nonfreezing synthetic lubricants like Anderol or WD-40 are mandatory. The latter is also the best rust preventive I've found.

Any shotgunner, whether a wildfowler or not, will benefit from good books on the subject. For a starter, the National Rifle Association's *Shotgun Handbook* is excellent. The price is a modest $3, less to NRA members—which is only one of thirty-seven reasons why, as a hunter, you should belong to the NRA.

BIRD DOGS

BY JEROME B. ROBINSON

Despite smaller bag limits, dwindling access to public hunting lands and shorter hunting seasons, it is one of life's many paradoxes that more good hunting dogs are being bred today than ever in history. More men hunt with dogs than ever before, and the general level of excellence among those dogs has never been so high.

The modern upland-bird or waterfowl hunter has a broader selection of dogs to meet his individual requirements and tastes than his forebears ever had—but fewer opportunities to reap the benefits of his dog's inherent ability to endure long hours in the field, find birds unerringly and bring large numbers of fallen game to his master's hand.

Bird-dog and retriever breeds were developed to help man find and harvest more birds with less effort. Yet today, when hunting dogs are better endowed than ever, game-bird and waterfowl harvests have been so limited that few men honestly need a hunting dog.

In the last century the hunter's outlook has been reversed. A man no longer *needs* a hunting dog so much as he *wants* one. A modern sportsman is more interested in how his dog works than in how many birds fall to his gun. Today's bird-dog man is more excited by the style with which his dog handles birds than in how many birds he finds. Likewise, the waterfowler takes his pleasure from his dog's manners, marking ability and stylish retrieves, and overlooks the fact that he could have rowed out and picked up his meager daily bag without having to feed, house and train a dog all year.

For generations, hunting dogs have been bred to fill the requirements of the men who would use them in the field. The Chesapeake Bay retriever, for example, was developed as a market hunter's utility dog in a day when canvasback ducks brought $5 a brace and there was no limit on how many a man could shoot. The market hunter needed a dog of endless endurance who could swim through the roughest seas, breaking ice all the way, and whose determination to retrieve every duck that fell knew no limits. The Chesapeake was a workhorse, and the man who had one brought home more ducks to sell on the market.

Today, the Chesapeake retriever's popularity has suffered for the simple reason that the modern duck hunter's requirements

Today, the Labrador retriever is a breed of immense popularity. A fine performer in the water, it also works extremely well in the uplands, as here.

have changed. Today's duck hunter wants a companion dog of happy disposition who will take training well, be good with the kids and make his fewer retrieves memorable because of the style with which he marks the falls and delivers the game.

The slower, more determined but also more stubborn Chessy has given way in popularity to the Labrador retriever, a breed of immense happiness, easy trainability, stylish speed and entertaining eagerness.

Similar changes are afoot among bird-dog breeds. It used to be popular to breed bird dogs that would go to the horizon to find birds if that was where the birds were. But how many hunters nowadays know places where they can run a dog that goes that wide? Modern hunters are faced with posted land, and open spaces are smaller every year. Today's hunter wants a closer-working bird dog that he can control easily. He wants stylish work on birds, classy points and fast retrieves, but he has neither the room nor the inclination to run a bird dog whose natural range eats up more space than is contained on the piece of land on which he has permission to hunt.

To fit the new requirements, modern hunters are turning in ever-increasing numbers to European breeds which were developed for hunting in countryside where open space was more confined. That is why the Brittany spaniel is soaring in popularity. The Brit was developed as a poacher's dog in France when hunting as sport was restricted to rich landowners. The peasants who

The classic example of the "big-going" (wide-ranging) upland dog is the English pointer. When there is a lot of ground to be covered, this is the breed that can do it.

The German short-haired pointer, a close-working and deliberate breed, is not as stylish as the English pointer, but is gaining popularity because it better fits today's hunting conditions.

poached game on the lands of the rich needed small dogs that they could control in the field without much yelling at them, yet that found game quickly and held it until the poacher arrived with his gun. When not hunting, the dogs had to serve as house pets, and the fact that they were small and ate little made them all the more attractive. Close-working, easy to control, good in the house—these are increasingly the necessary characteristics in a dog for the modern "land-poor" hunter; hence the Brittany is more popular than ever before.

Currently, only field trialers are breeding the wide-going pointers and setters that were a man's best bet for finding birds when the country was young and one knew no limits to his hunting land. Few other than major-circuit field trialers ride horseback behind bird dogs today, and even the big-circuit field trials are now outnumbered by a new rash of smaller stakes in which closer-working pointers and setters vie for honors with Brittany spaniels, German short-haired pointers and other Continental breeds.

With more and better hunting dogs to choose from, it naturally follows that there are more professional dog trainers than ever before. Also, the modern dog trainer is better equipped to do his job; he has all the knowledge of the generations of men who preceded him. Great progress was made in methods of training bird dogs and retrievers as interest in field trials grew early in the twentieth century. The great trainers of that era discovered and perfected methods that really worked—and the biggest boon of all was that they passed their knowledge along. Today anyone can read volumes of expert instruction on training bird dogs and retrievers, written by men who really know how. The deep, dark secrets are out in the open, and there are enough dogs to train so that even the best of the pros will talk publicly about how they do their work. The result is that the average man's goals have been heightened and the standards he wants his dogs to attain have been refined.

The breeders, the trainers and the men who hunt with dogs have all benefited from this broadened knowledge about training and field standards. The increasing number of men who buy hunting dogs want better performance than they can usually get by trying to completely train the dogs themselves. Reputable breeders of good hunting dogs find a huge market waiting for their pups, and good trainers have all the business they can handle.

It is unlikely that two men have ever agreed on every detail of what makes the perfect bird dog. For every man who loves to see a dashing pointer or setter exhibiting a nose that works as fast as the dog's legs can run, there is another who believes that the only bird dog worth feeding never goes more than 40 yards away, hunts at a trot and is totally subservient to his master. It is easier to agree over how a retriever should perform, yet there are plenty of retriever owners who are exceptionally proud of dogs another man wouldn't allow in a duck blind.

I was once invited to hunt with a man whose Labrador retriever, Old Pete, was said to be truly exceptional. All the way to the hunting area we heard stories about Pete's performances. It sounded as though Pete could find ducks no other dog would ever get, swim farther and never come back without the duck. No dog ever had a more dedicated and enthusiastic owner than did Old Pete.

"You don't have to watch for ducks coming in," Pete's owner told me once we had the decoys out. "Old Pete'll let you know when they're coming."

This proved to be the understatement of all time. Pete watched the sky intently, and within minutes he was whining, slobbering, barking and threatening to leap out of the blind. "Get ready," Pete's owner told me; "he sees some."

A bunch of whistlers was boring up the shoreline, and Pete was going out of his mind. "You shoot," the owner said. He obviously had both hands full trying to keep Pete from charging out to meet the oncoming flock. As the birds slid in over the decoys, Pete's owner got the dog in a half-nelson and clamped his muzzle shut with the other hand. The dog's muffled, strangling sounds were all I heard as I rose to shoot.

My shot had barely cleared the gun when Pete's owner let go, and Old Pete knocked half the front out of the blind as he took off in a mad rush to the water's edge.

"You gotta admit, he's eager," Pete's old man confided.

But there was Pete at the water's edge, tail going a mile a minute, barking his fool head off.

"He doesn't see the duck yet," said Pete's owner. "He won't go into the water till he's got that duck marked for use. Gimme a shotgun shell."

I handed over a live round, and Pete's owner yelled, "Watch it, boy!" and skimmed the shell out over the water, where it splashed down in the dead duck's vicinity. Pete barked louder than ever and raced up and down the shoreline. "Damn," his owner said; "he didn't see the splash. Gimme another shell."

As it turned out, it took three or four thrown shells to get Pete into the water and a few more (we later switched to rocks) to steer him out to the duck. Once there, he clamped down on his bird with a powerful chomp and swam back toward shore, conscientiously avoiding the spot where we stood waiting.

"One thing about Old Pete," his proud owner chuckled; "he'll bring the ducks in to shore, but that's where his job stops. You gotta go pick the bird up yourself."

Pete hit the shore a good 50 yards from us, dropped the duck at the edge and ran to his master for congratulations. He wasn't disappointed. His owner swooned all over Pete, patting him and thanking him for bringing in that duck. Then the owner walked up the shoreline to finish Pete's retrieve.

Back in the blind, Pete got a rubdown with a towel.

"You better hide that duck under some rocks," Pete's owner

warned me. "Old Pete likes to eat duck just about as much as I do myself, don't you boy?" A few minutes later he was strangling the dog again to keep him quiet as another flock of whistlers came to the decoys.

I don't need a dog like that and neither do you, but Pete's owner thought the world of that dog and wouldn't have had him any other way. There are dogs that need men like that, and luckily for Pete, he'd found one.

Selecting the dog that is right for you is not that tough if you know the choices you have available and are honest with yourself about how much time, effort and money you are willing to invest to get what you want. Be realistic about the kind of hunting you will be doing and the kind of work that you want from the dog. Another thing: Don't take unnecessary chances. Let others do the experimenting.

For instance, if you live where good duck hunting is available and pheasant inhabit the upland coverts, the dog that will probably bring you the most pleasure with the least trouble and expense is a Labrador retriever.

You can train a Lab yourself to do basic water retrieves and to hunt under control as a flushing dog on upland birds. You need only a copy of James Lamb Free's excellent book *Training Your Retriever* (Coward-McCann, 1970). It is the retriever owner's bible and tells you all you need to know about what a retriever should be expected to do and how to make him do it.

On the other hand, training a pointing dog to handle wild cock pheasant with consistent style takes a lot of work, a lot of time and a lot of wild birds. For most people, this means sending the dog to a pro. Let's face it: most pointing dogs used on pheasant bump a lot more birds than they point. Why not settle for a flushing dog that will also excel in water work?

Before choosing a bird-dog breed, you should analyze what kind of cover you will be hunting. Will you be hunting quail in the big grainfields and soil-bank lands of the Midwest, where you can see a dog a long distance away? If so, you'll need a dog with the endurance to run all day and the boldness to reach out to find birds. A pointer or setter of top field-trial blood could be the dog for you.

But if your hunting will be done in thick overgrown farmland or the hillside tangles of New England, you won't be happy with a wide-ranging dog. A Brittany spaniel or German short-haired pointer might be a good choice; or if you like the classic grace of pointers or setters, you should be careful to buy one of stock that has been used successfully in the type of country you plan to hunt. You don't want a dog whose ancestors have been wide-ranging champions if you are planning to hunt woodcock and grouse in confined cover. Use your common sense and don't be swayed by some dog jockey who is trying to sell you one of his dogs regardless of your specific requirements.

Field-trial background can tell you a lot about the ancestry of the dog you choose. But be careful to study what *kind* of trials your dog's ancestors were winning.

If your choice is a retriever, you'll have an easier time finding the dog you want if you stick strictly to field-trial stock. Retriever field trials are true measures of the qualities you want to find in any retriever used for hunting. Pups from champion retriever stock will be the best bets for whatever kind of hunting you intend.

Training a hunting dog is a big thing in a man's life, but it should not be taken so seriously that the fun is lost. Like all the other trappings of modern living, the behavior of a man's hunting dog is in some way a measure of the man himself. But it's surprising how often a man who can successfully hold down a good job, raise a gang of kids, figure out how to meet all his monthly payments and live harmoniously with his wife gets all in a clutch when it comes to training a dog.

Let's face it, if he's worth his salt, a well-bred bird dog is going to point his birds, a retriever will naturally want to bring you whatever falls from the sky and a spaniel will naturally flush and retrieve. These are inherited traits, and generations of careful breeding have instilled them so deeply that they have become instinctive in hunting breeds. With calm, thoughtful encouragement from his owner, the well-bred hunting dog will learn to do his field work in a manner that makes him a good companion and a good hunting dog.

It takes a lot of refined training to develop a dog that will win in competition, where standards are tough, but training a decent gun dog is easy if you don't sweat it. Men who succeed in daily life do so because they know how to gain the respect of those around them and they go out of their way to make people like them.

Dog training demands the same accomplishments. Make the dog respect you and like you. From then on, training is a simple matter of logical instruction—and it should be fun.

Look at it this way: A well-bred pup from one of the pointing breeds is going to point his birds naturally unless you confuse him to such a degree that his natural instincts are addled. He's going to break and chase, too, that's for sure. But instinct will stop him on point once he learns to discriminate between scents and realizes that unseen birds are ahead.

Your job is to encourage him to hold his points for longer and longer periods of time, to let you come progressively closer to him before he breaks and busts the bird out of there.

When you simplify the trainer's role to this extent, the job doesn't seem so difficult. The dog's natural instincts are in your favor. Your job is simply to show the dog how he can gain your affection and avoid your wrath by channeling his instincts.

It's the same with retrievers. Any eight-week-old retriever pup will drag a rolled-up sock back to you if you first tease him with it and then toss it a short distance away. Generations of breeding have built into him an overwhelming desire to bring things to you. Your job is to show him how to retrieve with style—delivering to hand, marking accurately, taking hand signals to unmarked falls, etc.

Before you can train effectively, you've got to learn to look at problems from the dog's point of view. You've got to train yourself to ask, "Does the dog understand what I mean? If not, why?" Most dog owners who fail in training do so because they have never learned to show the dog what they want him to do before they begin harassing him for not doing it.

Anyone who can raise children and help teach them the meaning of an entire vocabulary of English words certainly knows how to convey the meaning of a little dog lingo like "Good boy," "No!," "Come," "Sit," "Heel."

If the dog is around you a lot, as he should be, you will have occasion to use those commands every day, and the dog will automatically become quick in responding to them, so long as you demand that he respond properly *every* time. If you let him get away with sloppy responses, he'll automatically get sloppier. Demand absolute obedience, and you'll get it.

At the same time, your relationship with your dog will become more casual and you'll find that you are not as nervous and he is not as tense when it comes to the refining of his field work.

It's really not very hard to come up with a controllable, pleasing hunting dog if you have established a good rapport with him in the first place. The big step from yard work to field work can be much less awesome for you and more understandable to the dog if you have played logical backyard games with him regularly.

For instance, every bird-dog owner should have an old glass fly rod mounted with 6 or 8 feet of line and an old game-bird wing tied on the end. From your dog's puppyhood through his veteran years, this training tool will be effective in helping you convey to him the desired responses—and you'll both have fun with it.

When he's no more than ten weeks old, a bird-dog pup will sight point the wing-on-the-string. Twitch the wing in front of him and get him chasing it. Start doubling back over him, being careful not to let him grab the wing and making him fall over backward in his rush to catch it.

When he begins to tire and stops with his tongue lolling, drop the wing on the ground in plain view. His expression will intensify, his tail will stiffen and he'll begin to stalk the wing. As he takes his first step, twitch the wing slightly; if he rushes it, twitch the wing away. Keep doing this until he gives up and stops in his stalking pose, rigidly studying the wing. There you have it: his first sight point!

"Good boy," you tell him.

Do this a few times a week as the pup grows up and he'll soon exhibit a pointing habit that will please you immensely. By the time he's six months old, you can add a little check cord to his collar. Now when he stops on point, lay the fly rod down and work your way up the cord to the pup, restraining him if he tries to leap in.

Get your hands on him and stroke his back. Push his haunches toward the wing, causing him to stiffen. "Good boy," you repeat softly.

When he rushes, and he will, restrain him with the check cord and caution, "No!" No rough stuff—just tone of voice and firm restraint.

When the dog is older and is going into the field with you to hunt and chase birds and butterflies, precede his runs with a few minutes of wing-on-the-string games. Lay the wing on the ground and lead him up to it on a check cord. If he doesn't point automatically, stop him and pose him in a pointing position. Hold him that way several minutes. Praise him. You are conveying to him that pointing is good. Later on, this will help.

Even an older bird dog that has tired of wing-on-the-string games can be taught new tricks. Before trying to steady him in the field, try this: Set him up pointing the wing. He may flag his tail to indicate that he knows this is just a game, that the real stuff happens in the field.

Don't worry about his tail. Just make him stand still. Then, with an upward swing of the fly rod, make the wing flush in front of him and yell, "Bang!" He'll break, right? Now start correcting his tendency to break.

Restrain him with a check cord and work with him every day or so until you've got him where he will stand still and not break even when you flush the wing from his feet and yell.

You'll find that this background game will make him understand more quickly when you start teaching him that he's not to chase when birds flush in the field.

Every retriever owner should have at least three canvas or tough-plastic dummies for use in backyard games. Before he graduates to working with live pigeons and ducks, the retriever's lessons can all be taught with dummies.

You teach him to retrieve at top speed by running away from him when he slows down on his return with the dummy. You encourage him to deliver to hand by running away and taking the dummy from his mouth as he comes alongside.

He learns to mark the places where dummies fall at longer distances. Double and triple retrieves help develop his memory of where things fell. All of this will help when he's in the duck blind with you.

The retrieving part he will do automatically; the trainer's biggest problem will be to steady the dog and prevent him from breaking to make the retrieve before he is sent by command.

Tie a stout, 25-foot check cord to the base of a rigid stake or solid tree. Then attach the other end to the dog's collar and make him sit at the base of the tree or stake. Now throw the dummy, but do not command him to retrieve. When he breaks, he will hit the end of the check cord at full tilt and be jerked over backward.

There is no need to say anything. Just keep repeating this until he stands still when you throw the dummy. Now say "No!" if he starts to move. Make him sit and mark the fallen dummy. Without being observed, detach the check cord. Command him to fetch.

Consistent repetition of this backyard game will teach the dog that he must not rush out to make a retrieve until you send him. Backyard practice like this will do much to prepare him for being steadied in the same manner when real birds start falling.

Once he is steady on dummies in the backyard, do everything you can think of to tempt him to break before the command is given, and *always* reprimand him when he does break. Before he

The pointer at the left is "staunch," holding his point in the midst of a covey rise, but the younger dog at right is beginning to bolt. Staunchness in a dog is not natural; it comes only after long and patient training.

will be controllable in a duck blind he must realize that he cannot break no matter how he is tempted.

The same kind of backyard practice applies to flushing spaniels, who also are taught to retrieve with dummies in yard sessions. Later you can begin schooling them to "Hup" or sit on command in the midst of their rush to retrieve a thrown dummy.

If you are going to train a pup yourself, understand from the beginning that the first pup you buy may not be the one you want to keep. If you just can't seem to get anywhere in training the pup and are convinced you have not made serious training mistakes, get rid of that pup and buy another. In the long run, it's both cheaper and much more rewarding to write off the expense of a pup you can't train than to justify the expense of several years of unhappiness and high cost that result from a dog that will never amount to much.

Once you have a pup that shows promise, be prepared to spend some money on his schooling. You'll need birds. Unless you really have a good native supply of wild birds, realize from the start that

The natural inclination of the English springer spaniel is to leap at birds and put them into the air. Unless the dog has been trained to "hup" or sit until the gunner is in range, he'll probably bust the covey prematurely, as is happening here.

you will need a recall pen and a couple of dozen quail on hand. If you must travel to get to a good training area, make arrangements to be able to keep birds there for liberation during training sessions.

It may be necessary for you to do your training at a game preserve. Before you buy a pup, be sure you know where you are going to train and how you are going to provide your dog with a steady supply of birds during training sessions. You can't train a bird dog without them.

You must school yourself as fully as possible in the principles of dog training. The pros will tell you that you can't learn to train from a book, and it's true that books won't give you all the understanding that professional trainers acquire through years of experience with many different dogs. But books can teach you a lot. Good ones will give you knowledge of common problems that you will have to face with your pup and will acquaint you with various proved methods of overcoming them. Frankly, I have never known a professional trainer who lacked an ample library of training books.

Three that I think are mandatory reading for anyone who contemplates training a bird dog are *Training Your Own Bird Dog* by Henry P. Davis (G. P. Putnam's Sons, 1970), *Wing & Shot* by Robert G. Wehle (Country Press, 1964) and *Gun Dog* by Richard A. Wolters (E. P. Dutton & Co., 1961). These books are currently in print and are available through local bookstores or may be purchased through the mail from various sporting-dog-supply houses.

Just as surely as a man must assert himself as boss to train a hunting dog, he must also become that dog's friend. This is the great advantage the owner has over the professional trainer: He can devote his attention to just one dog at a time and become that dog's buddy as well as his boss.

The best hunting dogs respond to training with an eagerness to please their masters. Eagerness to please, not fear of punishment, makes the great dogs respond to training with a total desire to learn to do the job right.

The bird dog that stays steady on point because he wants to please his master is less apt to run off and bust birds for himself than the dog who stays in only because he knows he'll get a beat-

The pointer, at right, is executing a beautiful point, while the setter is "honoring," or backing, it, stopping cold in its tracks whether it has smelled birds or not. This sort of performance can be gotten only through expert training.

ing if he bolts. Punishment is necessary in training, but the dogs that really want to please their masters will need punishment less frequently and in smaller doses.

A dog that is in training quickly becomes proud of his ability to respond to commands. Be fair to the dog and do not punish him unless you are sure that he understands his misdeed clearly and has disobeyed intentionally. If that course is followed, the dog will respond to commands happily. He has learned most of all to want your praise. For that reason, it is important to have him with you much of the time. Let him know he has pleased you every time he responds to your commands. He will grow to value that praise above all else.

It is important that a dog live by a set of rules, but I think it helps to relax the rules from time to time as a form of special praise. For instance, my setter, Ed, spends most of his nights out in the kennel, but he gets bedroom privileges on an incredible number of nights during bird season, and he spends some part of every day in the house or in the car with us. It's good for him to be outside most of the time, but he loves his hours with people, and it is from them that he learns to want to please.

Like fine paintings, good hunting dogs sometimes sell for much more than the price of the time and material that went into making them. The really big money goes for field-trial winners that can earn a good return in stud fees. Occasionally, dogs sell for incredible prices simply because someone wealthy enough not to let money matter decides that he has to have a certain one.

Nevertheless, the average hunting-dog buyer is a hunter, not a field trialer or breeder. He's looking for a dog that will enhance his very best times in the field, not an animal with which he hopes to make money or even improve the breed.

Prices of $750 and more are commonly paid for bird dogs that handle easily and are staunch on game, regardless of whether they are steady to wing and shot. In most cases, gun-dog owners do not maintain a dog's steadiness once they own him anyway. If the dog does not break until his birds are flushed by someone else, he's already more staunch than the vast majority of gun dogs.

Steadiness to wing and shot is talked about a lot more than it is ever seen among hunting dogs. It is one thing to have a dog steady during training sessions, and quite something else to keep him steady when guns start going off and birds are falling. Even top all-age-field-trial dogs that are consistently steady under competitive conditions will often break on shot when they are being hunted.

Field-trial standards are helpful. They spell out the accomplishments that all of us should try to attain in training our own dogs. But remember that the dogs that fulfill those standards are champions. And here we're examining the price of average gun dogs, not champions.

A good dog that is the product of a trainer's ability is worth a price that must include fair recompense for the time it took to train the dog as well as the cost of the dog's feed, medical attention and housing plus its original value.

Even at bulk feed prices, it costs $75 a year to feed a dog, and any pup from a good breeding is worth at least $75 at eight weeks. Medical attention will have cost at least $25. That means someone has at least a $250 investment in a two-year-old dog that has had no training at all. Add training time (and figure to pay a fair hourly rate for scores of hours) and you begin to see why trained hunting dogs bring the prices they do.

A well-trained three-year-old bird dog of average ability has cost someone a minimum of $350 in actual cash outlay, plus training time. Dogs that handle easily in the field and hold their birds staunchly have not been sitting in the kennel all year. They've been worked.

Even if the dog has had no more than one hundred hours of actual training in its lifetime (and that's not much), the trainer's time is a sizable investment. Call it $4 an hour—and a good trainer is worth more than that.

At that rate, a well-trained three-year-old bird dog of only average ability could sell for $750 and still not pay any profit on the trainer's investment in kennel, training area, birds and general maintenance.

But in the long run, buying a fully trained dog is often the least expensive route. You know what you are getting from the start. Assuming that you have taken the opportunity to hunt with the dog several times before buying him, you know that he reacts the way you want him to, his pace suits yours, he handles birds nicely and he has a good nose and a general appearance and personality that please you.

Unless you have lots of time and a good training area, often the best way to get top performance out of a hunting dog you bought as a pup is to send it to a professional. A good trainer has the confidence, the experience, the training grounds and the *birds* that make all the difference in whether a gun dog learns to turn out sloppy performances in the field or thrills his owner with consistently classy work.

A good professional can get a dog to work at the height of its capabilities. He can get an average dog to turn in better-than-average work and can make a better-than-average dog look great. Because of his experience, his sense of timing and his knowledge of dogs, a good pro can make a few months of training really pay off.

This is not to say that you can't turn out a perfectly serviceable dog on your own. He will get you game, he will behave in a competent manner and you'll both enjoy yourselves. A trainer, however, will elevate your dog's performance to a much higher level, which you will be able to appreciate fully only if you are fairly experienced in dog work yourself. Look at it this way: If you have a child, you can teach him to swim well enough to do the basic strokes correctly. But if you want the youngster to make an Olympic squad someday, that's a job for a professional.

But there is more to getting the most out of a pro-trained gun dog than simply sending your dog to a professional and paying the training bills.

Very often you hear an owner complain, "The dog was great when he came back from the pro, but now he's forgotten everything he learned." Another mid-hunting-season refrain goes: "My dog works for the pro, but he won't do a damned thing for me."

Too often owners proceed under the mistaken belief that once a dog is trained by a professional it will perform at peak capacity ever after. Nothing could be further from the truth.

When you send a dog to a pro, you incur a responsibility to both the dog and the trainer. To get the same performance the pro gets from your dog, you must learn to handle it the same way the pro does. The dog will learn to respond to the trainer's commands and attitudes. You must learn the same commands and develop similar attitudes before your dog will respond to you with equal alacrity.

Dogs test people. If the dog finds you will put up with sloppy work, he'll start doing a sloppy job. At the same time, he may respond perfectly when the pro works him, because he has learned to respect the pro as someone who demands that a good job be done.

The man who sends his dog to a professional trainer should realize that a three-way relationship must develop. Dog and owner must learn from the pro; owner and pro must each earn the dog's respect; dog and pro must each work for the owner.

An owner can learn a lot about how to handle his dog in the field if he is careful to choose a gun-dog trainer who is willing to teach him the do's and don'ts of handling his particular dog. The top gun-dog trainers encourage this sort of thing for obvious reasons—they want the owner to be satisfied with their work.

Most pros prefer that owners stay away when their dogs are undergoing initial field training. The trainer must assert himself during the early sessions as someone the dog likes, respects and wants to please. Too often a dog will revert to his old ways if his master shows up on the scene, reminding the dog of the fun he had in his reckless, carefree days.

But once he has the dog working well, standing his points stylishly and confident of his role as birds are shot over him day after day, a trainer should welcome having the owner come for a day or two when both of them can go out and shoot over the dog.

It is during this "parent's-day" indoctrination that a trainer can really show an owner what to expect from the dog and how to get the best performance out of him. Furthermore, the pro can help spot some of the owner's handling mistakes and show him how to correct them before the dog finds his owner's weak spots and begins to exploit them.

Until a few years ago, it sometimes made sense for hunting-dog owners to mix and cook their dog's food. Today the top commercial dog foods are so perfectly balanced that it is impossible for an owner to mix a ration that will give his dog a more efficient diet.

The amount of research and experimentation in dog nutrition that has been undertaken in the past fifteen years has pinpointed exactly what normal dogs need in their diets, depending on their situations. Working dogs, pregnant bitches, growing pups, dogs that loaf in kennels all have specific nutritional requirements. These have been filled by various commercial dog foods which are available at feed stores and supermarkets.

The proper feeding of hunting dogs that are being worked hard every day is a specific problem which dog nutritionists have analyzed carefully. The problem is this: Because he is using tremendous amounts of energy, the working dog needs a much greater nutritional intake than a dog that loafs in the kennel or house. But, also because he is working hard and is in top physical condition, the working dog has a tight, small stomach with a smaller capacity for food. In order to give him a larger energy intake, the food must be concentrated. His diet must be made denser and more potent.

Tests have shown that dogs prefer that dry dog foods be moistened with water. If working hard, the dog should be given all of the moistened dry-concentrate dog food he wants. Feeding once a day is ample unless the dog begins to look thin; then twice-a-day feeding may be necessary. Usually the best time to feed is in the evening. Dogs should not be fed just prior to a workout. If a hard-working dog does not stay in good condition on a regular dry food, then it is recommended that up to 20 percent meat be added. The meat does not affect the nutritional balance of good dry food, but in most cases it will increase the palatability of the food and encourage the dog to eat more, thus increasing the nutritional intake.

No hunting dog's value to his owner can be measured in dollars. Once your dog has thrilled you in the field a few times, you stop thinking of him in cash terms. When dogs enter, your whole way of life is influenced, and you will never be again exactly as you were before.

You may be a vigorous hunter who wants a fast, dashing bird dog of infinite grace and style; or you may want a hunting dog simply as a reason to get outside more and thus will be satisfied with a slower canine companion.

Regardless of your requirements, the dog that meets them may be expensive to buy, difficult to train and costly to keep—but if he pleases you, you'll never mind a penny of it; for he will have added a dimension to your life that will be infinitely valuable.

ABOUT THE AUTHORS

JIM BRADY has been writing on all outdoor subjects for a decade. Prior to becoming a full-time writer and photographer, he became acquainted with the backwoods as a Treasury agent, searching for illegal whiskey stills. Jim is a director of the Hudson River Fisherman's Association and is the author of the recently published book *Modern Turkey Hunting*.

BOB BRISTER is the Shooting Editor of *Field & Stream* magazine. For twenty years he was the outdoor columnist for the *Houston Chronicle* and received numerous awards for both his outdoor writing and his coverage of major news stories. Bob has been both a professional hunting and a professional fishing guide and is a live-bird shooter of international caliber. He is the author of *Moss, Mallards and Mules,* a collection of hunting and fishing stories.

JIM CARMICHEL is the Shooting Editor of *Outdoor Life* magazine. An avid hunter since his teens, Jim put himself through school on the basis of his gunsmithing talents and, after graduating, served with the Tennessee Game Commission. He has hunted all over the United States and recently completed an African safari. Prior to joining the staff of *Outdoor Life,* he was a regular columnist for *Rifle* magazine.

BYRON W. DALRYMPLE has been for more than two decades one of our most prolific and widely published outdoor writers. An expert hunter and fisherman, he has written more than two thousand magazine articles. His books include *Fundamentals of Fishing and Hunting* and *Doves and Dove Shooting*. Most recently, he has authored *Hunting Across North America*.

GEORGE BIRD EVANS began his career as a magazine illustrator but, in 1939, forsook the studio and New York for a West Virginia farm surrounded by superb grouse and woodcock cover. In addition to breeding his own strain of English setters, Evans has found time to write four mysteries, a novel and many magazine articles. His outdoor books include *The Upland Shooting Life* and *The Best of Nash Buckingham*.

NORM NELSON is a forester by profession and a waterfowl hunter by obsession. He has been published in virtually all of the major outdoor magazines and is a regular contributor to *The American Rifleman*.

DAVID E. PETZAL, the Editor of this volume, is also Managing Editor of *Field & Stream* magazine. Dave has written widely on many aspects of hunting and shooting. He edited the first volume of this series, *The Experts' Book of the Shooting Sports*, and is the author of *The .22 Rifle*.

GEORGE REIGER is on the mastheads of both *Field & Stream*—as Conservation Editor—and *National Wildlife*—as Associate Editor. Although only in his early thirties, George is the author of many magazine articles and has two books to his credit.

JEROME B. ROBINSON has been the Gundogs Editor of *Sports Afield* magazine since 1970. A former newspaper reporter, he has hunted and fished over all of the United States and Canada. He admits a fondness for English setters, Labradors and beagles.

NORMAN STRUNG is another outdoor writer whose achievements far exceed his years. A former college English professor, he is a professional hunting and fishing guide, a director of the Outdoor Writers' Association of America and the author of scores of magazine articles. His book titles include *Camping in Comfort* and, most recently, *Deer Hunting*.

ZACK TAYLOR is known primarily as the Boating Editor of *Sports Afield* magazine. In addition to being an expert skipper and salt-water angler, Zack is also a devoted hunter of waterfowl and has written many articles on that subject. He is editor of the book *Tales of the Old Duck Hunter, and Other Drivel.*

CHARLES F. WATERMAN is an outdoorsman of vast experience and a prolific writer. His magazine articles can be counted by the hundreds, and he is the author of many books on the outdoors, the most recent of which are *The Hunter's World* and *Hunting in America.*

FRANK WOOLNER has diverse interests in the outdoor field, and high on his list is upland hunting. He hosts his own television program in his home state of Massachusetts, has written widely in outdoor magazines and has authored the books *Grouse and Grouse Hunting* and *My New England.*

INDEX

307